THE SUPREME SOVIET: POLITICS AND THE LEGISLATIVE
PROCESS IN THE SOVIET POLITICAL SYSTEM

THE SUPREME SOVIET: POLITICS AND THE LEGISLATIVE PROCESS IN THE SOVIET POLITICAL SYSTEM

PETER VANNEMAN

DUKE UNIVERSITY PRESS, DURHAM, NORTH CAROLINA 1977

To Paula

CONTENTS

Foreword   ix

Preface   xi

INTRODUCTION   3

1. THE RUSSIAN AND SOVIET INSTITUTIONAL
HERITAGE   11

2. THE SUPREME SOVIET AS THE CONSTITUTIONAL
CENTERPIECE OF THE SOVIET JURIDICAL ORDER   37

3. COMPOSITION, ELECTIONS, AND LEGITIMACY   61

4. HOW THE SUPREME SOVIET WORKS: INTERNAL
PROCEDURES AND SESSIONS   81

5. THE NATURE OF THE SUPREME SOVIET: LEGISLATIVE
OR ADMINISTRATIVE ASSEMBLY?   101

6. THE EVOLUTION, ORGANIZATION, AND FUNCTIONING OF
THE COMMISSION SYSTEM OF THE SUPREME SOVIET   119

7. THE FUNCTIONS OF THE SUPREME SOVIET IN THE SOVIET
POLITICAL SYSTEM   151

8. THE PRESIDIUM OF THE SUPREME SOVIET: EXECUTIVE
LEGISLATIVE CONFLICT IN THE SOVIET SYSTEM   177

9. THE COMMUNIST PARTY AND THE
SUPREME SOVIET   201

10. PROSPECTUS: FUTURE TRENDS   227

Notes   237

Index   255

FOREWORD

In recent years we have seen the spread of comparative legislative studies to many countries in Asia, Africa, and Latin America, as well as the Western world, but there has been very little attention to countries in the Communist world. Most Communist countries have political institutions that are formally defined as legislatures, though they do not generally appear to exercise real decision-making authority in legislating. However, we have begun to suspect that legislative institutions that have persisted over time must play some useful role in a political system, and we have recognized that legislatures may carry out a number of significant functions in addition to law-making. These conclusions, based on a number of studies in the developing countries, suggest that we should examine more carefully the legislatures of Communist countries.

Professor Vanneman's study of the Supreme Soviet of the USSR is a major step in that direction. He describes in some detail the historical and legal background of the Supreme Soviet, and he also explores the confusing and frequently confused theories of Soviet scholars concerning the relationships between the Supreme Soviet and other political institutions. He suggests a number of functions that the Supreme Soviet plays, many of which are comparable to functions defined by students of other legislative bodies. He traces the relationships between the Supreme Soviet and its Presidium and the Communist Party and provides evidence that the Party leadership is using the Supreme Soviet as a vehicle for strengthening its control over the administrative machinery of the state. He describes the development of the commission system, used for preparing legislation and carrying out oversight—commissions that are apparently much more active than the Supreme Soviet itself. Professor Vanneman's conclusions are judicious and balanced. He does not believe that the Supreme Soviet has become a powerful independent body, but he foresees the gradual enhancement of its power because of the growing importance of its functions: legitimizing party policies, enhancing popular support, and facilitating stability and rationality in the Soviet system.

This study should encourage in-depth studies of legislative bodies in other Communist societies, in several of which there appear to be even stronger trends toward enhancing the power and enlarging the functions of the legislature. More broadly, this study is important because of the new dimensions it adds to our understanding of the variety of functions that legislatures may play and the complex relationships that can develop between legislatures and other political institutions.

Malcolm E. Jewell
General Editor, Comparative
Legislative Studies Series

PREFACE

Since the literature in the Soviet field in recent years has devoted little attention to the evolving role and significance of the Supreme Soviet in the context of Soviet politics, this study seeks to help fill that gap. In addition, the burgeoning sub-field of comparative legislatures has produced little on the nature of the legislative process in Communist countries, and it is hoped that this study will make a contribution here also.

The author would like to acknowledge his debt to Dr. Vernon V. Aspaturian, Director of the Soviet and Slavic Language and Area Center and a Distinguished Research Professor at the Pennsylvania State University, who made available all of the substantial resources of that institution for this research. His encouragement, guidance, and material support made this work possible; however, he of course bears no responsibility whatsoever for errors of fact or judgment which may have crept in.

The author also owes a special debt to Professor Jerry Hough of Duke University and Professor Malcolm Jewell, Editor of the Comparative Legislative Studies Series whose wise advice, experience and patience greatly facilitated the final revisions of the manuscript. The assistance of Professor Cyril Black of Princeton University also proved quite valuable.

The author also gratefully acknowledges the support of President Charles Bishop, Provost Charles Leone, Dean Robbin Anderson of the College of Liberal Arts, Dean Aubrey Harvey, Co-ordinator of Research, and Dr. Thomas Bellows, Chairman of the Political Science Department, all of the University of Arkansas. Thanks also to Kelly Carithers, an outstanding research assistant, who bore the main burden of proofreading.

The assistance of Ashbel G. Brice, Director, and Joanne Ferguson, Assistant Editor, Duke University Press proved invaluable in the final stages of preparing the manuscript for the printer, and was much appreciated.

The encouragement of Dr. Robert Friedman, Chairman of the Political Science Department, Dr. J. Cudd Brown, Dr. Trond Gilberg, and Dr. George Enteen, all of the Pennsylvania State University, is also gratefully acknowledged.

Above all, the greatest contribution to this work came from my family.

Peter Vanneman

THE SUPREME SOVIET: POLITICS AND THE LEGISLATIVE PROCESS IN THE SOVIET POLITICAL SYSTEM

INTRODUCTION

"The highest organ of *state* power in the USSR," reads the 1936 Constitution, "is the Supreme Soviet of the USSR." This seemingly extravagant use of words to describe the authority of the Supreme Soviet has been in part responsible for generating widely divergent appraisals of its function, ranging from non-Soviet characterizations of it as a fraudulent facade—a juridical Potemkin village—to Soviet exaltations of the body as the supreme manifestation of democratic-representative government. Much of the controversy arises from a misconstruing of the Soviet Constitution, which assigns supreme *state* power to the Supreme Soviet in contradistinction to supreme *political* power, which resides in the Communist Party of the Soviet Union (CPSU) and its central organs.

The Soviet dichotomy between *state* and *political* power, while seemingly distinguishing juridical structures from power structures with fastidious precision, nevertheless has created two overlapping and increasingly competitive sources of legitimacy in the Soviet system. Although the Party supposedly represents the ultimate repository of a higher ideological legitimacy in the Soviet system, and the Supreme Soviet represents a lesser juridical or legal legitimacy, the two may increasingly collide as factional conflict within the Soviet elite impels various factions to employ both structures in their political struggles to enhance both the legitimacy and the legality of their power and policies. Increasingly, law and politics intersect in the Soviet system to create a vortex into which the Supreme Soviet has been drawn and from which it may emerge to play a fundamentally different role than originally envisaged. The Supreme Soviet need not necessarily be reshaped as a democratic parliament in order to become a more effective political structure, since its "politicization" by the Party, while the latter is simultaneously "legalized" by the Supreme Soviet, can transform the body into a main arena for factional debate and struggles as the regime attempts to resolve the existing tensions between "legality" and "legitimacy."[1]

[3]

During the past fifteen years the Supreme Soviet has been gradually but systematically moved closer to the center of political conflict and resolution as the tension between "legality" and "legitimacy" increasingly represents competing political forces. This process has been euphemistically described as "strengthening" the Supreme Soviet and all the lesser soviets, although it appears to strengthen certain forces in Soviet society more than others in the process. Thus, some of the questions to which this study addresses itself are: Who benefits in the Soviet system from the upgrading of the Supreme Soviet? Who calls for the "strengthening" process? Who supports it? Why? How? What are the ramifications for Soviet society as a whole if the institutional equilibrium between Party and state is seriously disturbed as a result?

Since the fall of Malenkov in 1955, the leadership of the Soviet Union has expended much time and effort to activate every aspect of the Supreme Soviet. The Supreme Soviet has held more sessions, the sessions are longer; there are more deputies and more permanent commissions; the Supreme Soviet and its Presidium pass more laws, while the deputies are more energetic as ombudsmen and high officials of the CPSU apparatus seem more active in the Supreme Soviet and its associated bodies; the Supreme Soviet receives more publicity; more books and articles are written about it, and there even appears to be more vitality in the perfunctory atmosphere of the proceedings at Supreme Soviet sessions.

Despite all this activity, there is no comprehensive study of the evolution of the Supreme Soviet and its associated bodies, nor any analysis of the significance of this institutional evolution for the polity as a whole. Nor has there been an attempt to discern institutional antecedents in Russian and Soviet history which might provide insights into the present nature and future direction of this evolutionary process. Since institutional development in the Soviet polity is a fragile and tenuous process, always subject to arrest and even extinction, this description and analysis of the Supreme Soviet of necessity focuses on tendencies and directions of institutional evolution in an endeavor to make sense out of a highly fluid and evolving process. Arthur Bentley, in discussing the problems of describing and analyzing tendencies and directions in the governmental process, put it this way: "We have one great moving process to study and of this great moving process it is impossible to state any parts except as valued in terms of other parts."[2] The evolution of the Supreme Soviet is "one great moving process" in constant flux with no terminal stage in sight, incorporating many conflicting tendencies and directions. Nevertheless, some tendencies appear more salient than others and therefore deserve greater attention.

Previous interpretations and characterizations of the Supreme Soviet have run the gamut from non-Soviet appraisals of it as a mere facade for manipulating the populace to the exalted Soviet version of it as the institutional expression of the moral and political spirit of Soviet society. In his book on the organs of state power in the USSR, M. G. Kirichenko, a Soviet jurist, advanced the official Soviet characterization of the Supreme Soviet: "The Supreme Soviet of the USSR is the living embodiment of the moral and political unity of Soviet society. It expresses the united interests of all our people—workers, peasants and intelligentsia."[3]

In contrast to this glowing Soviet account is that of W. W. Kulski who flatly rejects all Soviet claims that the Supreme Soviet embodies any democratic practices and brands it a facade.[4] Derek Scott's interpretation is somewhat less harsh, but in the same vein; he dwells on the manner in which the sessions are completely staged by the Party *apparat.*[5] Merle Fainsod and John Hazard both argue that the staging is not so much for internal but for external consumption.[6] Their focus is primarily on the unveiling of the Constitution by Stalin in 1936, when his foreign policy required better relations with the democratic Western nations in view of the rise of Hitler. Undoubtedly, this democratic facade was one of Stalin's multiple motives for fostering the 1936 Soviet Constitution which created the Supreme Soviet.

A few Western scholars have interpreted the creation of the Supreme Soviet as the harbinger of parliamentary democracy in the Soviet Union. Sidney and Beatrice Webb were the most optimistic of these, although their view suffers from the fact that they saw no contradiction between the simultaneous conduct of the purges and the introduction of a "democratic" constitution.[7]

Another Western scholar, George Carson, in his analysis of the Soviet elections, envisioned a gradual evolution toward parliamentary democracy based on his conviction that involvement in democratic forms like the Supreme Soviet and the election system develops its own momentum.[8] The existence and extent of this momentum constitutes another thread running through this study.

Two other Western scholars writing two decades apart pointed without disparagement to the function of placing the stamp of legality on the decisions of the regime as the most important, although certainly limited, function of the Supreme Soviet. In 1947 Julian Towster described the Supreme Soviet as primarily a "ratifying and propagating body."[9] In other words, he viewed it as a representative body that confirms the policy of the leadership through a highly symbolic process which is widely publicized. An analysis of this symbolism and process also forms a part of this study. Writing in 1967, just as the system of permanent commissions was being expanded, Leonard Schapiro reached a conclusion similar to Towster's two decades before: "The Supreme Soviet is therefore at most a confirming body and can play little if any part as a sounding board for opinion in the country."[10]

While all of these interpretations of the Supreme Soviet are discussed when appropriate throughout this study, the central focus is on describing and analyzing the activation of the constitutional provisions relevant to the structure and functions of the Supreme Soviet, for as Vernon Aspaturian has warned:

> The possibility, no matter how remote it may appear at the moment, that ritual and ceremony may some day be replaced with substance should not be ignored. Lifeless legal bodies playing a ritualistic role sometimes come to life under certain conditions and circumstances.[11]

Underlying the description of the process of dormant legal forms coming to life is the question of the extent to which this evolutionary momentum derives from organic legal processes rather than political forces. Another student of the Supreme Soviet, Peter Juviler, writing in 1959, implicitly rejected the possibility of legal forms developing their own life independent of political forces when he concluded that "parliamentary forms will not in themselves generate pressure for parliamentary change."[12] A leading student of Soviet law, Harold Berman, has argued that the Russian-Soviet legal tradition is fundamentally distinguished from Western law by the former's lack of an organic, living tradition and by its apparently arbitrary, ad hoc qualities:

> Finally, the Western principle that law is a living, growing process, moving into the future with its eye on the past, though it made important strides, was never firmly established in prerevolutionary Russian legal development. . . . Above all, the polarity of Russian and Western history over the past thousand years poses the question of the relationship between the law way and other ways of ordering the affairs of society. The West has exalted law, with its principles of Reason, Conscience, and Growth; it has fostered the doctrines of the supremacy and completeness of law, its basis in equality, its organic continuity.[13]

Without denigrating the essential correctness of Berman's insight, this study seeks to identify some emerging characteristics of an organic legal system such as a typology and hierarchy of legal norms and a science of constitutional interpretation. The study asks to what extent a hierarchy of legal norms exists, and explores the theoretical position of legal acts of the Supreme Soviet in relation to acts of other state organs such as the Presidium, the Council of Ministers, the ministries, and state committees. It also attempts to classify joint acts of Party and state bodies in relation to legal acts of the Supreme Soviet. Even Soviet legal scholars are extremely reluctant to pursue the problem of classifying legal norms with meaningful precision, in all probability because of the potential political implications of such an exercise. As a consequence, the hierarchy synthesized herein represents perhaps the first comprehensive attempt at legal typology for the Soviet system in either Soviet or Western literature.[14]

Since the USSR Constitution stipulates that all state organs, including the Presidium of the Supreme Soviet, the Council of Ministers, and to a lesser extent the powerful Procuracy, are accountable to the Supreme Soviet in law, the analysis attempts to assess the extent and nature of this legal control in practice, which is again relevant to the theme of reviving relatively dormant legal forms. This involves an exploration of the distinctive and overlapping functions of the Supreme Soviet and other political organs, both in theory and practice.

The juridical debates surrounding the fleshing out of constitutional provisions relevant to the Supreme Soviet exacerbated a long-standing and fundamental tension between the organs of the Party, representing structures of ideological legitimacy, and the organs of the state, representing structures of legality. A central query here is to what extent the Party remains above the law; or, in other words, to what extent the evolution of the Supreme Soviet has impinged upon the Party's freedom from the restraints of law as expressed below by Andrei Vyshinksy:

> The dictatorship of the proletariat is authority unlimited by any statutes whatever. But the dictatorship of the proletariat creates its own laws and makes use of them, demands that they be observed, and punishes breach of them. Dictatorship of the proletariat does not signify anarchy and disorder, but, on the contrary, strict order and firm authority.[15]

If the Party's immunity from the law is gradually being circumscribed, then perhaps the dual system of what Berman termed law and unlaw is also being subtly altered, which would erode a substantial impediment to the development of an organic legal system.[16] A significant amelioration of the ad hoc, arbitrary quality of Soviet law would represent a fundamental break with both Russian and Soviet legal traditions and would perhaps portend a significant transformation in the polity.

Turning from juridical and theoretical concerns, the study analyzes the composition of the Supreme Soviet to determine who sits in it and who is represented in it, which involves contrasting the representative image that the regime attempts to project with the elitist composition in reality. Further on, the representation of groups in the Supreme Soviet is compared and contrasted with the representation of groups in the CPSU Central Committee in an effort to discern to what extent the Supreme Soviet might constitute an alternative arena separate and distinct from higher Party arenas. This involves an analysis of the evolution of the composition of the Supreme Soviet over time, and an analysis of the process of selecting deputies to the Supreme Soviet. Whether the changes in the composition of the Supreme Soviet reflect policy changes is also explored somewhat.

While the compositional pattern of the Supreme Soviet appears to be deliberately symbolic in order to enhance the legitimacy of the regime, whether the involvement of the populace in the activities of the Supreme Soviet and its associated bodies is meaningful in any significant sense is another question. Thus, an attempt is made to determine whether the different levels and kinds of involvement in the Supreme Soviet encourage participation in the governmental processes. In other words, does this involvement have the effect of socializing those involved to participate; does it induce a more positive attitude toward the regime, which also enhances its legitimacy? Or, on the other hand, is this involvement viewed as just another effort to manipulate the populace? Again, we confront the caveat that we are studying an ongoing process in its infancy and, therefore, we are analyzing tendencies and directions rather than terminal processes. A potentially important example of this ongoing evolution that is particularly relevant to the legitimating function of the Supreme Soviet is the tendency for deputies to perform an ombudsman function. This grievance-complaint function has been buttressed by a major draft law which outlines the rights and duties of deputies to all Soviets.

Although the individual deputy's role may soon be strengthened substantially, perhaps the major developments in the institutional evolution of the Supreme Soviet are the expansion of the activities and mechanisms of the Presidium of the Supreme Soviet and the system of permanent commissions of the Supreme Soviet, which this study analyzes and describes in detail in order to assess their impact on the relationship of the Supreme Soviet to other state organs and to the Party apparatus. Thus, there is an extended exploration of the overlapping and interlocking personnel in state and Party bodies, which supplements the more formalistic juridical-theoretical exegesis. The analysis also attempts to distinguish the executive, legislative, and judicial functions of the Supreme Soviet and its associated bodies from the roles and functions of other state bodies and, at the same time, it seeks to identify the overlapping areas of jurisdiction and competence among the various bodies. In particular, an effort is made to describe the role of the Supreme Soviet in the legislative process with respect to the various kinds of legal norms, which leads to an analysis of the evolution of the Supreme Soviet's expanded legislative activity and its impact on the polity as a whole.

Finally, the study proceeds to an extensive examination of the relationship between the Supreme Soviet and the CPSU in all its ramifications—theoretical, legal, and political. This involves an explanation of how the CPSU apparatus seeks to resolve the inherent tension and duality between itself as a structure of ideological legitimacy and the state, headed by the Supreme Soviet, as a structure of legality. This raises the question of how the CPSU apparatus controls the Supreme Soviet, which involves an analysis of their overlapping and interlocking membership, particularly in the most important official positions of the Supreme Soviet and its associated bodies. Lastly, the study of this relationship requires an explanation of the utility of the Supreme Soviet to the regime; in other words, why has the ruling elite activated the Supreme Soviet? This, of course, leads to an explanation of how various groups and factions within and outside of the Party apparatus might benefit from the expansion of the Supreme Soviet. Thus, the study turns from a descriptive analysis of how the Supreme Soviet has evolved to explore briefly what political forces have given momentum to its evolution, and to suggest some possible avenues of development within the juridical framework of the USSR Constitution and the more organic jurisprudence interpreting it.

While the study explores various avenues of analysis, it is primarily a descriptive study, since nowhere else has there been a clearly stated description of the Supreme Soviet which is, after all, the constitutional centerpiece of the Soviet juridical order. The expansion and activation of the Supreme Soviet's multiple structures and functions suggest that this institution which is the legal-constitutional source of all state power—executive, legislative and judicial—may be acquiring considerable importance in the context of Soviet politics, and thus a descriptive analysis of the Supreme Soviet is long overdue.

Chapter 1

THE RUSSIAN AND SOVIET INSTITUTIONAL HERITAGE

THE SUPREME SOVIET IN THE SOVIET
CONSTITUTIONAL ORDER: AN OVERVIEW

Before analyzing the institutional antecedents of the Supreme Soviet, a brief outline of its place in the Soviet constitutional order is appropriate.[1] It is the largest bicameral legislature in the world, with 1,517 deputies in the two combined chambers. One chamber, called the Soviet of the Union, is elected directly by the people from relatively equal districts, while the other, the Soviet of the Nationalities, is elected from the various federal and multinational units—union republics, autonomous republics, oblasts, and okrugs. Each chamber has a Chairman and four Vice-chairmen who preside over its sessions and coordinate its activities.

The composition of the Supreme Soviet virtually duplicates the social membership and the actual personnel of the Party, state, military, and economic bureaucracies. About two-thirds of each convocation (elected every four years) are new members with the continuity representing a core of the leadership of the regime. In one sense the Supreme Soviet is a forum of relatively prominent personages before which the regime airs its policies. By law two sessions of the Supreme Soviet are required per year, but only since 1966 has this been adhered to, and in any case sessions seldom last longer than five days.

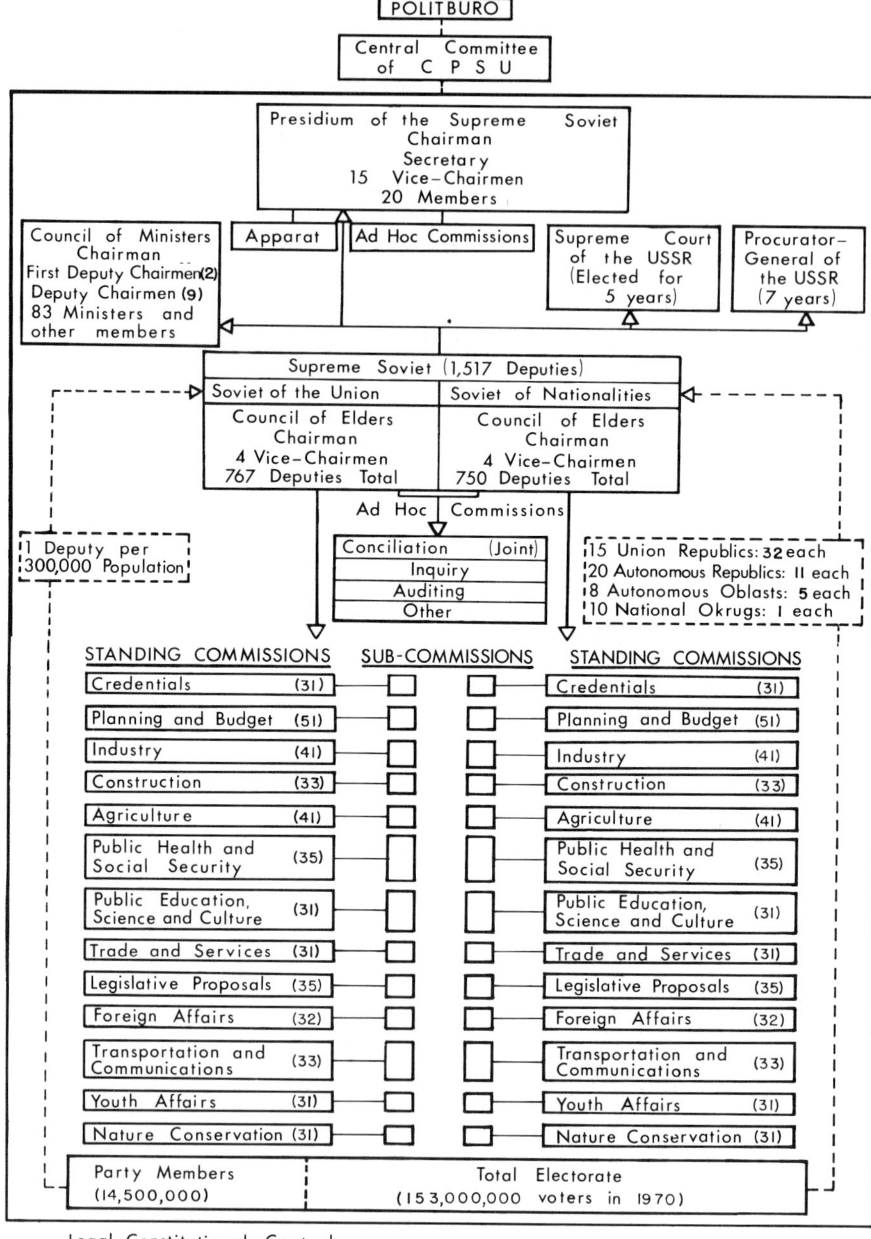

Figure 1.1: THE SUPREME SOVIET IN THE SOVIET CONSTITUTIONAL ORDER
Source: V. Aspaturian (1972) "The Soviet Constitutional Order," in Modern Political Systems: Europe, R. C. Macridis and R. E. Ward (eds.) 3rd ed. (Englewood Cliffs, N.J.: Prentice-Hall), as modified by author

Since the regime carefully controls elections to the Supreme Soviet, they do not serve the function of choosing a government, which, of course, mitigates the legitimacy of its act. Instead the elections serve to disseminate propaganda at home and abroad and, to some extent, to measure dissatisfaction with the regime and impart a sense of involvement; and perhaps they also tend to conjure up an image of legality and legitimacy.

Deputies are elected after highly publicized ceremonial "campaigns" where the leadership appears for speech-making. They are nominated at their place of work, and only one name appears on the ballot.

According to the Soviet Constitution, the Supreme Soviet appoints the government of the USSR, known as the Council of Ministers, many of whom sit in it, thus creating the superficial appearance of the classic parliamentary system with its principle of ministerial responsibility. The Supreme Soviet also elects the Supreme Court and appoints the Procurator General, who supervises the Soviet legal system.

The Supreme Soviet further elects its own Presidium which acts in the place of the Supreme Soviet when it is not in session. The precise demarcation of authority between the Supreme Soviet and its Presidium, both in theory and practice, is unclear, and the constitution itself appears to be deliberately ambiguous in this respect. While it is clear that the Presidium serves exclusively as the symbolic collective Head of State, and that the Supreme Soviet possesses the exclusive power to amend the constitution, the exact nature of their apparently concurrent legislative powers is the subject of debate, as is the extent of their respective authority over the twenty-six standing commissions of the Supreme Soviet.

Although authorized by the constitution in the late thirties, most of these specialized commissions have only recently (1967) been created, perhaps the most significant event in the history of the evolution of the Supreme Soviet. Their two chief functions are monitoring the state apparatus and assisting in the drafting of complex legislation, both important functions which have drawn them into the power struggle.

A somewhat secret body known as the Council of Elders seems to act as a sort of pre-sessional stage manager for Supreme Soviet sessions as well as a symbolic link with those authoritative figures of the Russian past, "the elders." It may, however, perform a more substantial role, since some effort is made to portray it as a representative body.

Legally the Soviet Constitution (Article 126) assigns the CPSU a mere "guiding" role in the Supreme Soviet, but in fact personnel of the higher Party organs (the Politburo and Central Committee) hold almost every official position in the Supreme Soviet and its Presidium. This overlapping and interlocking of personnel is the key to Party control of the Supreme Soviet. About two-thirds of the Supreme Soviet deputies are Communists, and approximately one-third are high Party and government officials who constitute an unchanging inner core reelected at each session (unlike the other two-thirds).

Since Party rules require Party members to support the instructions of higher Party organs, these higher Party organs in effect make the policy which is transformed into law by the Supreme Soviet. In a sense, the Supreme Soviet is a parliamentary system with one strong Party and with power in the hands of a strong extra-parliamentary Party.

It is becoming increasingly clear that the activation of the Supreme Soviet and its associated bodies is primarily motivated by the Party apparatus' interest in strengthening its hold over the somewhat recalcitrant State bureaucracy. The Supreme Soviet provides the Party with a new channel of "legal" supervision over the State bureaucracy supplementing the Party's "ideological" supervision. It provides an alternative legal norm-creating mechanism to the State bureaucracy's pervasive administrative regulations. And finally, in addition to ideological legitimacy imparted to the regime by the CPSU, the Supreme Soviet adds legality and some degree of political participation to the bases of the regime's legitimacy. With this general outline of the Supreme Soviet and its place in the Soviet political and constitutional order in mind, let us turn to explore some of its institutional predecessors.

THE TSARIST LEGISLATIVE HERITAGE

The institutional antecedents of the Supreme Soviet emanate from three generic sources in Russian-Soviet history—"old" Russia, the Western influence embodied in the nineteenth-century reform proposals which culminated in the Duma of 1905, and the revolutionary

tradition of workers' and peasants' councils, called soviets. An awareness of the Russian and Soviet concepts of state and law prior to the
promulgation of the present constitution facilitates a more balanced
view of the institutional origins of the Supreme Soviet.

In focusing on pre-revolutionary political institutions which resem-
ble legislatures, an attempt is made to avoid exaggerating their
importance within the polity, while at the same time presenting a
somewhat detailed portrait of the institutional forms. There are two
further purposes for the detailed treatment. The first is to assess the
significance of legislative forms in Russian history as one gauge
among many of the potential of that modern form, the Supreme
Soviet. The second is to set the stage for contrasting the roles of such
legislative forms at several stages of political development, especially
the pre-modern stage of the *Zemsky Sobor* and the modern stage of
the Supreme Soviet.

VECHES: THE EXTINCTION OF DIRECT DEMOCRACY IN MEDIEVAL RUSSIA

The first Russian assemblies, called Veches, emerged in the medieval Russian principalities such as Pskov and Novgorod as early as the
year 862. Although their forms and practices varied from principality
to principality, they were indigenous popular assemblies of free adult
male heads of household. Custom rather than law ordained that
either the prince or the people might call these town meetings where
decisions were arrived at by unanimous vote, taken orally without
secret ballot. The Veches were strong enough to force covenants
upon their princes which guaranteed certain rights, and resembled a
primitive institutional charter.[2]
First the Tartar invasions, then the Muscovite annexations extinguished this loose federation of medieval Russian principalities, ruled
to varying degrees by these popular assemblies. The absolutism and
administrative centralization of the period of Mongol domination
from the early thirteenth to late fourteenth centuries (the so-called
appanage period), the later Byzantine Cesaro-papism, and then of the
Muscovite princes, virtually expunged the idea that the legitimacy of
government derived to some extent from popular assemblies. The
Tsarist system was based on the principle that the security of
Muscovy required a strong centralized state headed by an absolute
prince whose legitimate authority derived from God rather than
popular sovereignty.

THE ZEMSKY SOBOR: THE ARRESTED EVOLUTION OF THE FIRST REPRESENTATIVE ASSEMBLIES

Analyzing the rise and demise of the Muscovite Zemsky Sobor (Assembly of the Land) provides some insight into the nature, role, and function of assemblies in the Russian context. The first of these representative assemblies was convened by Ivan IV in 1546. Other such gatherings met sporadically until 1613 when a Sobor elected the first Romanov Tsar. From 1613 to 1650 the Sobor met continually. Thereafter, it was convened infrequently until Peter the Great abolished it in 1700.[3]

Originally, the Tsar alone could convene the Sobor, which he did primarily to decide important issues of war or finance, or to mobilize support for crucial decisions. The composition of the Sobor was designed to meet these objectives. It was determined by custom and the will of the Tsar rather than by law. As a result, its form and composition varied considerably from time to time.

During the reign of Ivan IV the Sobor served as an arm of the Tsar, who gradually packed it with newly appointed supporters from the lesser nobility; these were given a small piece of land in return for supporting the Tsar against his external and internal enemies. From 1549 until the abolition of the Sobor, these appointed "gentry servitors" increased their strength at the expense of the landed nobility (boyars) in the Duma of Boyars. (Some confusion over the authority of the Zemsky Sobor stems from the fact that Ivan IV manipulated it to facilitate his rule—especially the gatherings of 1550 and 1566—while in 1613 it elected a Tsar). In general, the Sobor remained subservient to the Tsar, but when anarchy threatened, it played a considerable role in ruling Muscovy.[4] Conjuring up a kind of residual legitimacy, it proceeded to crown a new Tsar, thus instituting the Romanov dynasty.

Likewise the Supreme Soviet has always apparently served as an instrument of the regime; however, Vernon Aspaturian speculates that factional conflict may have spawned a resort to a kind of residual legitimacy in 1964: "Thus, Khrushchev, when confronted with a demand to resign, may have countered that, since he was accountable only to the Supreme Soviet as premier, that body should be convened, but constitutional niceties were swept away as his colleagues refused to provide him with a forum to override their decision."[5]

Ivan the Terrible in 1549 greatly strengthened the Zemsky Sobor to counterbalance the growing power of the boyars. Under his rule there were essentially three groups represented, which often met separately like the French Estates-General. They were the boyars (nobles), the clergy, and the gentry servitors of the Tsar. The power and influence of the first two groups declined under later Tsars.

In 1613 peasants attended the lower house as well as townspeople and delegates from the provinces. Representation in the lower house, was eventually based on two principles of representation—occupation and geography. Later assemblies of the Sobor were comprised primarily of lesser nobility, upper clergy, landed gentry, and some merchant elements. Later Tsars further increased the gentry servitors, an appointed element, who aided in the administration of the government and were rewarded for their services with small land grants.[6]

Not until the Time of Troubles (1584–1613) did this elective principle emerge. Then the Zemsky Sobor became the highest authority, electing a new Tsar in 1613 and meeting continuously during the first part of his reign. Thus, ironically, an institution designed to buttress the legitimacy of the Tsar ultimately offered the greatest threat to his authority by conjuring up a concept of residual legitimacy residing in the people when princely authority disintegrated.[7] It was this notion of residual legitimacy that the Slavophiles later idealized and exaggerated.[8]

Historians disagree on the scope of authority and power of the Zemsky Sobor in the Muscovite order of things. The Sobor reached its zenith under two circumstances: first, when internal political divisions threatened anarchy; and second, when foreign invasion threatened. This zenith of power and authority covered the twenty-nine year period of the Time of Troubles and the early part of the reign of Michael Romanov when he was consolidating his position.

During this time, the Sobor administered and ruled Muscovy, elected a new Tsar, codified existing Russian law in the Ulozhenie of 1649, decided questions of war and peace, and raised revenues. It had the earmarks of an embryonic parliament, but its evolution was arrested by Alexis, and its existence extinguished by Peter the Great.

The Sobor's authority never was buttressed by a constitution or a covenant with the prince as in the case of the Veches. In fact, the question of restricting the sovereign's authority never arose at its gatherings.[9]

A seat in the Zemsky Sobor represented primarily an obligation of service to the sovereign rather than a right and privilege restricting his authority.[10] The Cesaro-papism of the Orthodox Church plus the Tartar administrative tradition placed sovereignty in the Tsar and left little room for popular deliberation. For similar reasons neither a class of feudal barons nor an independent church emerged to hedge the power of the Tsar. Russia never developed the strong legal estates which buttressed the Estates-General against the French crown. The nobility was constantly divided by the principles of birthright and service, the clergy never enjoyed the high status of its Western counterpart, and the peasantry was enslaved by the Zemsky Sobor itself in the codification of 1649, the Ulozhenie which remained law until 1833. In this code, the lesser landed gentry, who controlled the Sobor, bound the peasants in serfdom tightly to the land, thus enlarging and protecting their most immediate economic interests.[11] In short, the Byzantine and Tartar traditions facilitated the Tsars' ability to manipulate society—a condition identified more recently in the Soviet era as a hallmark of totalitarianism.

The composition of the Sobor represented primarily an elite of landed gentry, and gradually it became a retrogressive force, resisting change, foreign trade, contacts with the West, and modernization in general.[12] A strong merchant class would have threatened the landed gentry's economic interests. No exceptionally strong merchant class emerged in Russia as it did in England to form the backbone of the Whigs who so fervently fostered parliamentary supremacy.

This resistance to the introduction of science and technology came to represent a threat to the security of the state in the eyes of Peter the Great who formally abolished the Sobor as an integral part of his Westernization program, which relied heavily on a new class of picked fellows whom he molded into a centralized civil service bent on modernizing Russia.

To retain some perspective, one must recall that when Peter the Great was touring seventeenth-century Europe, the process of modernization was taking its toll among European representative assemblies. For example, in 1614 the French Estates-General held its last meeting prior to the Revolution. After the Treaty of Westphalia (1648), the German Reichstag lost political importance, as did the Cortes of Aragon and Castile and the provincial diets of Hungary and Bohemia. What Peter saw was the decline of continental European legislatures in the face of modernizing monarchs.[13] Of course, the Polish Sejm and the English Parliament were exceptions to this rule.

In a sense, the Zemsky Sobor of 1649 served as the first codification commission in Russian history. Foreign incursions into Russia had retarded the gradual evolution of an organic legal system such as England's while simultaneously fostering a more arbitrary, capricious rule by strong-willed leaders. Codification represented an attempt to ameliorate the mercurial nature of the polity by providing some rudimentary personal security in legal norms. Thus it sought to mitigate not only the Tsar's caprice, but also the intermittent popular upheavals stemming from reactions to his arbitrary rule.

Codification did not serve as a vehicle of modernization either except by providing a degree of stability. For example, serfdom might be viewed as a modernizing step in offering a source of manpower for the army. Generally, however, an awareness of the utility of law and codification as a positive instrument of modernization grew very slowly in Russia. Thus codifying efforts of the Sobor bear the earmarks of much that became characteristic in Russian law and legislation.

The significance of the Zemsky Sobor for this study is twofold: it was functionally conservative in most respects, but in exercising a kind of residual legitimacy it suggested the radical potential of legislative assemblies in the Russian context. In fact by the late seventeenth century it emerged as a rather conservative force representing the elites of the time, despite Slavophiles' idealizations to the contrary. It represented the forces of order and consolidation, not the forces of radical change. Its chief functions were consultation, mobilization, and codification and, to a very small extent, amelioration of grievances.[14]

The Zemsky Sobor did implicitly embody the concept of residual legitimacy residing in a legislative body. It was for this communal spirit of the people (*Sobornost*), allegedly embodied in and expressed through a representative assembly, that the Slavophiles yearned. It was this notion of residual legitimacy that came to challenge the authority of the Tsar, who originally created the Zemsky Sobor as his own instrument of rule. Whether a similar idea embodied in the Supreme Soviet could seriously present an alternative to the CPSU is a question for the future. Suffice it to say that this sense of residual legitimacy has persisted under various guises throughout Russian-Soviet history.

The conscious historical-intellectual links between the Sobor and the Supreme Soviet remain implicit rather than explicit. One can, of course, cite Stalin's well-known penchant for emulating the "creator" of the Sobor Ivan IV and also the place of Herzen, an idealizer of the Sobor, in the Soviet hagiography. Nevertheless, to what extent the Supreme Soviet might evolve as the Sobor must remain somewhat speculative.

THE RUSSIAN EMPIRE'S FIRST REPRESENTATIVE ASSEMBLY

The Russian Empire's first representative assembly, the National State Duma, was born out of war (the Russo-Japanese War) and internal political division (the Revolution of 1905)—which prompted Nicholas II to call the Duma, as Ivan the Terrible had assembled the Zemsky Sobor in somewhat similar circumstances.[15] The significance of the Duma in Russian history has been much debated. Since these debates and discussions are beyond the scope of this study, only a few selective aspects of its abortive career commend themselves.

The lack of parliamentary experience among the deputies, and the obstructive revolutionary mission of some parties, subverted the Duma from within and rendered it malleable to the Tsar's ministers. While the Constitutional Democrats remained the only party dedicated to creating a working parliament, the parties of the right and left sought to destroy the parliament for various reasons.

Nevertheless, the Second Duma groped toward developing two important devices of parliamentary power—specialized committees, and the right to invite experts to advise on legislative matters. One leading authority on the Duma argues that the Tsar curbed the Second Duma precisely at the time when these devices began to accumulate real power for the Duma.[16]

The implication of the Duma experience is that even without clear ministerial responsibility, without any notion of popular sovereignty, without viable parliamentary parties, and under all the formal structural restraints in the Russian political culture, a representative assembly buttressed by specialized committees and access to technical expertise can accumulate significant power and thereby plant the kernel of a potentially viable parliament. This assumes particular relevance in light of the fact that the Supreme Soviet has recently acquired through formal juridical acts a system of specialized commissions composed substantially of experts.

THE SPIRIT OF RUSSIAN LEGISLATION

Since the Supreme Soviet as supreme organ of Soviet state power is the primary instrument for converting political decisions into the fundamental law, called *zakon,* an examination of the nature and spirit of the zakon in Russian history appears relevant.[17] Russian law has never been a gradual emanation from custom or sociological fact. It is primarily the inorganic quality and spirit of Russian law which distinguish it from Anglo-Saxon tradition, the model of which is Great Britain and, to a lesser extent, the United States. Though Russian law was to some extent a civil law system, it is distinguished from the Western civil law tradition by a relative absence of the rule of law—that is, the equal, rational, non-arbitrary application of legal norms.[18]

Russian law took two basic forms: the decree of the Tsar (*ukaz*) and the more fundamental law or zakon. Both ukaz and zakon reflect the Roman concept of law as legislation. However, the Roman concept included the notion that law derived from popular consent, as expressed and ratified by the Roman Senate and other bodies representing the enfranchised citizenry. Russian reform proposals embodied the concept of a formal process of creating law through a ratifying body such as a representative assembly, but excluded the notion that its source was popular consent. The source of Russian law always remained the Tsar, the interpreter and voice of divine law. Thus, Russian law always carried with it the notion of law as a detailed reflection of an official messianic orthodoxy.

Tartar practice instilled the notion of law as the edict or command of the sovereign, requiring no further ratification but rather immediate obedience. The ukaz reflects Tartar influence. The ukaz became the intermittent, ad hoc rule or norm concerned primarily with details of administration rather than fundamental principles or social policy.

Throughout Russian history, the ukaz, because of its ease of promulgation, proliferated, lending an arbitrary, capricious quality to Russian law which the Tsars periodically sought to ameliorate by codifying the ukaz. These attempts to systematize law usually degenerated into a massive writing down of every ukaz which, in an illiterate society often under censorship and dominated by a huge bureaucracy, seldom led to any appreciable increase in the rule of law. Nevertheless, the very existence of codes, or zakon, further publicized and disseminated the notion that a more important kind of law existed than the imperial edict or ukaz.

The nineteenth-century reformers injected into the Russian legal tradition the Enlightenment concept of law as a rational code of fundamental principles designed to improve the welfare of the people. When coupled with Peter the Great's ideal of the Tsar as servant of the people, this principle conjured up the view of law as a positive instrument of the Tsar—not a restraint upon him—for the purpose, in theory at least, of improving the lot of his subjects.

While in the West, where highly developed organic legal systems had already emerged, the rational precept of the Enlightenment had the effect of reducing arbitrary, ad hoc tendencies of increasingly rigid legal systems, the rational principle introduced into a retarded, inorganic system such as that of imperial Russia made it more rigid.

In summarizing the spirit of the Russian legal tradition, one must recall that it developed in an ad hoc, inorganic fashion as an adjunct of administration. The source of Russian law was neither popular consent nor the evolution of custom, but the decree of the Tsar. The two formal mechanisms for creating law were edicts of the Tsar, and codification commissions which merely published vast comprehensive compendiums of previous ukazes. To a very minor extent, these codes served to rationalize the legal system, but the continuing proliferation of the ukaz and bureaucratic inflexibility thwarted both better coordination of government and amelioration of the arbitrary, ad hoc quality of Russian law.

THE DEVELOPMENT OF THE SOVIETS

THE SOVIETS AT THE MATRIX OF THE BOLSHEVIK CONCEPTS OF STATE, LAW, AND LEGISLATURES

Turning now to the soviet tradition, let us examine the origins and early functioning of the system of soviets. The soviets emanated from three revolutions, the Paris rising of 1871 and its famous Commune, and the Russian Revolutions of 1905 and February 1917. Thus, like their antecedent assemblies, the Zemsky Sobor and the State Duma, the soviets emerged, thrived, and reached the zenith of their power under conditions of war and internal strife. As these conditions disappeared, so did much of the influence of these councils.

The soviets emerged spontaneously, not as the result of any preconceived plan or ideology. Both Marx's and Lenin's concept of the dictatorship of the proletariat remained without a precise institutional focus until they discovered in the Paris Commune and in the soviets an institutional device to usher in and administer the socialist state.[19] Marx and Lenin adopted the soviets as the institutional form of the dictatorship of the proletariat.

The spontaneous origins of the soviets in the 1905 Revolution reflects their anti-bureaucratic character. They were a sophisticated reaction to that bureaucratic wall between Tsar and people which stifled nineteenth-century attempts to endow Russia with political institutions capable of modernizing the state. Composed largely of workers in the major cities, they sought primarily economic gains and only resorted to violence as a last resort.[20] They were led by Mensheviks whose credo, true to Marx, envisioned a bourgeois state as a predecessor to the socialist one. In 1905 the Bolsheviks' interest in the soviets was minimal and belated.

In 1917, after the February Revolution, substantial power passed from the Provisional Government to the soviets, which assumed an antiparliamentary character. The soviets were antiparliamentary in many senses. Parliamentarianism in the Duma and among the nineteenth-century liberal reformers had resulted in deliberation and delay. Deliberation took on the aspect of another bureaucratic tactic to foil the aspirations of the masses. Thus, deliberation was impugned by the Bolsheviks, who called for direct action. Legislating and executing on the spot without debate or delay reflected the spirit of the early concept of soviets.

Antiparliamentarism also meant rejection of any theory of checks and balances or divisions of government along functional lines as a means for regulating clashes of interest within society. After all, Bolshevism in 1917 foresaw the immediate triumph of one class, the proletariat. That class would rule directly. It would both legislate and administer. There would be no distinction between legislative and executive functions.

Lenin, who was, of course, a Russian lawyer, saw in the soviets a sort of direct democracy not unlike the spirit of the old Veches in the sense that legislation through the soviets took on the character of direct popular initiative. Even representative democracy was denigrated as bourgeois. Lenin's utopian faith in the people's initiative is reflected in the organization of the soviets. The higher soviets were elected from the lower ones, thus preserving the image of direct popular initiative even in the higher soviets.[21]

The concept of the amateur-deputy to the higher soviets, loudly trumpeted until recently, derives from the original notion of the soviets as spontaneous councils of workers legislating and executing laws to meet their needs and then returning to their manual chores.

The contrast between this legislator and the eloquent, bedecked, and bewigged British member of Parliament appears to be direct and deliberate.

In sum, the Bolshevik concept of soviets was distinctive in form and content. It was proletarian in content and in form was a reaction to Western bourgeois parliamentarism and to Russia's endemic bureaucratization. It was a reaction against parliamentary deliberation and debate, which appeared to be another of Russia's seemingly interminable excuses for delaying reform. The soviets emerged in time of war and internal political division. Unlike their predecessor assembly, the State Duma, but like the old Veches and Zemsky Sobor, the soviets possessed substantial power.

THE SOVIETS AS SYMBOL AND TACTICAL WEAPON

When Lenin confronted the task of administering the largest state in the world and thus of spelling out in detail the daily functions of the soviets vis-à-vis the other political organs, such as the Council of People's Commissars (henceforth *Sovnarkom*) and the Party itself, he began to view the soviets as a school of self-administration rather than as a tactical weapon to seize power. One must recall that this view evolved amidst both a major international war and a brutal, multifaceted civil war. Thus, in the onrush of events Lenin's functional conceptualization did not necessarily conform to the actual reality of institutional evolution; that is, the soviets for some time were more than a mere tool of the Party.

The Bolshevik vision, of course, foresaw the withering away of the socialist state as the masses became imbued with the ethic of giving from each according to his ability to each according to his needs. An important function of the Party was to eradicate those classes—the bourgeois in particular—who opposed this revolutionary course.[22]

While in the Civil War the Party focused on the negative function of eliminating its class opposition, Lenin clearly envisioned the soviets as a major instrument of preparing the masses for the withering away of the state. In effect, by participating in the soviets the masses would learn to actually administer the state. The soviets would habituate the Russian populace, which heretofore had such a dearth of self-governing experience, to govern themselves and eventually to become so imbued with the Marxist ethic that formal institutional state structures would cease to exist. The superstructure would and should cease to exist because resistance to its ends had vanished.

Naturally, this utopia did not materialize and, in theory at least, the Soviet Union is still in the transition stage from socialism to communism. The important role in this transition process assigned to the soviets by Lenin has received lip service continually in Soviet history and constitutes a major theoretical bulwark of the aura of legitimacy surrounding the pyramid of soviets, capped by the Supreme Soviet.

THE SOVIETS AS INSTRUMENTS OF SOCIALIZATION

Gradually, as the Party consolidated its power through the Sovnarkom, it converted the functions of the soviets (in the ideological guise of teaching the masses self-government) into socializing and public-opinion sampling organs. Stalin eventually saw the soviets as just one instrument among many for manipulating the masses, a hollow shell to be converted to whatever purpose suited the Party and ultimately Stalin himself. In Stalin's own words:

> The soviets are only a *form* of organization—true enough, a socialist form, but only a *form* of organization for all that. Everything depends upon the *content* that is put into this form. We know of cases when soviets . . . for a certain time supported the counter-revolution against the revolution. . . . Hence, it is not only a matter of soviets as a form. . . . It is primarily a matter of the content of the work in the soviets; it is a matter of the character of the work of the soviets; it is a matter of who leads the soviets. . . . We must assume that the anti-soviet elements take all this into account . . . and use these as a screen for their underground organizations. . . . The soviets, taken as a form of organization, are a weapon and a weapon only. Under certain conditions this weapon may be turned against the revolution. . . . It all depends upon who wields this weapon and against whom it is directed.[23]

Socializing meant imbuing the participants in the soviets with Bolshevik values, ideology and methods. It became a major function of the soviets. Socialization is a long-range process of instilling fundamentally new attitudes, as distinct from mobilization which envisions harnessing public energies for the more immediate, less essential shifts of policy and tactics for which Lenin first adopted the soviets.

THE SOVIETS AS BAROMETERS OF PUBLIC OPINION

Gradually, as the Civil War subsided and Stalin emerged, the Party grew to appreciate the soviets as barometers of public opinion, as instruments through which the Party could listen to public sentiment and then determine to what degree it must be satisfied and to what degree it must be refashioned. In a sense, the soviets served the Party as the nineteenth-century reformers hoped their proposals would serve the Tsar, as a bridge across which the people could transmit information concerning their wants and needs—in other words, as a vital informational policy input into the decision-making, as a conduit through the murky bureaucracy to the supreme authority. Formally the soviets appeared to fulfill a major revolutionary demand. One might view the socializing and barometer functions as informational inputs and outputs from the decision-making organ.[24]

THE STRUCTURE AND FUNCTIONING OF
THE SOVIET PYRAMID TO 1936

The Constitution of 1918 regularized and formalized institutions which had emerged under revolutionary conditions and which then confronted the task of governing under civil war conditions. Supreme power was formally vested in an All-Russian Congress of Soviets, composed of representatives of city soviets on the basis of one deputy for every 125,000 inhabitants. The Congress elected the All-Russian Central Executive Committee (CEC), a body of not more than 200 members, which exercised all powers of the Congress when the Congress was not in session. The CEC appointed the Council of People's Commissars or Sovnarkom, whose function was the general administration of the affairs of the Russian Soviet Federated Socialist Republic but extended also to the issuing of decrees according to the Constitution.

When the Bolsheviks took power on November 7, 1917, there was no Presidium of the CEC. Its existence was later recognized in Party and Congress announcements and finally formalized in the Constitution of 1922. The CEC established a small unofficial body of seven or eight persons soon after the Bolshevik seizure of power; however, its duties were not mentioned among the organs of power in the 1918 Constitution.[25]

A brief review of the highlights of the birth and functioning of the CEC and the Congresses prior to the 1918 Constitution illuminates the process of institutional evolution in the Soviet Union and the origins of the Supreme Soviet.

The soviets sprang up in the major cities as revolutionary councils of workers controlled largely by Mensheviks. Although they held substantial independent power, they continued to cooperate with the Provisional Government. In his April Theses, Lenin called for the soviets to take power and rejected cooperation with the Provisional Government.[26] It is important to note that in Lenin's mind, the soviets were clearly extra-legal bodies. Their legitimacy derived from direct popular initiative, not from law enacted by some formal legislative mechanism.[27]

After the Party's April Conference, it worked to transfer all power to the soviets and to achieve Bolshevik majorities in them. Soon thereafter, a conference of Petrograd factory workers in May yielded a Bolshevik majority. At the First All-Russian Congress of Soviets in June 1917 Lenin asserted that the Bolsheviks, as distinguished from any other party, were prepared to take power.[28]

The Congress was composed of delegates from the city soviets representing all parties. It elected a CEC whose decisions would be binding on all soviets in the intervals between Congresses, thus centralizing the power which had emanated from decentralized sources—that is, the cities. Each party held the same proportion of seats in the CEC as it held in the Congress. After the attempted military coup by Kornilov in August 1917, the Bolsheviks secured majorities in the Petrograd and Moscow soviets, though the Socialist Revolutionaries (a radical peasant party) and Mensheviks controlled the CEC.

By late November 1917, the CEC had become a center of some state power in which the Bolsheviks had formed a coalition to maintain control. The elections to the Constituent Assembly followed, yielding a majority which threatened Bolshevik rule. Well aware of this, the by now Bolshevik-controlled CEC summoned the Third All-Russian Congress of Soviets to torpedo the Constituent Assembly.

The CEC, guided by its Bolshevik leadership, directed the campaign to eradicate the Constituent Assembly. Sverdlov opened the Assembly in the name of the CEC and presented a resolution drafted by the CEC which amounted to an abdication of power by the Assembly to the soviets. The Assembly never met after debating this resolution and the CEC decreed its dissolution the next day. Thus, when the Third All-Russian Congress of Soviets met shortly thereafter, it naturally succeeded as heir to the Constituent Assembly. It confirmed the CEC resolution vesting power in the soviets and instructed the CEC to draft what became the Constitution of 1918.[29]

THE CONGRESS OF SOVIETS

The 1918 and 1922 Constitutions formally designated the Congress of Soviets as the supreme state authority. It appears to have been a continuously operating constituent assembly rather than a legislature like the CEC. Through time the number of its delegates rose substantially, thus rendering it unwieldly as a deliberative parliamentary body; however, until 1919 there were non-Bolshevik members in it and debates were often sharp. In fact, it never exercised its authority in many areas within its competence. In foreign affairs it was used primarily as a propaganda forum from which the Sovnarkom could make pronouncements to foreign powers and the Soviet masses. The Supreme Soviet serves the same function today. The early functions of the Congresses consisted in ratifying and propagating policy of the Party and the CEC or the Sovnarkom with respect to consolidating the regime (in the early period) and economic problems (in the late twenties and early thirties). As Stalin rose to power its significance and frequency of convocation fell, although the number of participants in debate increased, more to vindicate than contest Party policy.

THE CENTRAL EXECUTIVE COMMITTEE

From the experience of the bicameral Central Executive Committee comes much of the formal structural-functional pattern of the Supreme Soviet and its auxiliary bodies. The CEC passed through considerable metamorphoses from its inception in June 1917 to its extinction by the Stalin Constitution in 1936. Its struggles with the Sovnarkom will be discussed further. What follows is a short review of the formal structures and functions assigned to it by the 1918 and 1924 Constitutions.

The CEC was conceived of as the supreme organ of state power in periods between the meetings of the Congress of Soviets. It was functionally both legislative and executive. Its membership rose from 200 to 386 to 751, then declined slightly to 509 at its last convocation in 1935. As its power declined, so did the frequency and length of its sessions. Until 1927 CEC members received remuneration for their work, but after that they were allowed to earn only what they could have earned at work, plus free rail and river travel, thus moving further away from the professional parliamentarian concept toward the amateur-deputy concept, which lies at the core of the unified executive-legislative working assembly concept of the soviet assemblies and which buttresses their legitimacy.[30]

Most of the CEC membership consisted of people from the localities—local soviet deputies. Unlike the Supreme Soviet commission systems for which it served as a partial model, the CEC permitted government (Sovnarkom) officials to serve on it. A "Council of Elders," a sort of steering committee of Bolsheviks, helped select CEC members to assure representation of women, workers and peasants, and all parts of the Union.[31]

The CEC had the right to form committees, both temporary and permanent, to aid it in its legislative work. On paper it had extraordinary supervisory power over its own Presidium, the Sovnarkom, local soviets, and the Supreme Court, all of which gradually atrophied with the rise of the Sovnarkom and the Party.

In short, the CEC exercised some power in its early days and possessed vast formal powers on paper, powers which dissipated over time to other bodies. From 1931 on, its proceedings exhibited complete unanimity. Henceforth, like the Congress of Soviets, it acted primarily as a policy-ratifying and propagating body.

THE PRESIDIUM OF THE CEC

The Presidium of the Central Executive Committee constitutes another example of a powerful political institution whose structures and functions fully emerged prior to its sanctification by legal instruments. The CEC created it shortly after the October Revolution to prepare materials for its sessions and to supervise its commissions. An unofficial body of seven or eight, its membership rose to fifteen in 1921 and finally to twenty-seven. It soon achieved the not insubstantial power of editing CEC decrees. It also reportedly determined the composition of the first constitutional commission.[32]

The Eighth All-Russian Congress formally granted it the power to annul decisions of the Sovnarkom and also to issue decrees in the name of the CEC.[33] In May 1921 the CEC also assigned the Presidium the role of supervising the local soviets. In this role the Presidium investigated conditions in the localities and resolved conflicts between central institutions and local organs. It was the government's chief source of information on local sentiment. The Presidium also supervised the permanent commissions of the CEC. The Ninth All-Russian Congress of Soviets in December 1921 provided that members of the Presidium should serve as chairmen of these commissions.

The legislative authority of the CEC and its Presidium was never precisely demarcated. While some Soviet jurists pointed to the CEC's power to veto Presidium decrees, others noted the Presidium's authority rested on the criteria of urgency and importance, such authority being almost unlimited for the former but more restricted for the latter. The exact limits were never specified.

Although the Constitution of 1918 barely mentioned the Presidium, and the Constitution of 1924 listed only the Congress of Soviets and the Central Executive Committee as the supreme organs of power, its functions as enumerated, plus its small, manageable size, frequency of sessions, and prestigious membership rendered it the most powerful body vis-à-vis the Congress of Soviets or the CEC, although not the Sovnarkom or the Party. Its relation to the latter two institutions is explored next.

THE RISE OF THE SOVNARKOM

The contest for political-institutional power between the Sovnarkom (Council of People's Commissars) and the Central Executive Committee further illuminates the process of institutional evolution in the Soviet Union. Since the two bodies are the precursors of the Council of Ministers and the Supreme Soviet, an examination of this contest peculiarly lends itself to this study.

The decree creating the Sovnarkom granted control over it to the CEC. Four days thereafter, the Sovnarkom declared that the CEC "has a right at any time to suspend, modify, or annul any decision of the government." Since the CEC had existed and functioned since June, this early deference appeared natural, but encroachment soon commenced.

On November 17, 1917, the CEC itself stated that "the Soviet Parliament [that is, the Central Executive Committee] cannot deny the Sovnarkom the right to issue decrees of immediate necessity in the spirit of the general program of the All-Russian Congress of Soviets without first submitting them to the Central Executive Committee."[34] The use of the words "Soviet Parliament" reflects the powerful non-Bolshevik influence remaining in the CEC. The Mensheviks in the CEC favored a traditional separation of powers along bourgeois lines in order to preserve their influence. For them, the CEC most nearly approximated a parliament and the Sovnarkom a rudimentary cabinet. This notion lingered as late as March-April 1922 at the Eleventh Party Congress, when Lenin rejected Osinsky's proposal to create a "cabinet system," concentrating the legislative function exclusively in the CEC, with the cabinet function residing in the Sovnarkom.

The early efforts (November 1917) to strengthen the CEC vis-à-vis the Sovnarkom, composed of the major Bolshevik figures led by Lenin, represented a challenge to the Bolshevik control of the polity. The Mensheviks in the CEC were attempting to shift the decision-making process to an arena where their influence was significant. On the other hand, a proposal by one Osinsky was an effort by a faction of Bolshevik leaders, the Democratic Centrists, to acquire more influence in the decision-making process by strengthening the CEC.[35] As we shall see, the use of different institutional arenas by factions within the Party to enhance their influence persists. This tactic of attempting to shift at least increments of the decision-making process to various institutional arenas has influenced the evolution of the Supreme Soviet in a multiplicity of ways.

The early recognition of the Sovnarkom's right to issue decrees (*postanovlenie*) without previous CEC discussion opened the floodgates, especially under the dire necessity of civil war. By 1925 the pattern was well established, with the Sovnarkom enacting the major part of the legislation. Apparently, the CEC quickly recognized its error. Complaints concerning the Sovnarkom's abuse of its legislative authority pervaded every CEC session in November and December 1917. Within two weeks of its delegation of legislative authority, the CEC sought to remedy the situation by passing a new resolution attempting to clarify its position. The resolution called for each Sovnarkom commission to account weekly to the CEC.[36] It further granted the CEC the right of interpellation, which had proved so dangerous to the government of Stolypin in the hands of the Duma. This interpellation required immediate replies. Finally, the resolution specified the content of the legislative authority delegated to the Sovnarkom. The Sovnarkom could adopt measures against counter-revolution without reference to the CEC, but "all legislative acts and ordinances of major political importance must be submitted to the Central Executive Committee for confirmation."[37]

In civil war conditions, the breadth of the legitimate definition of counter-revolutionary measures could be considerable. The loophole remained.

Little came of the accounting and control provisions of the CEC resolution. The power of interpellation, which is primarily a negative power, served to strengthen the CEC very little where circumstances called for immediate decisive action. Oral interpellations so customary in Western parliaments never found their way into Soviet practice. Delegates of the Congress of Soviets could submit written inquiries to the Presidium of the CEC at the end of a session, and the Presidium, at its discretion, would determine whether or not to make them public, thus circumventing the CEC. However, interpellations signed by 100 or more delegates had to be announced by the Presidium immediately, although no debate on them was permitted. These devices reflected the Party's growing power in the Congress of Soviets and the Presidium of the CEC which gradually whittled away the impact of the procedural right of interpellation. These maneuvers exemplify the gradual emasculation of the CEC by the Party and the Sovnarkom.

The text of the 1918 Constitution reflected the Sovnarkom-CEC dispute but did little to resolve it. The CEC remained formally the supreme legislative and administrative body in the state.

Shortly after the Constitution went into effect, the CEC's military and peasantry commissions were fused with the relevant commissariats. These specialized working technical arms, which might have become the germs of a powerful supervisory institution vis-à-vis the Sovnarkom, were converted by the Sovnarkom to its own use, thus facilitating its acquisitions of institutional power. The Constitution of 1924 perpetuated the facade of supreme power residing in the Central Executive Committee, although by then most of its power had actually passed to other bodies.

THE PRESIDIUM OF THE CEC AND THE SOVNARKOM

The gradual evolution of the Presidium of the Central Executive Committee and the Sovnarkom confused even contemporary jurists and observers. The role of both institutions in performing both legislative and executive functions was especially confusing. It was argued that the Presidium was the government and the Sovnarkom a managing department, or that a diarchy or bicameral system was emerging without a functional differentiation. Professor M. A. Reisner likened the Presidium to the old Tsarist Senate or State Council as the guardian of legality. Professor Engel saw the Presidium as possessing higher legislative authority than the Sovnarkom, but lower than the CEC. Professor Gurvich saw both the Presidium and the Sovnarkom as dependent auxiliary bodies of the CEC, with the Sovnarkom specializing in administration and the Presidium in legislation.[38]

Some observers were substantially misled by the formal juridical acts. Webb saw the Presidium as the most influential organ under the Constitution (1924). Batsell saw it as the real source of constitutional authority, dominating the Sovnarkom. He also argued that the Congress of Soviets and the CEC acted only on matters already decided by the Presidium of the CEC. Against this, of course, stands the fact that the Sovnarkom served as the initial source of most major legislation passed by any of the three organs in the soviet pyramid, and that the Sovnarkom passed much legislation without even seeking soviet ratification under its urgency authority.[39]

The locus of legislative authority was also the subject of much debate. No precise formulations as to the jurisdictional limits of each organ's legislative competence appeared. However, it was widely argued that the Presidium's legislative prerogatives were limited by the CEC's ultimate veto power—a rather specious argument adopted by legal scholars in the 1960s when a similar dispute arose over the legislative authority of the Supreme Soviet vis-à-vis its Presidium.[40]

One authority from a juridical, but not political, view came closest to reality when he asserted that importance and urgency constituted the criteria establishing the locus of legislative authority. In the early days, power to act on *important* legislation rested with the Congress of Soviets, the Central Executive Committee, the CEC's Presidium, and the Sovnarkom, in that order, while the power to act on *urgent* legislation rested with the same organs in the opposite order.

From the point of view of real political power, the Party soon made it quite clear that the CEC's authority over the Sovnarkom, composed of the Bolsheviks' highest leadership including Lenin himself, was more formal than real. The Party thwarted an attempt to make the Rabkrin's predecessor a department of the CEC rather than a commissariat of the Sovnarkom. This represented a fundamental blow to the CEC, for Lenin until his last days regarded the Rabkrin as an alternative weapon for combating bureaucracy.[41]

The Party also forced the CEC to include the appropriate Sovnarkom representatives on the commissions dealing with the CEC's agenda problems. In contrast, the 1967 statute governing the commissions of the Supreme Soviet specifically seeks to forbid such interlocking between the Supreme Soviet commissions and the Council of Ministers.

When the Presidium of the CEC objected to the encroachments on its power, the Party Central Committee replied:

> The comrades will perhaps point out that by the resolution of the Seventh Congress of Soviets the Presidium C.E.C. was given the right to confirm certain decisions of the Sovnarkom and suspend the execution of others in the name of the C.E.C. Quite right. [But] exceptional cases were envisioned here, [cases] where the Central Committee of our party, which controls and directs the work of the [Soviet] organs, comes to the conclusion that on account of its importance this or that decree should have been passed by the C.E.C., the plenum of which could not be convoked in time for technical reasons. . . . When a given decision of the Sovnarkom must be annulled or suspended, the Central Committee does it through the Presidium of the C.E.C. Therein lies the fundamental aim of the above right of confirmation and suspension, and not in any independent [power of] decreeing concerning decisions of the Sovnarkom given the Presidium C.E.C. by the Seventh Congress.[42]

This illustrates the Party's increasing manipulation of the several organs of state and government for its own purposes, as well as its increasing preference for the Sovnarkom as an instrument of legislation and administration. Perhaps this preference is being reversed today.

In summary, one discerns in the institutional power struggle following the Bolshevik Revolution several themes especially relevant to analyzing the evolution of the Supreme Soviet. Most obvious is the multiplicity of institutional forms in the polity. Their structures and functions as well as their relations to each other remained fluid and volatile throughout this period, a general pattern inherited from Tsarist days, but especially exaggerated in this period of civil war.

Second is the pattern of emerging informal organs with real power, existing simultaneously with organs formally sanctioned by juridical instruments—such as the soviets and CEC before the Revolution, and the CEC and its Presidium up to 1924. Thus, the actual legal (de jure) creation of political institutions by constitution, decree, zakon, or whatever, appeared to follow the de facto emergence and functioning of such institutions, occasionally by years.

Third, where genuine struggles for power between institutions exist, formal legal tests seldom appear to resolve the contest, which continues behind the scenes usually within the higher Party organs.

Finally, the soviets have derived considerable legitimacy from Lenin's endorsement of them as agents for inculcating Bolshevik values and attitudes, a sort of socialization for the utopian withering away of the state. They also appear to have retained their anti-parliamentary and antibureaucratic character.

THE SUPREME SOVIET AS THE CONSTITUTIONAL CENTERPIECE OF THE SOVIET JURIDICAL ORDER

If the multi-dimensional complex of juridical-theoretical forms and institutional systems allegedly accountable to the Supreme Soviet ever acquired a vigorous life from what is now a multiplicity of mere trappings, the Supreme Soviet would dominate the Soviet polity.

The Soviet literature on state and law theory is voluminous, overlapping, vague, and contradictory. Nevertheless, an effort is made here to illuminate the central thrust of this literature in order to identify the juridical-theoretical trappings relevant to the Supreme Soviet's evolution that might acquire substance with the passage of time.

THE BASES OF THE SUPREME SOVIET'S AUTHORITY

Article 30

The highest organ of state power in the USSR is the Supreme Soviet of the USSR.

Article 32

The legislative power of the USSR is exercised exclusively by the Supreme Soviet of the USSR.[1]

These provisions of the Soviet Constitution establish the juridical basis for the Supreme Soviet's authority over the entire system of state and law in the USSR. They identify the Supreme Soviet as both the head of the Soviet state and the chief lawmaker therein. This places it at the pinnacle of a system of institutions identified as "state" organs. It also provides the juridical foundation for the supremacy of Supreme Soviet enactments over a vast, complex hierarchy of legal norms.

Article 1

The Union of Soviet Socialist Republics is a socialist state of workers and peasants.[2]

Traditional Marxists viewed law and the state as reflections of the socioeconomic class structure of society. As such it was by nature bourgeois and exploitative. The very concepts of law and state were suspect because of their social foundations. Prior to 1936 the Bolsheviks impugned these concepts, claiming they were bourgeois remnants which the Party must eradicate. By fiat the 1936 Constitution declared that socialism was built and bourgeois elements in society were erased. The Soviet concepts of law and the state were declared to be law and state of a new type, which meant, primarily, law and state based on a new social foundation.

From a theoretical viewpoint, the concepts of state and law took on a new legitimacy as the formal embodiments of the will of the new social foundations of Soviet society, the proletariat. Here, in theory, was proletarian law in a proletarian state. The socioeconomic foundations conjured up their reflection in a proletarian superstructure. Thus, it was argued that state and law represent the sovereignty of the people. Power resides in the people, the state and law reflect their foundation; therefore, the power and sovereignty of the people reside in the formal concepts of state and law, now legitimized by the creation of a proletarian social foundation. The highest institution in the new proletarianized state was the Supreme Soviet, whose laws embodied the sovereignty of the people.

Under the new Constitution, the very nature of the concepts of state and law were transformed. Law and the state were viewed as positive instruments of the leadership for building communism, rather than as negative instruments for destroying the bourgeois machine. In theory they became tools to aid the regime in its declared ultimate objective—building communism.

From a theoretical viewpoint, then, state and law emerged as conceptual forms designed to help perform two functions essential to the building of communism: (1) to build the economic and technical base for communism; and (2) to serve as vehicles for teaching self-administration in the communist society. Lenin had always foreseen the latter as the major function of the soviets after the Revolution. The recent economic reforms have underlined the former.[3] In theory, then, the Supreme Soviet emerged as the institutional focus of this new normative view of state and law. As the pinnacle of the Soviet system of state and law, in theory all institutional efforts within that system to achieve the ultimate goals of communism converged on the Supreme Soviet.

The precise nature of the Supreme Soviet's relationship to its subordinate and auxiliary bodies (both actual and theoretical) within the system of state and law remains to be explored further on. However, this central theoretical role, as the leading organ of the Soviet system of state and law in the process of achieving the ultimate goal of communism, casts a powerful aura of legitimacy on the Supreme Soviet as an institution. As an institutional focus of so many fundamental concepts in Marxist-Leninist theory, the Supreme Soviet acquires a very considerable influence and prestige regardless of actual institutional relations and the realities of power.

THE INSTITUTION OF THE STATE

An amendment to the Constitution in 1947 provided the first clue that a process culminating in the development of a vast system of institutions called state organs was beginning.[4] In the important jurisdictional clause of Article 14, the words "higher organs of *state* power" (our italics) replaced the words "higher organs of power." Ever since, the relatively hollow forms of the "Stalin" (1936) Constitution have been acquiring substance as a system of "state" institutions. The following outlines the theoretical-juridical relations of the Supreme Soviet to the institutions of the state system.

THE STATE AND THE POLITICAL SYSTEM

In theory the CPSU is not a state institution, but it is a part of the political system. As the director of the Soviet Institute of Law and Government put it:

> In dealing with some of the general propositions concerning the state we said that while the state was the most important it was not the only element in the political organization of society. What then are the parts that go to make up the political organization of socialist society?

> In the most general terms, it may be said to be a system of mass organizations—state and non-state (mass)—uniting various sections of the working population. It includes the state, the Party, the trade unions, cooperatives, young people's leagues and other mass organizations of working people.[5]

In other words, the state is one among many political organizations in the Soviet political system; the other political organizations are the Party and a system of mass organizations. Although Professor Chkikvadze treats the Party as one among many mass or non-state organizations, the Party and mass organizations are usually treated as two separate systems by Soviet scholars.[6]

These sub-systems, the Party system, the system of mass organizations, and the state system—which together comprise the political system—overlap in fact if not in theory. The fluctuating relations of these systems in theory and in fact reveal much about the nature of the Soviet polity, the dynamics of its institutional evolution, and the authority of the Supreme Soviet. In fact, it is only quite recently that Soviet sources appear reluctant to admit that the state's competence encompasses political, not just cultural and economic, matters.

The meaning of the word political in Marxist-Leninist jargon has shifted considerably over time. For Lenin it meant policy and decision-making, involving the class struggle and the process of destroying the bourgeois class. Announcement of the Stalin Constitution marked the theoretical end of the bourgeois class, and Khrushchev's announcement of the All-People's State suggested a further proletarianization of Soviet society in theory. This confronted theorists with the dilemma of identifying and demarcating the role and functions of the Party and the state. Most literature on state and law stressed the end of the emphasis on coercion which distinguished the Stalin period of the "personality cult."

The literature almost universally stresses building the economic base for communism. Second and third in order of priority are eradicating survivals of capitalism at home and abroad. The respective roles of Party and state in achieving these goals are quite unclear.

The statement that economic planning is increasingly free from politics implies that responsibility for it may shift from the Party to the state. It indicates that the major task of the All-People's State is increasingly apolitical, thus implying perhaps a subordinate role for the Party whose chief tasks would relate to foreign policy and propagandistic efforts to erase capitalistic survivals.[7] In fact, the expansion of the Supreme Soviet in the decade of the sixties appears to be clearly motivated in a large part by the economic reform—both to centralize and to facilitate it.

The early literature on the All-People's State implies that the chief spheres of activity henceforth will be in the economic and cultural areas, formerly the areas to which the state apparatus had been limited.[8] Realizing that its early theoretical pronouncements on state and law undermined its authority, the Party began to modify its stand by 1966. It warned against underestimating the state coercive function. It stressed the political nature of the leading role of the working class, as embodied in the Party. It admitted that while economic and organizational functions of the state were increasing, political factors were still important. It thus underlined the guiding, central role of the Party vis-à-vis the state without establishing any clear line of demarcation between their roles.[9]

Since Krushchev's fall, the theoretical demarcation of Party and state spheres of competence has been increasingly blurred. This probably represents both theoretical and actual confusion concerning their respective roles.

The most significant development for the Supreme Soviet is the appearance of scholarly opinion openly identifying state power with political power, thus impinging on a sphere formerly reserved for the Party. It also implies the use of the word political in a non-Marxian sense, connoting decision-making, not class struggle.[10]

The reemphasis of "political" factors in Soviet society is usually identified with the simultaneous increase of the roles of both the Party and the organs of state power at the expense of the mass organs and organs of state administration.[11] As we shall see, this reflects the trend of actual institutional development also.

Some Soviet sources speak of the state as the central element of the socialist political system:

> But the state and its bodies are, of course, the central element of socialist society's political system, and the representative organs of state power are foremost among them. These constitute the political basis of the socialist state system, and are a direct and immediate embodiment of popular sovereignty.[12]

The precise relationship of Party and state with regard to the Supreme Soviet will be examined in detail further on. What is important here is that from a juridical viewpoint, there is no overlapping of Party and state as institutions. They are both part of the political system. In theory the Party guides and directs the work of state institutions. In fact many of the personnel in state institutions are members of the CPSU, but in law the CPSU is neither the subordinate of the state nor the superior of the state. In short, the CPSU in Soviet state and law theory is not a part of the state system.

This is seldom explicitly stated; rather, it is implied when discussing other concepts, as exemplified in the following:

> But the sovereignty of the state is obviously a political and juridical expression of the plenary powers of the class which has gained dominion over society and whose will the state expresses through its organs. Other specific features of the state determined by its social nature are: (a) it is an organization of the whole ruling class (and not of any section of it, *as a political party is*); and (b) its decrees (those of its organs) are binding on the entire population.[13]

Another example of this implicit exclusion of the CPSU from the legal system is found in the distinction between legal and mass legislative initiative. The Party implicitly does not have legal legislative initiative, although it exercises "direct" initiative in important questions.[14]

In Soviet legal theory, then, the relationship between the state and Party from a juridical viewpoint remains quite vague. The two are treated as separate entities except for the incessant incantation that the Party is the guiding force in society.

STATE POWER AND POPULAR SOVEREIGNTY

Article 30 of the Soviet constitution designates the Supreme Soviet as the highest organ of state power. Thus, it is directly granted authority over the system of organs of state power, which are the soviets at all levels. The concept of state power refers to the power of the people. In theory the soviets are composed of representatives, elected by the now proletarianized people. State power means popular sovereignty. In theory, it is a major source of the legitimating authority of the Supreme Soviet and lower soviets.[15]

At the top of this system of organs of state power sits the Supreme Soviet, the embodiment of the will of the people of the entire Soviet Union. As Vyshinsky put it, "personified in the highest organs of state authority, the will of the people—of the masses of millions of workers, peasants and intellectuals—finds expression."[16] The very concept of state power, to say nothing of the vast institutional complex embodying it, raises the prospect of a duality of power in the Soviet Union. If state power represents the will of the people, who does the Party represent? In theory and in law, the Party merely *guides* the state and the people. Its influence is persuasive, not binding and coercive, as is state power.

The 1936 Constitution conjured up a notion of popular sovereignty, located it exclusively in the Supreme Soviet, and designated the statute, or zakon, as the highest vehicle for expression of that popular will.

> In socialist society a statute is the highest act of state authority, responsive to the interests of the consciousness of the masses which augments the force of a Soviet statute. In contrast to the ever-increasing part played in capitalist countries by executive authority at the expense of legislative authority, the Stalin Constitution emphasizes the supremacy of the socialist statute as expressing the will of the sovereign Soviet people.[17]

Though the Party apparatus stands behind Supreme Soviet legislation in fact, in theory the gnawing query remains: Where does legitimacy lie should popular will depart from the will of the Party apparatus? This duality is not new in Russian history. The Slavophiles had posited a kind of "residual legitimacy" in their glorification of "Sobornost," which viewed the communal spirit of the Russian people as the ultimate repository of legitimacy should the Tsar fail in his obligation to provide for the welfare of his people.

In summary, the Stalin Constitution reflected a new perception of law as a positive instrument for building communism, and for the first time in Russian history identified a legislature as the locus of sovereignty—*popular* sovereignty—thus raising the prospect of dual legitimacy within the Soviet Union. At the same time, law itself acquired a new aura of legitimacy, both because of its alleged suitability in building communism and its source in the popular will.

INSTITUTIONS OF THE STATE SYSTEM

The state system comprises a vast number of institutions, excluding the Party, which are juridically accountable in varying degrees to the Supreme Soviet. In effect, the Supreme Soviet sits at the apex of many different systems of institutions within the state system. Some are the organs of state power, the organs of state administration, the judicial organs (the courts) and the organs supervising the observance of the law (the Procuracy), and perhaps even the election system. Each of these systems is a pyramid of organs extending from the All-Union level down to the localities.

As elective organs representing the will of the people, the system of state representative organs (soviets) at all levels exercises authority over the other three institutional systems comprising the Soviet state system:

> In the USSR, they are called soviets, which are massive and representative organizations of the working people and which have the features of both state and mass organization.[18]

The concepts of state power and popular sovereignty are the juridical-theoretical bases of the Supreme Soviet's paramountcy over the other systems of state institutions within the state system.

Each of these systems performs a different function. The nature of their function and their precise juridical relationships to the Supreme Soviet will be described further on. The Supreme Soviet appears to be gradually extending its juridical and actual control over this vast apparatus of institutions, a fact which might prove in the long run to be the most significant trend in the institutional evolution of the Supreme Soviet.

JURISDICTION AND COMPETENCE OF THE SUPREME SOVIET AND ITS PRESIDIUM

There appear to be three views of the jurisdiction of the Supreme Soviet and its Presidium:

(1) The jurisdiction is coextensive;[19]
(2) The Presidium possesses independent jurisdiction;[20]
(3) The jurisdiction is coextensive, but the Presidium has narrow independent competence.[21]

Each view has some basis in the actual wording of the Constitution; thus proponents of each view concentrate on the articles supporting their views.

COEXTENSIVE JURISDICTION

The proponents of the coextensive view focus on Article 14, which treats both the Supreme Soviet and its Presidium, the two higher organs of state power, as institutions with the same jurisdiction over the matters listed below:

Economics. Determination of the national economic plan; approval of the consolidated state budget; allocations of taxes and revenue between Union and local budgets; determination of land tenure and use of natural resources; administration, organization, and/or direction of banks, financial, credit, and monetary institutions; administration of economic enterprises, transport, communications, state insurance, and the organization of the uniform system of natural-economic statistics.

Education and welfare. Determination of the "basic principles" of education and public health; determination of the principles of labor legislation.

Foreign affairs and national security. Representation of the USSR in international relations; conclusion, ratification, and denunciation of treaties; questions of war and peace; organization of national defense and security; direction of foreign trade on the basis of a state monopoly.

Constitutions. Control over the observance of the Constitution and insuring the conformity of the Union Republic constitutions with the All-Union document; admission of new Republics; confirmation of boundary changes between Union Republics and other administrative-territorial boundary alterations.

In this view, Article 30 designating the Supreme Soviet as the "highest" organ of state power refers only to its power to enact the highest form of legal norm, not to the scope of matters which it may consider—i.e., its jurisdiction.

Likewise, Article 32 vesting exclusive legislative power in the Supreme Soviet refers to the power to enact zakons, the highest form of law, not to a separate jurisdiction or scope of matters which might be called legislative jurisdiction. This view tends to ignore the inscrutable Article 31, which implies a separate jurisdiction for the Presidium as well as the Council of Ministers and the ministries.

Article 31

The Supreme Soviet of the USSR exercises all rights vested in the Union of Soviet Socialist Republics in accordance with Article 14 of the Constitution, in so far as they do not, by virtue of the Constitution, come within the jurisdiction of organs of the USSR that are accountable to the Supreme Soviet of the USSR, the Council of Ministers of the USSR, and the Ministries of the USSR.

INDEPENDENT JURISDICTION

The view that the Presidium possesses an independent jurisdiction focuses on Articles 31 and 49. Article 31 authorizes the separate jurisdiction and Article 49 spells it out, listing the separate jurisdictions.

In this view, all of the enumerated powers listed in Article 49 represent independent powers of the Presidium which the Supreme Soviet may not infringe upon. Most admit that sections (g) through (r) represent power to act only in the interval between sessions. However, this independent jurisdiction view is reluctant to concede the Supreme Soviet's right to ratify action on items included within the separate jurisdiction. Thus is justified the de facto legislating of the Presidium.

Even the power to issue decrees in section (b) is considered a separate power to issue legal norms of a non-concretizing nature.

Both the coextensive view and the independent jurisdiction view do not draw much distinction between competence and jurisdiction. The notions of scope and power are combined. Their differing views derive, juridically at least, from the focus and emphasis on different sections of the Constitution.

THE KUZNETSOV HERESY

The third and most sophisticated juridical view distinguishes between jurisdiction and competence. It views the jurisdiction of the Supreme Soviet and its Presidium as coextensive, but not their competence. It distinguishes between the constitutionally authorized power to act and the constitutionally authorized power to establish the legal-juridical basis for acting.[22] In this view, the scope of matters (typological and territorial) which may be considered is the same, but the manner or nature of the way in which the institution may act is different.

The manner in which the Supreme Soviet may act is legislative and normative in Kuznetsov's view. This is the import of Article 32 on the Supreme Soviet's exclusive legislative power. In other words, the Supreme Soviet's competence is legislative and normative because that is the nature of it as an institution—it legislates broad general norms of the highest order. The nature of the Presidium is implementive or executive, although Soviet theorists scrupulously avoid the legislative-executive dichotomy as bourgeois.

In Kuznetsov's view the Supreme Soviet inherently as implied in Article 32 has the power to establish (*utverzhdat*) the legal basis for acting, while the Presidium possesses only the competence to act upon that legal basis, which is what Article 49 is all about.[23]

Thus, in this view Article 14 grants coextensive jurisdiction; Article 31 acknowledges separate competence on the part of each body; Article 32 identifies the nature of the Supreme Soviet's competence; Article 49 identifies the areas of competence of the Presidium for which the Supreme Soviet may establish normative guidelines for the Presidium's action.[24]

Curiously, Kuznetsov hints at a separate jurisdiction and competence for the Supreme Soviet with respect to one narrow area, the awarding of medals. He points to the two powers to establish medals in Article 9 (i) and to award them in Article 49 (z). Perhaps this is just an illustrative passage to demonstrate the concept of competence. He does not repeat this in his later book, where his notion of competence is elucidated in detail.[25]

Kuznetsov's view of competence is not a majority view among jurists. The practical implications of Kuznetsov's approach are akin to the view of the Presidium, adhered to by Stalinist jurists, as a mere executive committee of the Supreme Soviet.[26]

In practice, Kuznetsov's and Stalin's view would curb the apparently growing power and utility of the Presidium to the regime. That Kuznetsov has not been the subject of wide criticism is probably due to the broad latitude in interpreting what action is authorized by zakons as well as the practice of issuing ukazes for later verification by the Supreme Soviet. Both leave the Presidium the practical power of legislating almost at will. However, one must not discount the delicacy and sophistication of Kuznetsov's argument, which is difficult to refute logically.

JURISDICTION AND COMPETENCE OF THE COUNCIL
OF MINISTERS AND THE SUPREME SOVIET

The preamble of Article 14 establishes that the jurisdiction of the organs of state power and state administration are coextensive throughout the entire USSR. The highest organ of state administration is the Council of Ministers (Article 64). The scope of matters which they may consider is the same. The territory within which they consider these matters is the same—that is, the entire Soviet Union.

However, the competence of the two organs is different, because their inherent nature is different. This difference is reflected in the names given to the two systems which they head, state power and state administration. In theory the Council of Ministers and the ministries are administrative organs. Their inherent nature is to execute, to implement, to carry out. Their nature in theory limits their power. They do not, in theory, perform a legislative function— that is, they do not, in theory, create new behavioral norms.

The normative function of the Council of Ministers is limited to elaborating and concretizing zakons, not to creating new norms.[27] In theory, this means issuing administrative regulations filling in the details required to implement statutes. The authority for this is Article 66. These concretized administrative regulations are binding throughout the Soviet Union (Article 67), just like zakons of the Supreme Soviet. Regulations of the ministries are binding only in the sector of the economy over which the respective ministry has authority.

The Council of Ministers is responsible and accountable to the Supreme Soviet (Article 65) primarily in the sense that its competence is designed to give effect to the competence of the Supreme Soviet, and to the Presidium when the Supreme Soviet is not in session. The theoretically distinctive juridical nature of the Council of Ministers in Soviet jurisprudence is illustrated by contrasting it to the Presidium of the Supreme Soviet.

The Presidium can annul acts of the Council of Ministers, but the reverse is not true. The Council of Ministers is accountable to the Presidium between sessions of the Supreme Soviet, but the Presidium is not accountable to the Council of Ministers under any circumstances.

While in theory all Soviet political institutions represent the will of the people, some are more equal than others from the juridical viewpoint of Kuznetsov because of the principles upon which they are created. Both the Council of Ministers and the Presidium are accountable to the Supreme Soviet and the latter is theoretically somewhat representative since it has a Vice-president from each union republic.[28] Thus, its nature, as Kuznetsov would have it, partakes more directly of the will of the people, being elected and representative like the supreme organ, the Supreme Soviet, rather than appointed like the Council of Ministers. The authority of the Council of Ministers to issue legal norms is clearly delegated, that is, derived from a higher norm, the zakon; the Presidium of the Supreme Soviet derives some of its authority from its inherent nature, competence. Perhaps this illustrates why Soviet jurists debate the competence of the Presidium from a juridical-constitutional viewpoint much more than that of the Council of Ministers.

CONSTITUTIONAL FEDERALISM AND MULTINATIONALISM

Even from a juridical point of view, the Supreme Soviet is a major instrument limiting Soviet constitutional federalism and multinationalism. Democratic centralism of the Party and Russianization have long been recognized as the key vehicles circumscribing the federal, multinational principles in the Soviet party. Now a third vehicle supplements these—the law.

Both fundamental purposes for the Soviet regime's stress on legality—control of the polity and efficiency of the economy— militate against federalism and multinationalism. Yet federalism and multinationalism have been declared to be backbones of Soviet constitutionalism.

LEGAL CENTRALIZATION

From the point of view of normative subordination, all laws of union republics or autonomous republics must conform to zakons of the Supreme Soviet, even the constitutions of the union republics and autonomous republics (Articles 16, 19, 21, and 60 [a-1], [b-1]). Thus, from this juridical perspective the Supreme Soviet has the legal power to abolish Soviet federalism piecemeal or even, theoretically, with one blow. This is constitutionally authorized and inheres in the nature of the zakon.[29] In fact, the Supreme Soviet and its Presidium abolished autonomous republics during World War II and retrograded the Karelo-Finnish Union Republic to an autonomous republic in 1955.

The piecemeal approach has proved adequate enough. The proliferation of all-Union fundamentals of legislation authorized in Article 14 has chopped away the republics' theoretical juridical power considerably. Ordinary and current zakons, though theoretically not possessed of the same normative spread, can chip away also since all law must conform to the zakon. It is the highest form of law. The greater geographical scope of a Supreme Soviet zakon means it represents a greater segment of the people and is thus superior to the zakon of republics.

The competence of republic supreme soviets is the same as the All-Union Supreme Soviet. They are both elected, representative institutions which legislate. Although there is no question that their territorial jurisdiction is different, there is controversy over whether the scope of matters within their typological jurisdiction is the same. This controversy centers around Article 15:

> The sovereignty of the Union Republics is limited only in the spheres defined in Article 14 of the Constitution of the USSR. Outside of these spheres each Union Republic exercises state authority independently. The USSR protects the sovereign rights of the Union Republics.

Do these words grant independent typological jurisdiction to the Union Republics? Is this equivalent to a reserved powers clause? Soviet jurists are equivocal. They cite the article as evidence for the existence of a federal system without citing specific powers exercised under this clause. For all practical purposes the point is relatively moot since the principle of normative subordination when applied through Article 14 can virtually erase any independent jurisdiction of the republics even from a purely juridical viewpoint.

ADMINISTRATIVE DECENTRALIZATION

There never has been much question that the highly centralized control of the Council of Ministers over administration of the government apparatus, and particularly the economic apparatus, undermines the fictions of federalism and multinationalism. The constitutional accountability of the Council of Ministers to the Supreme Soviet, plus the normative subordination of all organs both of state power and state administration, further weakens the facade of federalism.

In theory the local soviets have long been viewed as the base of two pyramids, the pyramid of state power and the pyramid of state administration. As such, in theory they are legally and administratively subordinate to the Supreme Soviet.

Since the promulgation of the Party Programme, a concerted effort has been made to increase the powers of the local soviets. The impact of this decentralization appears to be a weakening of federalism, since the powers given to the local soviets are in effect subtracted from the powers of the intermediate level supreme soviets of the union and autonomous republics. In short, decentralization has facilitated the decline of federalism, while being vindicated as more democratic and efficient economically.

MULTINATIONALISM IN THE SUPREME SOVIET

The Supreme Soviet is the focus of the multinational principle in the seventies; at one time that focus lay in the republics themselves. As mentioned before, the rigid centralization of the Party, the gradual Russianization of some republics, and more recently the decline of federalism through legal centralization and decentralization has shifted the focus of the multinational principle in law as well as in practice from the republican state organs to the Supreme Soviet where, as we shall see, it is also quite circumscribed. In short, the decline of federalism is not synonymous with the demise of multinationalism; however, the focus of the latter appears to be shifting to the Supreme Soviet.

The core of the multinational principle in the Soviet constitution lies in the purported equality of the two chambers of the Supreme Soviet as secured in theory by many clauses. Four constitutional practices of the Supreme Soviet have severely circumscribed the multinational principle. They are:

(1) Joint sessions of the Supreme Soviet;
(2) Legislative unanimity between chambers;
(3) The principle of sectionalism in the Supreme Soviet commission system; and
(4) The power of the Presidium of the Supreme Soviet.

The Supreme Soviet elects its Presidium at a joint session of both the Council of the Union and the Council of Nationalities, according to Article 48. Thus, the choice of these increasingly powerful figures rests with a body dominated by Russians and other Slavs (as we shall see), in clear contravention of the principles of multinationality.

That fifteen members of the Presidium (the Vice-presidents) are presidents of the presidiums of the increasingly Russianized union republics—which possess only unicameral supreme soviets that elect these union republic presidiums—is clearly no protection of multinational rights. Likewise, joint sessions appoint the Council of Ministers, according to Article 56. Thus, this institutional head of the vast, highly centralized administrative system is not subject even in law to multinational review. In these two important areas of choosing the personnel of powerful state organs, the Supreme Soviet becomes in effect a unicameral legislature dominated by Slavic nationalities. This de facto unicameralism deprives the Council of Nationalities of its veto right.

Article 47, though much touted by Vyshinsky, requires the two chambers of the Supreme Soviet to agree on all legislation. While this amounts to a veto of the Council of Nationalities over the Council of the Union, the reverse is also true. As the population of non-Russian nationalities grows proportionally, one must pause over the apparent equality of vetos.

Such disagreement conjures up the power of the Presidium to dissolve the Supreme Soviet and order new elections. In the meantime, the constitutional power to legislate and administer the state resides in two bodies not subject to veto by the non-Russian nationalities—the Council of Ministers and the Presidium of the Supreme Soviet.

As we shall see, the expansion of the system of permanent commissions of the Supreme Soviet has had the effect of further centralizing state power and curbing federalism. It also mitigated the multinational principle in the commission system itself. The Economic Commission of the Council of Nationalities, a virtual forum for multinational grievances in the budgetary process, was abolished. In its stead emerged a system of commissions organized along functional lines, with investigatory and auditing jurisdiction over various defined sectors of the economy.

The power to issue ukazes and to interpret laws by a Presidium over which the Council of Nationalities has little de facto control clearly reduces the equality of nationalities. The Presidium's power to dissolve (Article 47) and convene (Article 46) Supreme Soviet sessions and to exercise the powers of the Supreme Soviet between sessions (Articles 53 and 49) certainly holds the seeds for arbitrary contravention of initiatives by the nationalities.

In summary, the equality of nationalities, much circumvented by non-legal means, may also be contravened in a multiplicity of legal juridical ways within the Supreme Soviet system itself despite appearances to the contrary. Although the Supreme Soviet remains perhaps the chief forum for multinational interest articulation, it may also be a powerful institution for manipulating such pressures.[30]

ACTS OF THE SUPREME SOVIET
IN THE SOVIET HIERARCHY OF LAWS

The legal acts of the Supreme Soviet have long been considered the highest form of law, but only recently has so much stress been laid on their superior juridical force over other normative acts. This superiority is of two kinds:[31]

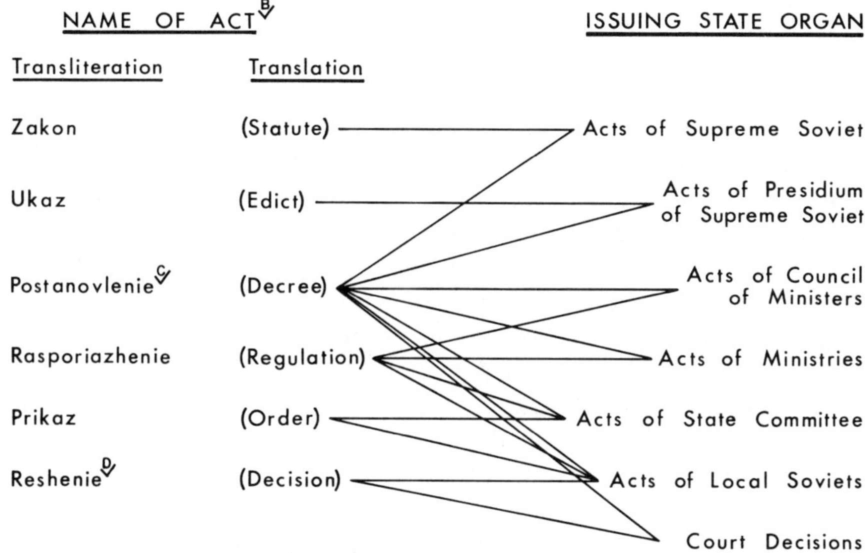

Figure 2.1: LEGAL ACTS OF STATE ORGANS[a]

> a. Miscellaneous legal acts: instruktsiia and ukazanie, both translatable as "Instruction," issued by ministries and departments to regulate internal agencies or individuals. A prikaz sometimes performs this function as well as other functions. An ustav is a charter; a polozhenie regulates the scope and authority of a lesser state organ.
>
> b. The legal nomenclature above applies to legal norms issued by republic organs, but they are restricted and subordinate in jurisdiction to acts of all-union organs.
>
> c. Postanovlenie issued by all state organs. Usually, they are procedural rules dealing with internal organizations, although when issued by the Council of Ministers and local soviets they usually have substantive impact.

(1) Supreme Soviet acts automatically rescind all previous acts not in conformity with them; and

(2) All subsequent legal acts must conform to Supreme Soviet acts. Much of the Supreme Soviet's real and potential power stems from its power to issue the highest juridical norms. Any study of the institution would be incomplete without an analysis of the interrelationships of the hierarchy of legal norms topped by acts of the Supreme Soviet.

Table 2.1 classifies Soviet legal acts (*pravovye akty*) according to four principles of normative subordination:[32]

(1) The nature of the institutional source;

(2) The nature of the act itself;

(3) The function of the act; and
(4) The geographical jurisdiction of the act.

The nature of the institutional source refers to whether it is elective or non-elective; acts of the latter are subordinate to the former. The nature of the act itself refers to whether it is a general fundamental norm or a detailed administrative regulation; the former is superior to the latter. The function of the act refers to the substantive-procedural dichotomy, the former being superior to the latter. The geographical jurisdiction of the act refers to the territorial extent of the act's coverage—the broader an act's geographical coverage, the more superior it is because of the principle of popular sovereignty, that is, more people are subject to the rule. These four principles establish the complex hierarchy of laws shown in Table 2.1.

Since the Supreme Soviet stands at the apex of the Soviet system of state and law, and since its zakons embody popular sovereignty, its legal enactments represent the highest form of legal norms in juridical theory. An analysis of the hierarchy of legal norms according to the principles of normative subordination in Soviet juridical theory is thus relevant to an analysis of the Supreme Soviet.

CONSTITUTIONAL LAW

The Supreme Soviet alone, according to Article 146 of the Constitution, may amend the Constitution by a two-thirds vote. In short, Soviet constitutional law is made by the Supreme Soviet: "The Constitution is the most important source of Soviet law and the highest type of law."[33] Soviet constitutional law is a mixture of general principles and specific detailed legislation. For example, changes in the industrial management apparatus require a constitutional amendment, which is hardly in the nature of a general principle of law.

Soviet constitutional law derives its importance, according to Soviet authorities, from the fact that it sets out the main features of the social and state system, defines the competence of state organs and the normative acts which they may issue, sets out the fundamental principles underlying the power of state bodies, and establishes the procedures governing modification of rules of law in every branch of law.

TABLE 2.1

A HIERARCHY OF SOVIET LAWS

**Legal acts (*Pravovye Akty*) of organs of
state power and administration**

Osnovnoi Zakon (basic fundamental law)
  Soviet Constitution
  Constitutional Amendments (2/3 vote of Supreme Soviet)

Zakon (statutes) (4 categories)
  Of Supreme Soviet
    Fundamentals of legislation
    Organic
    Ordinary or current
    Ukaz confirmed by zakon

Ukaz (edict)
  Of Presidium of Supreme Soviet

Postanovlenie (decrees)[a]
  Of Supreme Soviet (both chambers)
  Of Presidium of Supreme Soviet
  Of Council of Ministers
  Of Supreme Soviet (individual chambers)
  Of Supreme Soviet commissions (2 categories)[b]
    predlozhenia (proposal)
    recomendasia (recommendations)
  Of local soviets[c]

Rasporiazhenie (regulations)
  Of Council of Ministers
  Of ministries
  Of state committees and boards[d]
  Of mass organs[e]
  Of local soviets

Reshenie (decisions)
  Of courts[f]
  Of local soviets

---

a. Postanovlenie of all state organs are usually acts regulating internal procedure, except those of the Council of Ministers.
b. For the normative impact of predlozhenia and recomendasia see pp. 121–122.
c. Local soviets issue postanovlenie, rasporiazhenie, prikaz, and reshenie. The latter is most frequent.
d. These bodies sometimes issue legal acts called prikaz; their normative impact is in dispute.
e. Theoretically, mass organs such as trade unions are not state organs, although, if authorized, they may issue legal acts.
f. Theoretically, Soviet courts merely apply law, they do not interpret it; thus, in theory, they do not make it.

[55]

STATUTES (ZAKONS)

Since the Supreme Soviet has always voted unanimously, its enactments in effect modify the Constitution. It is not known where or
how the decision is made to publish a zakon as part of the Constitution. A constitutional amendment is, for all practical purposes, a
zakon.

Zakons other than constitutional amendments fall into four categories, according to Soviet sources, in the following order of importance:

(1) Fundamentals of legislation;
(2) Organic laws;
(3) Ordinary or current legislation; and
(4) Ukazes confirmed by zakons.

The fundamentals of legislation lay down the basic principles and
institutions of the legal system throughout the Union. The organic
laws regulate the procedures of state bodies. Current legislation deals
with policy matters such as marriage or pensions—in the common-
sense meaning of ordinary legislation.

CONSTITUTIONALITY AND LEGALITY OF UKAZ

Ukazes of the Presidium of the Supreme Soviet, which are later
ratified by the Supreme Soviet, are a subcategory of current legislation which is justified by its urgency, according to Soviet rationale.
Under the extraordinary conditions of World War II, the Presidium
even amended the Constitution by creating two commissariats.
Again, urgency was probably the rationale although, as we shall see
further on, this practice embarrasses some Soviet jurists who are
attacking it.[34]

The fundamentals of legislation are authorized by Article 14 of
the Constitution. The effect of passing many of these statutes over
the decades of the fifties and sixties was to centralize the Soviet legal
system considerably, since all other legal acts must conform to the
fundamentals.

As mentioned previously, the zakon derives its authority from the
fiction that it represents the will of the people, having been enacted
by an elected representative organ of the people. In theory, all
normative acts emanate from the will of the people in the sense that

their authority derives from zakons with which they must conform and which embody the will of the people as enacted by a representative body (the Supreme Soviet) for all of the Union. Authority to issue other normative acts is in a sense delegated by the Supreme Soviet pursuant to relevant constitutional provisions.

NORMATIVE ACTS OF THE PRESIDIUM: UKAZ AND POSTANOVLENIE

Most Soviet jurists view the norm-regulating activities of the Presidium of the Supreme Soviet as delegated authority from the Supreme Soviet, although there is growing debate from a juridical point of view, as we shall see further on.[35] The Presidium issues two kinds of normative acts: decrees (ukazes), as authorized by Article 49 of the Constitution; and resolutions (postanovlenie), which are implied from Article 49 of the Constitution and are procedural in nature. [36]

Ukazes actually set out behavioral norms. They fall into two categories: first, those which elaborate, concretize, or fill in the details of Supreme Soviet zakons—in effect, administrative regulations pursuant to Supreme Soviet statutes; and second, those which are in effect new laws which must be ratified subsequently by the Supreme Soviet.[37] Some Soviets jurists argue that the Presidium also has a third independent power to issue ukazes without Supreme Soviet ratification.[38] However, this violates the central juridical fiction that all law emanates from the will of the people as expressed through acts of an elected representative body. The juridical debates surrounding this controversy will be discussed further on also.

Postanovlenie (resolutions or decisions), the second kind of legal act issued by the Presidium of the Supreme Soviet, deal with procedural matters enumerated in Article 49, such as convening Supreme Soviet sessions, pardons, appointments to high office, awarding medals, conducting referendums, and dissolving the Supreme Soviet. In theory, they also are subordinate to the Supreme Soviet zakons, although some debate surrounds this as well.[39]

INTERNAL ACTS OF THE SUPREME SOVIET AND ITS AUXILIARY BODIES

There is a multiplicity of internal legal acts issued by the Supreme Soviet and its auxiliary bodies designed to accomplish one of two general purposes: first, postanovlenie to regulate the internal organization and procedure of the state bodies; second, *predlozhenia* (proposals) to facilitate fulfillment of the norms laid down by the zakon. If the acts involve major reorganization of the Supreme Soviet, such as the 1967 statute on the commission system, they are usually elevated to the status of zakon.[40]

Postanovlenie may be issued by vote of both houses of the Supreme Soviet or by an individual house. They are not normative acts; they regulate procedure and organization. The Presidium of the Supreme Soviet may also issue decrees regulating its own procedure and organization. Each decree applies only to the body which enacts it.

A second category of internal acts is proposals and recommendations of the commissions of the Supreme Soviet. These acts are issued to the Presidium of the Supreme Soviet, the Supreme Soviet itself, or to the Council of Ministers or the individual ministries. Their function is to point out inefficiencies or defaults in the fulfillment of norms established by zakon. Normally, these acts are merely recommendations, which can be reviewed and ignored by the bodies to which they are addressed.[41] The authority to issue such acts is implied from Article 51 of the Constitution which grants the Supreme Soviet the power to create commissions for investigation and audit. The Presidium may convert such recommendations into a ukaz under the power of concretizing—that is, in effect, issuing a further administrative regulation to facilitate faulty implementation of a zakon which has been uncovered by the commissions.

A predlozhenia from the Supreme Soviet commissions to the Council of Ministers is recommendatory unless converted to a ukaz by the Presidium of the Supreme Soviet. However, such a resolution to the ministries is legally binding and mandatory and must be carried out. Thus, the postanovlenie of a commission of the Supreme Soviet to one of the sectoral ministries take on the character of binding legal norms, although they are primarily investigatory in nature.[42]

A form of predlozhenia issued by commissions of republic supreme soviets, called a proposal, is now considered binding on republic councils of ministers, and a move is apparently afoot to make them binding at the all-Union level, which would give the Supreme Soviet commissions a rather extraordinary power to require the Council of Ministers to abide by its edict.[43] The theoretical justification for such power would be that the commissions were merely assuring that the zakons were properly administered. The power would be implied from Article 51, the audit power.

Another binding form of predlozhenia implied from Article 51

(and perhaps Article 71), which is procedural in nature, requires the
Council of Ministers and the ministries to submit to the commissions
all documents and materials necessary to any audit or investigation
of these bodies' activities in implementing a zakon. The 1967 zakon
on the commission system further implements this constitutional
power by requiring an answer from the Council of Ministers and the
ministries within one month. Article 71 requires a verbal or written
reply to a deputy's inquiry within three days, but has been ignored
until legally reinforced by a recent law.

Chapter 3

COMPOSITION, ELECTIONS, AND LEGITIMACY

Certainly a major reason for the existence of the Supreme Soviet is to provide an elaborate symbol of legality and democracy, which enhances the legitimacy of the regime. The Supreme Soviet satisfies only one of the usually accepted bases for parliamentary legitimacy; it possesses an unusually representative composition, although ironically here it falls short of the claims made for it in the Soviet tradition. The Supreme Soviet's legitimacy is derived primarily from its representativeness; thus, the regime is making an effort to improve that image in accordance with Soviet tradition. Since parliamentary traditions are weak in Russia, as we have seen, those traditions can only serve marginally to enhance its legitimacy. Similarly, although the USSR Constitution formally makes the government accountable to the Supreme Soviet, in fact it is relatively independent; thus, accountability to the Supreme Soviet is not a source of the regime's legitimacy. Finally, the elections of deputies to the Supreme Soviet are almost completely controlled by the Party apparatus; therefore, their utility in legitimizing the Supreme Soviet's acts and thus the regime is also marginal. In the last analysis, the representative image of the Supreme Soviet as a voice of the workers and peasants in a "proletarian society" appears to be the chief bulwark upon which the regime can rely in utilizing the Supreme Soviet to enhance its rule.

A workers' state should be ruled by workers, according to Soviet tradition, and thus the composition of its "parliament" should contain a large contingent of workers and peasants, the social foundation of the state. The dilemma of creating this representative image while still controlling the Supreme Soviet has tantalized the regime from the beginning.

Initially, the regime indulged in some fakery, listing as workers and peasants all those deputies whose social origin, but not present occupation, fit those proletarian categories. The evidence now indicates a trend by the regime to increase the proportion of actual workers and peasants by adding genuine proletarians who are occupied in proletarian work. At the same time, Soviet ideology has gradually accepted the white-collar intelligentsia as a "stratum" (not yet a class) deserving representation in the Soviet state, thus accomodating ideology to reality, and perhaps rendering the Supreme Soviet the most representative legislature in the world, one which falls short only of its own Soviet standards, that is, of the somewhat unrealistic Soviet claim that the social composition of a legislature should mirror that of society.

One other element of the Supreme Soviet's composition is worth mentioning before surveying the evolution of its composition, and that is its representation of the many Soviet nationalities. The non-Slavic nationalities are represented more heavily in the Supreme Soviet than in the major Party arenas, the Politburo and the Central Committee of the Communist Party. Symbolically and theoretically, then, it is in the Supreme Soviet that the nationalities could make their voices better heard, thus lending another increment of legitimacy to its acts.

The difficulty of analyzing Soviet data on the composition of the Supreme Soviet, especially in the Stalinist era, is compounded by some deliberate distortions and omissions to preserve ideological and political images. Another complexity involves the shifting categories in the format of the data over the years and from source to source.

There are six major sources of data on the composition of the Supreme Soviet:

(1) *Deputaty Verkhovnogo Soveta SSSR* (Deputies of the USSR Supreme Soviet, Moscow, 1959, 1962, 1966).

(2) *Pravda* and *Izvestia* reports of the Supreme Soviet Credentials Commissions at the first session of each convocation.

(3) *Zasedania Verkhovnogo Soveta SSSR,* Stenograficheski otchet. This is the stenographic record of Supreme Soviet sessions which is the source of *Pravda* and *Izvestia* material.

(4) N. Gradoboev, "Sostav Verkhovnogo Soveta SSSR," *Novyi Zhurnal* (non-Soviet), XXX (1952), 243–269. This is the third convocation.

(5) N. Gradoboev, "Sostav Verkhovnogo Soveta 1954 goda," *Vestnik Instituta po Izucheniiu istoriia i Kultura SSSR.,* IV, 11 (1954), 59–60.

(6) Miscellaneous reports in books, journals, pamphlets, and hand-outs which usually repeat the data and formats of the above, but occasionally provide additional categories.

The *Deputaty,* which includes detailed biographies of the deputies for the three convocations above (a fifth is at the press for the 1974 convocation), and which could be used to supplement the *Pravda* and *Izvestia* data, is highly inaccurate and thus must be supplemented itself by crosschecks with biographies appearing in the press and periodicals, a quite formidable task. For example, the *Deputaty* is often quite incomplete and quite inaccurate in specifying the jobs held by a deputy after entering Party work. This information is crucial to an assessment of the relation of the CPSU to the Supreme Soviet. The 1958 *Deputaty* merely states that the deputy was engaged in important soviet or Party work before his election without any indication of its nature. The precise post is not mentioned. Thus, analysis of the Party as a recruiting device over the years is impossible on the basis of *Deputaty* information. The 1962 and 1966 *Deputaty* frequently do list the precise posts held before election to the Supreme Soviet but withhold dates of service and often abbreviate the list. Post-election positions in the Party and State are frequently listed inaccurately. Another common distortion in the *Deputaty* is its reference to the substantial education of the deputy when in fact a crosscheck reveals a correspondence degree not unlike an American honorary degree.

The data from *Zasedania, Pravda,* and *Izvestia* include the following categories of information: occupation, sex, Party membership, education, nationality. There is considerable variance in the specificity of the occupational categories, which are the ones most subject to distortion for ideological purposes.

COMPOSITION: SOCIOECONOMIC AND PERSONAL CHARACTERISTICS

As Table 3.1 indicates, the proportion of intelligentsia in the Supreme Soviet seems to be declining; however, the distribution of elites within the intelligentsia has remained relatively constant. The managerial-technical group in the Supreme Soviet appears to have suffered the greatest among the intelligentsia. Slightly less than three-fourths of the deputies are male, and slightly more than that number are members of the Communist Party. Two-thirds of the membership changes at each election, and the remaining third is composed largely of the key officials in the regime. More than half of the deputies are over forty years old and have some higher education.

THE HIGH PROPORTION OF NON-ELITES

Soviet sources assert that approximately 50 percent of the Supreme Soviet is composed of actual workers and peasants, which buttresses their claim that it is a working assembly distinguished from Western parliaments—more representative of the masses and

TABLE 3.1

FUNCTIONAL AND SOCIAL COMPOSITION OF THE SUPREME SOVIET

	1966				1970			
	SU*	SN*	Total	Percentage	SU	SN	Total	Percentage
Intelligentsia	460	453	913	60.2	432	403	835	55.5
Party apparatus	160	129	289	19.1	152	109	261[a]	17.2
State apparatus	98	131	229	15.1	102	115	217	14.3
Managerial-Technical	104	83	187	12.3	91	63	154[b]	10.1
Cultural-Scientific	68	84	152	10.0	57	89	146	9.6
Armed forces	30	26	56	3.7	30	27	57	3.8
Workers	225	181	406	26.8	253	228	481	31.7
Collective farmers	72	105	177	11.7	82	119	201	13.3
Others	10	11	21	1.4	—	—	—	—
Women	222	203	425	28.0	230	231	463	30.5
Party membership	573	568	1,141	75.2	562	534	1,096	72.3
Elected for 1st time	482	533	1,015	66.9	404	442	846	55.8
Higher Education								
(complete & incomplete)	402	406	808	53.3	408	372	800	51.4
Secondary Education	141	132	275	18.1	224	224	448	29.5
Over 40 years of age	476	425	901	59.4	474	413	882	58.8

* SU = Soviet of Union; SN = Soviet of Nationalities.

a. Includes 20 trade union and Komsomol officials.

b. Includes 81 kolkhoz chairmen.

Source: V. Aspaturian (1972) "The Soviet Constitutional Order," in Modern Political Systems: Europe, Roy C. Macridis & Robert E. Ward (eds.) 3rd ed. (Englewood Cliffs, N.J.: Prentice-Hall).

thus more legitimate. Undoubtedly from a comparative perspective the high proportion of non-elites in the Supreme Soviet is perhaps the most striking feature of its composition. The exact proportion of workers and peasants has always been a subject of some controversy and is subject to interpretation.

In general it appears that the proportions of genuine workers and peasants are increasing. There is substantial evidence that Stalin confused social origin with occupation in order to present an image of the Supreme Soviet which would conform more to Marx-Leninist teachings and thus enhance the legitimacy of the Supreme Soviet's acts.

A forthcoming study argues cogently that the regime no longer resorts to fakery but is sending persons actually engaged in labor to the Supreme Soviet in increasing proportions:[1]

One finds that the assertion about 763 workers and kolkhozniki does not refer to social origin but to current occupation. The category "kolkhozniki" does include (as it should by Soviet—that is, government—definitions) 81 kolkhoz chairmen and 20 kolkhoz agronomists, etc. (but no sovkhoz directors and agronomists), as well as 90 brigadiers and farm heads and 57 link-leaders and *starshie* (usually shepherds) of both kolkhozy and sovkhozy. The worker category does include 6 foremen and 83 sub-foremen supervisors (and, of course, the sovkhoz non-technical, non-administrative personnel). Yet, this still leaves 144 rank-and-file kolkhozniki and sovkhozniki and 282 workers by the strictest definition. However, no Western census specifies foremen and sub-foremen supervisors as white collar, and surely the link leader-starshie categories in agriculture and the brigadier-starshie categories in industry are workers and peasants by any reasonable definition. (One might want to exclude foremen and agricultural brigadiers because these posts are gradually being reserved for technically-trained personnel in the Soviet Union). This would leave a "real" worker-peasant category of 567 persons, and a strong case could be made for adding at least those 55 of the 90 agricultural brigadiers and heads of farm who rose through the ranks.
Obviously if one wishes, one can emphasize that workers and peasants comprise only 37% of the deputies (or even 28%) instead of the advertised 50%. However, the question of trend is a different matter. If one compares 1962 and 1970 (as I am doing as part of an article I am writing), there is no trend whatsoever towards larger numbers of white collar deputies. In 1962 there were 114 peasants and 168 workers by the strictest definition or 192 peasants and 263 workers by the reasonable definition that excludes industrial foremen and agricultural brigadiers. Thus, the narrowly-defined worker-peasant category rose from 20% of the total in 1962 to 28% in 1970; the reasonably-defined workers and peasants rose from 32% to 37%.

The untrustworthiness of Stalin's statistics relating to the percentage of workers and peasants in the Supreme Soviet was exposed long ago.[2] Few of the alleged "toilers" were actually engaged in production or labor on the farms. Of 198 "peasants" in the second convocation (1946) in the Council of Nationalities, 75 held administrative posts as Party or Soviet officials, and 44 were chairmen of collective farms.[3] Eighty percent of the workers were fulltime administrators in one field or another. All workmen in the third convocation (1950) of the Supreme Soviet were Stakhanovites,[4] super-workmen who exceeded production quotas through sheer extra effort. The method of distortion was to confuse social origins with actual working occupation. Anyone who by any construction could be viewed as having been born a worker or peasant was included with the actual workers and peasants.

Another scholar, Peter Juviler, has analyzed the disparity between the actual and official figures included in the peasant, worker, and intelligentsia categories of the fourth convocation (1954).[5] The extent of the distortion there is evident when one considers that 80 percent of the "workers" at the second convocation were actually administrators or officials of some sort; or that only 17 percent, not 40 percent, of the deputies at the fourth convocation were actually workers.

The fifth convocation (1958) statistics began to distinguish between actual workers and peasants for the first time, thus suggesting a trend toward increasing the proportion of genuine proletarians in an effort to enhance the Supreme Soviet's utility as a device for legitimizing the regime.

THE BEST SONS AND DAUGHTERS: ELITES IN THE SUPREME SOVIET

As with all legislatures the Supreme Soviet does not mirror the populace. It is not an assembly of "common" men. Even Soviet spokesmen admit that it represents their best sons and daughters— not the most powerful necessarily, but the best, whether they be workers or bureaucrats, scientists or astronauts. It is clearly an elite group. By any standard it is comprised of the best, though certainly not all of the best, in the Soviet Union.

Many of the most prestigious persons in the Soviet Union sit in the Supreme Soviet. Altogether 1,163, or 76.7 percent of the seventh convocation (1966–70) were decorated with awards and medals.

As noted, every single genuine worker deputy in the 1950 Supreme Soviet was a Stakhanovite, the epitome of Stalin's industrial production drives. The Stakhanovite was a living symbol of the leadership's determination to industrialize. He was the best of Soviet workers.

The elite composition of the Supreme Soviet is further underscored by the high level of education among its membership. The level of education of the deputies has increased substantially since the second convocation, as shown in Table 3.2.

The Supreme Soviet is also composed of highly specialized and skilled persons in the trades and professions, as shown in Table 3.3.

OFFICIALDOM IN THE SUPREME SOVIET

The most highly overrepresented group of "best sons" in the Supreme Soviet is the officials of the Party and government bureaucracies, as one might expect, since they in effect constitute the leading core, as the chapter on the Party describes in detail. There are consistently over eighty times as many officials in the Supreme Soviet as there are in the population.

The Party and government officials also occupy a consistently high proportion of the Supreme Soviet itself—over one-third. However, this proportion has decreased about seven or eight percent since de-Stalinization, reflecting the regime's attempt to portray a more democratic image.

Except for the first convocation, the proportion of officials in the Party has exceeded the proportion of state officials in the Supreme Soviet by a few percentage points. In the eighth convocation Party-government proportional shares came within 2.9 percentage points,

TABLE 3.2

EDUCATIONAL LEVEL OF THE SUPREME SOVIET DEPUTIES

Convocation	2 (1946)		3 (1950)		4 (1954)		5 (1958)		6 (1962)		7 (1966)		8 (1970)	
	No.	%	No.	%	No.	%	No.	%	No.	%	No.	%	No.	%
Higher	445	33.2	517	39.3	651	48.3	591	42.9	705	48.8	761	50.2	734	48.4
Incomplete higher	71	5.3	94	7.1	95	7.1	80	5.8	56	3.9	47	3.4	46	3.0
Secondary	300	22.4	285	21.7	226	16.8	163	11.8	239	16.6	275	18.7	448	29.5
Incomplete secondary	a	a	a	a	136	10.1	278	20.2	291	20.2	344	22.7	252	16.6
Primary	523	39.1	420	31.9	239	17.7	266	19.3	152	10.5	90	5.9	37	2.5

a. Figures unavailable.

Source: Verkhovni Sovet (Vosmogosoziva), staticheskii sbornik (Moscow: 1970), pp. 40–41.

TABLE 3.3

MEMBERS OF THE SEVENTH SUPREME SOVIET OF THE USSR WITH SPECIAL QUALIFICATIONS

Trade or profession	Both chambers	Percent
Engineers and technicians	311	20.5
Agronomists, zootechnicians, and other farm specialists	177	11.7
Economists	16	1.1
Doctors	33	2.2
Lawyers	14	0.9
Teachers	132	8.7
Other specialists	190	12.5
TOTAL	873	57.6

Source: M. Saifulin (ed.), The Soviet Parliament (Moscow: Progress Publishers, 1967), p. 4.

the closest since the first convocation. The greatest gulf between their respective proportions emerged in 1950—eight and one-half points.

NON-PARTY AND NON-GOVERNMENT OFFICIALS

Approximately one-quarter of the Supreme Soviet is composed of non-Party and non-government officials, such as military officers, directors of state and collective farms, academicians, and others.

The number of collective farm heads has steadily declined. Military officers and construction foremen have remained stable. Academic officials have risen and fallen, while economic managers have fallen and risen.

While these sub-groups' proportional representation in the Supreme Soviet has fluctuated, the total proportion of all these officials vis-à-vis Party and state officials has steadily declined to less than one-quarter of the Supreme Soviet in the eighth convocation.

SEX AND AGE

The rise in proportion of women in the Supreme Soviet reflects another aspect of the regime's efforts to give the Supreme Soviet a more democratic image. The highest percentage jump since 1958 occurred in the 1970 eighth convocation, up 2.5 percent to a total of 30.5 percent.

TABLE 3.4
PROPORTIONS OF THREE CATEGORIES OF OFFICIALS IN THE SUPREME SOVIET

Convocation	Party	Government	Non-Party State
5th	19.0	16.0	28.0
6th	19.0	16.0	28.0
7th	18.0	15.1	26.0
8th	17.2	14.3	23.5

Source: Pravda and Izvestia.

If the proportion of women in each occupational category is examined, one finds a higher proportion of women among the workers than in the occupied population.[6] The contrary is the case among the government and Party groups, where women comprise a very small proportion of the deputies. Thus, among the most important groups women are decidedly outnumbered by men, an indication of their low level of influence.

When the various convocations of the Supreme Soviet are analyzed by age group, no general pattern appears (see Table 3.5). The first convocation was clearly the youngest; the eighth appears to be the most evenly distributed among age groups, but it is also the oldest with almost exactly one-third over 50. Since the third convocation those under 30 have increased, as have those over 60 since the second convocation. The 41-to-50 group has steadily declined. The 31-to-40 group has vacillated but is the lowest in the eighth convocation since the fifth. This reflects a pattern throughout the institutions of the Soviet political system, which is increasingly dominated by older men.

TABLE 3.5
DEPUTIES OF SUPREME SOVIET BY AGE GROUP

Convocation	Under 30 No.	Under 30 %	31 to 40 No.	31 to 40 %	41 to 50 No.	41 to 50 %	51 to 60 No.	51 to 60 %	Over 60 No.	Over 60 %
2	135	10.1	479	35.8	553	41.3	117	8.7	55	4.1
3	85	6.5	327	24.8	656	49.9	191	14.5	57	4.3
4	110	8.2	259	19.2	598	44.4	318	23.6	62	4.6
5	106	7.7	300	21.8	559	40.5	347	25.2	66	4.8
6	209	14.5	405	28.1	435	30.1	330	22.9	64	4.4
7	182	12.0	434	28.6	420	27.7	386	25.4	95	6.3
8	281	18.5	349	23.0	386	25.5	329	21.7	172	11.3

Source: Verkhovni Sovet (Vosmogosoziva), staticheskii sbornik (Moscow, 1970), p. 48.

COMPARING THE CHAMBERS OF THE SUPREME SOVIET

The Council of Nationalities represents the chief symbolic forum for the expression of nationality interests in the Soviet Union. Its alleged equality with the Council of the Union constitutes a major bulwark of the democratic image of the Supreme Soviet as the embodiment of popular sovereignty.

Analysis of the composition of the two chambers, like analysis of their purported juridical equality, reveals many inequalities as well as equalities.

Numerically, the chambers have always been roughly equal. The rising population had gradually increased the size of the Soviet of the Union until a constitutional amendment redressed the balance prior to the eighth convocation. The numbers of deputies in each age group, as noted, are also roughly equal; in addition, the members of the Presidium of the Supreme Soviet and of the Council of Ministers are distributed somewhat evenly between chambers.

The number of deputies who are Party members has remained roughly equal since 1958, although prior to that the Council of the Union had as much as 10 percent more Party members. The number of deputies bearing decorations in each chamber is roughly equal.

Apparently efforts are made even to maintain equality between the chambers in all categories of education. The Council of Nationalities usually has a slight edge in the number of deputies with a higher education, as well as in deputies who have completed only a primary education.

Both chambers have an almost equal percentage of specialists in trades and professions; however, in each category of specialization there are discrepancies. In the seventh Supreme Soviet, the Council of Nationalities had three times as many economists and twice as many teachers and lawyers. The Council of the Union had a few more doctors and many more engineers and agricultural specialists.

The Council of the Union normally includes more Party officials among its deputies, and the Council of Nationalities more government officials. Non-agricultural workers are usually more numerous in the Council of the Union and agricultural workers in the Council of Nationalities. Directors of enterprises in the fifth, sixth, and seventh convocations were most numerous in the Council of the Union. The military also has more deputies in the Council of the Union.

The entire Supreme Soviet is increasingly becoming a body dominated by older men, although the Council of Nationalities remains the younger body consistently.

As we shall see further on, in the commissions of the Supreme Soviet for the Council of the Union there seem to be consistently more CPSU Central Committee members—perhaps, the most significant indication of the actual inequality between chambers.

From this one might infer that one of the much-touted "equal" chambers is "more equal" than the other. The symbolic equality of the two chambers constitutes a significant bulwark of the Supreme Soviet's representative image and thus of its legitimacy. Nationality representation is constantly stressed. The number of nationalities represented in the Supreme Soviet increased from 58 in 1966 to 62 in 1970, allegedly reflecting the growing deference paid to the diverse nationality interests within the theoretically united will of the Soviet people. Although the two chambers do in fact appear to be unequal, and although that special forum for the expression of nationality interests, the Economic Commission of the Council of Nationalities, is now defunct, the Supreme Soviet and its auxiliary bodies nevertheless remain a significant political institution for airing nationality problems. Thus, it is not surprising that many of the calls for strengthening the legislative powers of the Supreme Soviet come from scholars in the non-Russian republics.

NATIONALITY REPRESENTATION IN THE SUPREME SOVIET

According to the constitution each nationality is represented in the Supreme Soviet through the federal nature of the Soviet state— that is, each union republic, autonomous republic, autonomous region, and national area has a quota of deputies. The statistics, however, do not reveal the actual nationality of each deputy; thus Kazakhstan may send many Russians to the Supreme Soviet, although the statistics seem to imply that they are all Kazakhs.

Several studies have sought to determine what proportion of the Supreme Soviet is occupied by deputies from each nationality.[7] The results shown in Table 3.6 indicate that the major Slavic nationalities (Russians, Ukrainians, Belorussians) are underrepresented when compared to the proportion of the working population they comprise. An analysis of earlier convocations of the Supreme Soviet comparing the Council of Nationalities alone with the 1939 census confirms the underrepresentation of the major Slavic nationalities and the over-representation of other nationalities. However, as we shall see further on, in the higher organs of the Party this representation pattern is reversed—major Slavic nationalities are overrepresented and the other nationalities are underrepresented.

COMPOSITION AS A MIRROR OF POLICY SHIFTS

One scholar argues that shifts of Party policy can often be detected, or are at least reflected, in changes of proportions of the Supreme Soviet comprised by various occupational groupings, since as a rule these proportions remain relatively consistent over time, but this appears to be a rather tenuous and unrewarding pursuit.[8] As an illustration, he points to substantial increases in the numbers of members of the Council of Ministers and ministry officials between 1958 and 1966, and the disappearance of Sovnarkhoz chairmen between 1962 and 1966 corresponding to the gradual revival of the ministries after the 1957 economic reform. The decline of police officials (for example, from 67 in 1937 to 15 in 1954) probably reflects the decline in terror as an instrument of rule, as well as the decline of the social status of the police. Also, the increased concern about Soviet agricultural policy was reflected by the appearance of farm heads in the seventh Supreme Soviet convocation, according to this scholar.

In summary, the composition of the Supreme Soviet is designed to project an image of representativeness which will enhance its own legitimacy, the legitimacy of its acts, and the legitimacy of the regime according to Soviet as well as Western standards. The Supreme Soviet's compositional pattern is a cross-section of the best in every occupation, nationality, and sex, and thus the basis is laid for the Soviet claim that theirs is the most representative assembly in the world. The Supreme Soviet does not mirror Soviet society, but neither does any other legislature. Like other Soviet organs it possesses a disproportionately high share of officialdom and intelligentsia.

Perhaps the most significant policy shift suggested by the composition of the Supreme Soviet is toward some greater concern for a more democratic image. This can be inferred from the greater proportion of genuine proletarians that appear to have been elected in the more recent convocations. However, the regime here is only injecting a greater degree of credibility into the Supreme Soviet's

TABLE 3.6

NATIONAL REPRESENTATION IN THE U.S.S.R. SUPREME SOVIET

| | Population 1959 | | Supreme Soviet 1962 | | 1966 | |
| | No. | | | | | |
Nationality	(thousands)	%	No.	%	No.	%
Russians	114,114	54.65	626	43.38	645	42.52
Ukrainians	37,253	17.84	211	14.62	200	13.18
Belorussians	7,913	3.79	54	3.74	56	3.69
Uzbeks	6,015	2.88	43	2.98	52	3.43
Georgians	2,692	1.29	46	3.19	50	3.30
Azerbaijanis	1,940	1.41	45	3.12	47	3.10
Lithuanians	2,326	1.11	30	2.08	32	2.11
Moldavians	2,214	1.06	19	1.32	22	1.45
Latvians	1,400	0.67	21	1.46	28	1.85
Kirghiz	967	0.46	19	1.32	23	1.52
Tadzhiks	1,397	0.67	28	1.94	35	2.32
Armenians	2,787	1.33	40	2.77	48	3.16
Turkmens	1,002	0.48	19	1.32	27	1.78
Estonians	989	0.47	27	1.87	29	1.91
Finns	93	0.04	2	0.14	1	0.07
Jews	2,268	1.09	5	0.35	5	0.33
Poles	1,380	0.66	4	0.28	5	0.33
Bashkirs	989	0.47	12	0.83	9	0.59
Buriats	253	0.12	8	0.55	9	0.59
Kabardinians	204	0.10	6	0.42	6	0.40
Kalmyks	106	0.05	6	0.42	6	0.40
Karolians	167	0.08	5	0.35	6	0.40
Komis	431	0.21	8	0.55	9	0.59
Maris	504	0.24	6	0.42	5	0.33
Mordvinians	1,285	0.62	7	0.49	7	0.46
Ossetians	413	0.20	13	0.90	14	0.92
Tatars	4,968	2.38	14	0.97	18	1.19
Tuvinians	100	0.05	8	0.55	8	0.53
Udmurts	625	0.30	6	0.42	6	0.40
Chechens	419	0.20	5	0.35	6	0.40
Chuvashes	1,470	0.70	9	0.62	8	0.53
Yakuts	237	0.11	8	0.55	5	0.33
Kara-Kalpaks	173	0.08	6	0.42	5	0.33
Abkhazians	65	0.03	7	0.49	7	0.46
Others	5,046	2.42	37	2.56	42	2.77
TOTAL	208,827	100.00	1,443	100.00	1,517	100.00

Source: Yaroslav Bilinsky, "The Rulers and the Ruled," Problems of Communism, 16, 5 (Sept.–Oct. 1967), 23.

image by replacing social origin with occupation as the test of its proletarian content. However, this credibility and thus the Supreme Soviet's legitimacy is somewhat diminished by the leadership's maintaining rigid control of the Supreme Soviet in a myriad of ways—even through the election process. Nevertheless, clearly the Supreme Soviet's representativeness is one major gauge of its legitimacy, and of its utility to the regime, and thus can be manipulated only within limits.

ELECTIONS TO THE SUPREME SOVIET

Although in neither theory or practice do they serve to choose a government, the elections to the Supreme Soviet perform several valuable functions for the regime which are, however, offset somewhat by the elaborate mechanism of controls which the regime maintains over the entire process.

Functionally Soviet elections serve, first of all, as an external propaganda device disseminating the image of a somewhat democratic society abroad, although the credibility of the image is probably negligible in nations that have relatively open elections free from corruption. It may be substantial in nations without elections at all. Secondly, the elections may serve as a barometer of public dissatisfaction, as a sort of warning device for the regime. Alternatively they may serve to impart a feeling of participation, of doing one's duty by supporting the candidates of the regime. Election speeches are ceremonial occasions in which the regime propagates its policies for external and internal consumption. Finally, elections are part of the facade of legitimacy and legality which the regime finds increasingly valuable for ratifying its policies and identifying its will with that of the masses.

AUTHORITY OF THE SUPREME SOVIET

It is not accidental that leading Soviet authorities in a standard work on state and law include the electoral system in a chapter entitled "How the Soviet State Is Administered."[9] Leading Western authorities agree that the electoral system is a major bulwark of the regime's control over the polity.[10] The electoral system is viewed herein both as another administrative pyramid over which the Supreme Soviet potentially exercises control and, alternatively as a key mechanism through which the regime may control the Supreme Soviet.

The Supreme Soviet elects its Presidium, which by law runs the election process.[11] Although such arguments have never been made public, one can imagine a legalistic debate over whether this power of the Presidium is an independent constitutional power. If so, its effect would be to virtually legalize the Presidium's control over the process of electing the deputies to the Supreme Soviet, which could in fact subordinate the Supreme Soviet to its Presidium. That was clearly not the original intent of the Constitution, although its evolution, as we shall see, has certainly been in that direction.

By law the Presidium of the Supreme Soviet must approve the selection of members of the electoral commissions which actually run the polling booths and approve the nominees. Members of the commissions are selected by meetings of mass organizations and at places of work. There is substantial evidence that the Party activists at these meetings as well as at the nomination meetings exercise control over the selection of personnel.

The electoral commissions carry out three functions: they (1) register candidates, (2) operate the polls, and (3) tally the results.

THE ELECTION PROCESS

The election process begins with the dissolution of the Supreme Soviet and the calling of elections by the Presidium of the Supreme Soviet.[12] Two months before the elections, the Presidium draws up election districts of roughly equal population. District election commissions are then selected by representatives of mass organs at places of work and the lists are submitted to the Presidium for approval.

Over 1,300,000 persons participate in the election commissions—a massive facade for the exercise of participatory democracy. Apparently the Party apparatus exercises some influence in determining the proportional composition of these commissions in order to maintain the democratic-representational image described below. The election commissions constitute a vast pyramid for carrying out the election of Supreme Soviet deputies (see Table 3.7).

The next step after the Presidium approves the composition of the election commissions is the nomination of deputies at their places of work.[13] Then the nominees are registered with the election commissions.[14]

TABLE 3.7

NUMBER AND COMPOSITION OF ELECTION COMMISSIONS FOR ELECTIONS TO THE SUPREME SOVIET

Election commissions	No. of commissions	No. of members	Men		Women		Party		Non-Party	
			No.	%	No.	%	No.	%	No.	%
Central Election Commission	1	27	19	70.4	8	29.6	20	74.1	7	25.9
Election commissions for Soviet of Nationalities	53	789	415	52.6	374	47.4	451	57.2	338	42.8
(No. of commissions in:)										
Union republics	15	265	147	55.5	118	44.5	165	62.3	100	37.7
Autonomous republics	20	294	155	52.7	139	47.3	164	55.8	48	44.2
Autonomous oblasts	8	102	52	51.0	50	49.0	54	52.9	48	47.1
National areas	10	128	61	47.7	67	52.3	63	53.1	60	46.9
District election commissions	1,517	16,687	8,463	50.7	8,224	49.3	8,695	52.0	7,992	47.9
(No. for:)										
Soviet of Union	767	8,437	4,323	51.2	4,114	48.8	4,432	52.5	4,005	47.5
Soviet of Nationalities	750	8,250	4,140	50.2	4,110	49.8	4,263	51.7	3,987	48.3

Source: Verkhovny sovet (Vosmogosoziva), statitcheskii sbornik (Moscow, 1970), pp. 40–41.

In the nomination of candidates for the election commissions and for the Supreme Soviet deputies, the Party *aktiv* is undoubtedly quite vigilant. There is evidence from the Smolensk archives, and from interviews with refugees, of NKVD interference in the nominations to the first convocation.[15] The latent shadow of the police must still hang over nomination meetings when the leading Party *apparatchik* in the district proposes a candidate.[16] Personnel selection has always been a bulwark of Party influence over the polity and must be even more crucial since the decline of terror inherent in de-Stalinization.

Following announcement of nominations, considerable speech-making by leading Party figures before rallies, which are widely and continuously reported, takes place. This "campaign" stressed primarily three themes in Stalin's era[17] : (1) personal glorification of Stalin, (2) the democratic nature of the Soviet polity, and (3) the imperative need to industrialize.

In short, the nominations and elections for the Supreme Soviet in Stalin's day served primarily to mobilize the populace and inculcate the notion that it was their civic duty to labor intensively to "build communism," which in that era meant working harder to increase labor productivity and thus facilitate the industrialization of the Soviet Union. More recently, election speeches have focused on foreign policy and aspects of economic reform.

After the speechmaking come the actual elections. In the elections, citizen participation is heavy due largely to considerable social and political pressure to vote. While voter participation in early elections was less than 50 percent, since 1937 it has averaged over 95 percent.[18] (See Table 3.8.) Citizens may vote yes or no for the one candidate. They may vote yes by simply dropping the ballot into the ballot box, or they may vote no by stepping into a secret booth and striking out the candidate's name.[19] This proved highly risky in Stalin's day. This procedure provides one illustration of the sublety of Party control at each stage of the election process. Most candidates are elected by an overwhelming majority, though occasionally candidates for local elections are rejected. In the 1966 election to the Supreme Soviet, 356,643 voted against the official candidates to the Council of the Union and 289,298 against the official candidates to the Council of Nationalities.

The missing one percent of those who are eligible to vote represents another form of dissent—individual abstentions. Both group dissent—that is, those who vote no—and individual dissent, reflected

TABLE 3.8
ELECTION RESULTS AND DATES

| | | | | No. & % Voting | |
Convocation	Date of election	Total electorate	No. & % voting	Soviet of the Union	Soviet of Nationalities
1	12/12/37	94,138,159	91,113,153 96.79	89,844,271 98.61	89,063,169 97.75
2	2/10/46	101,717,686	101,450,936 99.74	100,621,225 99.18	100,603,567 99.16
3	3/12/50	111,116,373	111,090,010 99.98	110,788,377 99.73	100,782,009 99.72
4	3/14/54	120,750,816	120,727,826 99.98	120,479,249 99.71	120,539,860 99.84
5	3/16/58	133,836,325	133,796,091 99.97	113,214,652 99.57	133,431,524 99.73
6	3/18/62	140,022,359	139,957,809 99.95	139,210,431 99.47	139,391,455 99.60
7	6/12/66	144,000,973	143,917,031 99.94	143,570,976 99.76	143,595,678 99.80
8	6/14/70	153,237,112	153,172,213 99.96	152,771,739 99.74	152,843,228 99.79

Source: Verkhovny sovet (Vosmogosoziva), statitcheskii sbornik (Moscow, 1970), pp. 48–49.

in the abstentions, have been declining since 1960, which indicates either some satisfaction with improving living conditions or a realization of the futility of such dissent against the powerful Party apparat.[20]

THE PARTY APPARAT AND THE ELECTION SYSTEM

A monolithic Party apparatus has a multiplicity of instruments at its disposal as vehicles for controlling the election of delegates to the Supreme Soviet and thus the Supreme Soviet itself. However, a fracturing of this monolith would provide mechanisms for avoiding and evading the will of the apparat. There are at least nine stages where the Party can exercise almost decisive influence over the election system, provided it possesses that all-important unity of will:

(1) Nomination of election commissions;
(2) Approval of election commissions by the Presidium;
(3) Nomination of deputies to the Supreme Soviet;

(4) Certification of nomination of deputies by election commissions;
(5) Certification of balloting by the election Commissions;
(6) Certification of credentials of deputies by Credentials Commission of the Supreme Soviet;
(7) Acceptance of report of Credentials Commission by the plenum of the Supreme Soviet;
(8) Gerrymandering the election districts by the Presidium;
(9) Recall of deputies by referendum.

This study does not pretend to be a thorough study of the Soviet electoral system. Much excellent work has already appeared on the subject. However, the list above should illustrate that the Party has many avenues, both legal and practical, of controlling the Supreme Soviet through personnel selection. Any radical or moderate attempt to wrest control from the apparat would have to confront these mechanisms.

The chief instrument and supervisor of the whole process appears to be the Presidium of the Supreme Soviet. This pyramid, the election system, is thus one more mechanism for facilitating the administration of Soviet society primarily through socializing the populace. From a legalistic point of view, it is another vast network of institutions nominally subordinate to the Supreme Soviet. From a practical viewpoint, the nine mechanisms above might be viewed as nine barometers (among many others) to be watched closely for signs of the weakening of the apparatus's grip and the gradual emergence of the Supreme Soviet as an independent organ. At present, one must admit that the perfunctory manner in which the polity carries out the nine stages provides no evidence of the potential of these trappings coming to life.

Chapter 4

HOW THE SUPREME SOVIET WORKS:
INTERNAL PROCEDURES AND SESSIONS

Descriptions of the meetings of the plenum of the Supreme Soviet have not occupied scholarly interest to any significant extent, largely because they appear to be perfunctory; in fact, a casual glance at the stenographic reports reveals a disarming sameness coupled with a "festival-like" atmosphere—an accusation about which the Soviets are quite sensitive.

This description of the physical setting and routine of Supreme Soviet meetings attempts to characterize the general tenor of each convocation, referring not only to sessional activities such as critiques of the Supreme Soviet in the press and law journals but also to leading Party statements on the role of the soviets. It also seeks to illuminate unique aspects of sessions in each convocation. With the routine aspects of the meetings as background, an attempt is made to discern trends and patterns of institutional evolution from these somewhat uncharacteristic events.

Each time a new Supreme Soviet is elected it is said to have been convoked, and a new convocation begins. Since World War II the Supreme Soviet has been convoked every four years pursuant to the Constitution. A convocation is similar to a United States Congress, except for its length of four years. Each convocation has a varying number of sessions. Since Stalin's death the number of sessions per convocation has substantially increased to about two per year. As we shall see, the number of days, hours, or even minutes which constitute a session varies considerably. The Council of Elders apparently establishes the number of sessions when it sets the agenda, and there is seldom a deviation from that schedule. A session is similar to a session of the U.S. Congress.

Stenographic copies, allegedly verbatim, of each Supreme Soviet session are issued soon after each session is complete.[1] Their name is *Zasedania Verkhovnogo Soveta SSSR*. *Pravda* and *Izvestia* also issue abbreviated reports of sessions. Some of the activities are reported in *Vedomosti Verkhovnogo Soveta SSSR*. It is difficult to determine to what extent *Zasedania* is edited, although, as we shall see, some of the speeches are toned down. In theory the sessions are open to the public; however, in fact it is quite difficult for a foreign scholar from a non-socialist country to gain access. This, plus the undoubted control of press coverage, renders the much-touted public sessions somewhat less than an open debating forum.

PHYSICAL LOGISTICS—THE SETTING

The Supreme Soviet has no home of its own, which some might argue reflects on its independence as an institution. In the seventh and eighth convocations it met in the new Kremlin Hall of Congresses, where the Party Congresses meet, as well as other large gatherings such as those of the trade unions or performances of ballets and operas. Prior to these convocations it met in the Great Hall of the Kremlin, also the scene of previous Party Congresses and other gatherings.

The commissions of the Supreme Soviet meet in Sverdlov Hall in the Kremlin, at least when all 26 commissions are in joint session. A joint session amounts to about two-thirds of the Supreme Soviet— approximately 912 members. These joint sessions seem to be a collection of the entire Supreme Soviet minus the genuine workers and peasants. That is, they are the elite core of officials and intellectuals and specialists. They meet in joint session just prior to the full sessions, as a sort of final review before the presentation of bills to the full Supreme Soviet for formal discussion and ratification.

In both the Great Hall and the Palace of Congresses the deputies sit in parallel rows, facing the front where the ten officers of the chambers sit. Behind them sit the Party and government leaders. Until the fifth convocation the Party and government leaders sat in balconies and lodges on either side of the halls and to the front. Whether this shift in locus signifies any major change in the institutions' status is a matter of speculation. Some might argue that it symbolizes the increasing utility of the Supreme Soviet for the regime.

Certainly, the seating pattern for the Supreme Soviet symbolizes its ratifying, executory character. In the English Parliament, the opposing parties face each other—a format which facilitates debate. Even the semicircle of the United States Congress facilitates debate more than the auditorium-like atmosphere of the Soviet "parliament."

Perhaps the huge, tense image of Lenin which looks down on the deputies in the Great Hall, where meetings of individual chambers are now held, symbolizes the importance of Party guidance. In any case, the seating pattern reflects the fundamental pattern of Supreme Soviet sessions: speeches from the leadership, followed by supporting speeches from the floor and—more often recently—mild criticisms from the floor usually of implementation of past programs by the ministries. There is no real debate in the sense of give-and-take, repartee. The seating arrangement does not encourage this and neither does the regime. The general impression created by the physical-logistical setting is one of a united body receiving the word so that it may return to spread it.

PROCEDURAL ROUTINES

FREQUENCY AND LENGTH OF SESSIONS

The frequency and length of Supreme Soviet sessions also seem to reflect its apparent increasing utility to the regime. Since Stalin's death the frequency and length of the sessions have increased. While Stalin lived, the Supreme Soviet met approximately only once in every year; since then, it has met about twice each year. (See Table 4.1.)

The duration of each session varies but it usually does not last longer than a week. The shortest session on record was the one confirming Stalin's death, which lasted only 67 minutes. Normally, the Supreme Soviet meets from 11 A.M. until 3 P.M., then reconvenes at 6 P.M. and adjourns at 10 P.M. This somewhat formalistic pattern again reflects the rather perfunctory nature of the sessions. The length of each individual meeting seldom varies.

The pattern of meetings does not change much either. The first

TABLE 4.1

**CONVOCATIONS AND SESSIONS OF THE
SUPREME SOVIET**

Convocation	Number of sessions	Years between convocations
1 (1938–46)	12	9
2 (1946–50)	5	4
3 (1950–54)	5	4
4 (1954–58)	9	4
5 (1958–62)	7	4
6 (1962–66)	7	4
7 (1966–70)	7	4
8 (1970–74)	7	4

meeting of each session makes appointments and elects officers (always unanimously); the next two or three meetings discuss the budget; and the remainder discuss whatever major legislation is presented and ratify the decrees of the Presidium of the Supreme Soviet.

Soviet sources explain the short sessions by pointing to the executive nature of the Supreme Soviet:

> The system of periodic sessions enables the deputies, who remain after their election actively employed in the national economy, science and culture, and the state apparatus, without being separated from their basic work and from the masses, to verify in a practical manner the actual execution of laws and to participate through their own activities in the fulfillment of the laws.[2]

Soviet sources are somewhat at pains to explain why Supreme Soviet sessions are more frequent, which implies more democracy, yet the number of meetings and the atmosphere surrounding them remains relatively stable. They are increasingly sensitive to Western critics of the somewhat robot-like performance at the sessions, as shown in the following:

> But back to the unanimity with which bills are adopted. We are usually taken to task for it by capitalist writers, who complain about the lack of debate. It is, indeed, a fact that the Supreme Soviet adopts laws unanimously. However, unanimity is not the point of departure but the effect of assiduous and, as we have just learned, drawn out effort.[3]

In effect, the argument is that sessions are somewhat perfunctory because the work and debate take place before the sessions. This is a relatively new admission. Previously, the fiction was maintained that unanimity displayed at sessions was spontaneous. Since the expansion of the commission system in 1966, the argument is that debate over Soviet legislation takes place in the commissions and at public meetings. As we shall see, there is substantial truth to this contention.

PRE-SESSIONAL ACTIVITIES

Since Stalin's death, pre-sessional activities of various auxiliary and Party bodies have increased considerably. There is almost always a meeting of the Party Central Committee prior to a Supreme Soviet session. There is always a meeting of the Council of Elders, a small body of supposedly experienced deputies whose prime function allegedly is to arrange the agenda. In fact, this could amount to a committee of Party leaders with responsibility for coordinating the sessions; its occupational composition is known but its deputies' names are not available. Many of the Supreme Soviet commissions meet one month before each session, ostensibly to put final touches on bills. The commissions meet separately or in joint session with their opposite number in the other chamber or as a combined session of all twenty-six commissions.

All of this activity is clearly designed to assure the festive air of unanimity and solidarity which surrounds the actual sessions. The vast increase in legislation by the Supreme Soviet since Khrushchev's ascent to power requires a more complex mechanism for coordinating general policy with the details of the legal norms enacted by the Supreme Soviet.

There is clearly more time devoted to legislative or ratificational activities at the sessions, as distinguished from the mobilizational and adulatory activities that dominated Stalin's Supreme Soviet sessions.

CONVENING THE SUPREME SOVIET

According to the Constitution, the Presidium of the Supreme Soviet convenes and dissolves the Supreme Soviet. The term of each Supreme Soviet is four years, although during the Great Patriotic War this role was suspended and the term of the first Supreme Soviet lasted for nine years. Since then, each term has lasted approximately four years.

When the term expires, the Presidium of the Supreme Soviet must order new elections within two months (Article 54). The Presidium of the Supreme Soviet formally dissolves the Supreme Soviet at the end of each four-year term (Article 53). It may also dissolve the Supreme Soviet under another set of circumstances. If the two chambers of the Supreme Soviet cannot agree on legislation, the disagreement is referred to a conciliation commission formed by both houses on an equal basis. If this commission cannot resolve the dispute, then the Presidium of the Supreme Soviet may dissolve the Supreme Soviet and hold new elections (Article 47).

Since there has almost never been a recorded "no" vote in the history of either chamber, this somewhat complex procedure appears somewhat ludicrous. However, it serves as a symbol of the Council of Nationalities' equality, and were the regime's monolithic control of the Supreme Soviet ever to relax, it could become quite significant.

The Presidium must convene new sessions of the Supreme Soviet within three months after elections (Article 55). This power to convene and dissolve the Supreme Soviet is an important instrument of control over the Supreme Soviet.

THE SEEDS OF REAL DEBATE

As we have seen, the one criticism of the Supreme Soviet which Soviet authorities seem most sensitive to is that there is no debate at the sessions. They point to the executive character of the assembly and to the debates in the commissions, at public meetings, and the press.

In fact, Western critics have not been quite fair to the Supreme Soviet, as one scholar has pointed out. The discussions in the Supreme Soviet of late do seem to show more "ginger."[4] Criticism of the ministries is on the rise. However, there are other forms of "semi-debate" than mild criticism of ministerial implementation of legislation. There are, for example, unscheduled speeches and proposals which are, in effect, an indirect form of disputing the regime's policy. Since Supreme Soviet sessions are highly regulated, there are three kinds of "debate," in effect, which take place on the floor: (1) unscheduled speeches; (2) unscheduled proposed amendments; and (3) scheduled criticism of ministries.

There appear to have been only two unscheduled speeches in the entire history of the Supreme Soviet.[5] At the first session of the first convocation a deputy objected to the Council of Nationalities meeting at night, and at the second session Stalin interrupted an academician, which was the only time Stalin ever spoke in the Supreme Soviet.

Perhaps the most dramatic "debate" in the history of the Supreme Soviet came in the seventh convocation discussion on the draft law on marriage and the family. The Supreme Soviet was in joint session with both chambers about to take the usual perfunctory vote, when a Lithuanian school teacher proposed some amendments to the law. Although the verbatim record *Zasedania* does not reveal the incident, there apparently was some consternation. The proposed amendments were considered so essential to the draft bill that discussion ensued which led to an almost unheard-of extension of the sitting beyond the usual time of adjournment. Eventually, the chairman of the session made the following statement: "Considering that several amendments to the various articles, of the draft have been proposed, it is suggested that the vote be postponed until tomorrow, giving the standing commissions time to discuss them."[6] Obviously, the Chair did not want to risk what might have been the first non-unanimous vote in the Supreme Soviet history. The relevant commissions did burn the midnight oil to hear jurists and scientists discuss the amendments. The commissions reported back to the plenum of the Supreme Soviet the next day in favor of the adoption of the schoolteacher's (Deputy V. I. Shimukonene) proposal. The amendments were carried unanimously.

It is perhaps symbolic of the somewhat new aura of democracy surrounding this institution that the Soviet writer who reported this incident did not treat it as an obviously unscheduled and potentially embarrassing episode but as an example of the democratic nature of the institution. That it was reported at all is significant, but that it should be identified as illustrative is quite intriguing.

The third form of "debate" in Supreme Soviet sessions is criticism which is specifically scheduled. It is usually ex post facto criticism of faculty implementation of policy by the ministries. It seldom involves criticism of the policy itself, although it is sometimes couched in disguised verbiage which implies criticism of policy and suggests quite indirectly a new course.

The first example of this kind of criticism occurred on the fifth day of the first session of the first convocation, when a high Party official criticized the foreign policy of the Commissar for Foreign Affairs, M. M. Litvinov. A. A. Zhdanov, First Secretary of the Leningrad Oblast Party Committee, delivered a broad attack on Litvinov's policy, citing his failure to recover a plane shot down over

Japan and his failure to close some foreign consulates in the USSR.[7] Shortly after this, V. M. Molotov defended the policy, and Litvinov fell from grace.[8] Molotov was, of course, at that time Chairman of the Council of Ministers.

A more characteristic form of criticism occurred at the second session of the seventh session (1967) when A. D. Nutetegryneh, a deputy of the Council of Nationalities, criticized the Ministry of Civil Aviation for its disregard of local airlines. In answer, at a later session of the Ministry of Civil Aviation, Y. F. Loginov, himself a deputy, reported on a long list of measures which his ministry was planning to take in order to improve the local airlines.[9] Here the emphasis was primarily on improving the implementation of an established policy.

Another more common form of criticism calls for better use of resources. This kind of complaint seems to have increasingly occupied the sessions of the seventh and eighth convocations. For example, at the same session and meeting described above, Deputy Y. V. Ilnitsky stressed the importance of working deposits of marble, tufa, and other building materials available in the Trans-Carpathian Region. Deputy A. Klychov proposed greater exploitation of oil deposits in the Turkmen Republic.[10]

The nature and function of criticism in the Supreme Soviet sessions is somewhat nebulous and difficult to identify. Undoubtedly, it serves varying functions which overlap and recombine from convocation to convocation. In the first convocation, criticism was sharp and personal, designed perhaps to facilitate the purges. Criticism after Stalin's death was mild and seemed to serve the function of airing some common administrative problems as a heuristic device for other bureaucrats who might be employing similar methods. In the more recent seventh and eighth convocations, the "kontrol" function appears to predominate, with perhaps some implicit policy criticism.

THE THEME AND TENOR
OF CONVOCATION
SESSIONS

The sessions at each convocation follow a general pattern, but the tenor, theme, or aura of each convocation, as distinguished from the purely procedural aspects of the convocation, does differ. What follows is a description of the general pattern, and an attempt to characterize some essential thematic differences in each convocation.

THE GENERAL PATTERN

Each first session is generally opened by the oldest deputy, "as instructed by the Council of Elders."[11] Then the officers of the chambers (four vice-chairmen and one chairman per chamber) are nominated by the motion of groups of deputies. The motions are always unanimously carried. Each chamber chairman presides over his respective chamber, and they alternate for joint sessions of both chambers. Under the new seating format, the chairman sits behind the speaker's platform at a sort of head table with his vice-chairmen on either side.

The next step is the unanimous approval of the standing orders, approved by the Council of Elders (their only known function), which is, in effect, an agenda for future sessions. With few exceptions this includes a budget session, a session for discussing other extraordinary legislation, and a session for approving the decrees of the Presidium of the Supreme Soviet. The standing orders also regulate joint and separate meetings of the Supreme Soviet.

Then a real agenda establishing the list of speakers is passed. Several kinds of speeches are permitted:[12]

(1) Reports: up to 90 minutes;
(2) Co-reports: 30 minutes, plus 15 minutes for "closing words";
(3) Discussion participants: 20 minutes, plus 5 minutes for "closing words";
(4) Explanation of vote: 3 minutes; and
(5) Independent speeches: 5 minutes.

The first three kinds of speeches are part of one process. A report is usually a long statement of policy by a high Party or government official. Co-reports are more detailed discussions of policy implementation by responsible officials, usually from the ministries. They follow the short comments by ordinary deputies on the matter being discussed. Both the co-reporters and the ordinary deputies have time for "closing words," which constitute in effect summary or rebuttal time. In fact, there is no evidence of the ordinary deputies ever making "closing words." Occasionally, co-reporters will use them to reply to explicit or implicit criticism leveled by ordinary deputies.

The three-minute explanation of vote rule has never been used, probably because of the general unanimity of voting. Although apparently superfluous, the rule does offer direction should unanimity be lacking.

Criticism emanates from two kinds of speeches, those of participants in scheduled discussions of reports, and scheduled five-minute independent speeches. However, a large proportion of these speeches is dominated by praise rather than criticism.

Following the approval of the agenda of scheduled speeches, a series of elections is efficiently rushed through in a matter of minutes. The Presidium of the Supreme Soviet is elected, the members of the commissions are approved, and the Council of Ministers is approved. This pattern is not invariable,[13] but each list usually carries with it the endorsement of the CPSU Central Committee and the Council of Elders.

This then is the general pattern of every first session: the opening, election of officers, vote of the standing orders, election of the Presidium, appointment of the government, appointment of commissions, and acceptance of the agenda.

The subsequent meetings and sessions follow the speech pattern outlined above: report, co-report, discussion, unanimous approval of proposed legislation or policy statement. Since the expansion of the commission system in 1966, the chairmen of the commissions have participated in the speechmaking extensively. The order of discussion in the agenda for the convocation invariably starts with the budget, which sometimes occupies many days, and usually the whole second session of any convocation. Other special legislation then is dealt with by the same speechmaking. Then Presidium decrees are ratified. The only other events which repeatedly occupy sessional time are foreign policy speeches which are interjected at almost any time. Such speeches seem to occupy less time proportionally in the more recent sessions and convocations. There is evidence that this de-emphasis is deliberate.[14]

While the procedural aspects of each convocation have not evolved much over time, one can discern significant shifts in the general tenor and aura surrounding each convocation, both within and outside the actual sessions. Table 4.2 attempts to characterize the themes of these internal and external events which give each convocation its own distinct image. This chart does not reflect clearly crystallized images, but rather overlapping processes from which an institutional pattern is emerging and from which some jurists might discern concepts of inherent powers.

TABLE 4.2
THE IMAGE OF EACH
CONVOCATION: CHARACTERIZING
THEIR TENOR

Convocation	Characterized aura-image
1 (1938–46)	Criticism and glorification
2 (1946–50)	Deification and mobilization
3 (1950–54)	Reconnoitering and regrouping
4 (1954–58)	Criticizing the institution
5 (1958–62)	Demarche
6 (1962–66)	Reforming the institution
7 (1966–70)	Economic reform and "kontrol"[a]
8 (1970–74)	"Kontrol" and economic reform

a. The concept of "kontrol" is discussed in Chapter 6

THE FIRST CONVOCATION: CRITICISM AND GLORIFICATION

The first convocation of the Supreme Soviet was unquestionably unique, which one might expect in the first operational gathering of a new political institution. Two themes predominated: first, there was sweeping and almost vitriolic criticism of certain personalities, which reflected the Great Purges then reaching a crescendo; second, there was inordinate glorification of Stalin—signifying the success of the purges—after the first session.

The first session opened with a speech praising the NKVD, in addition to the usual perfunctory remarks—a somewhat ironic and inauspicious beginning for the Supreme Soviet as the institutional paragon of socialist democracy.[15] On the fifth day of the first session, high-ranking Party officials commenced criticism of some ministers. The Litvinov case has been cited. It was the only time that foreign policy has been criticized in the Supreme Soviet, another unique feature of this session.[16] The brutal nature of some of the attacks on ministers is exemplified by A. A. Zhdanov's criticism of the Minister (then called Commissar) of Water Transport, N. I. Pakhomov:

The calm complacency which has largely overcome our . . . leadership must be overcome, and they must be warned that if such a state of affairs continues in water transport, then public patience may be exhausted, and if things are not corrected by the next session—the cuckoo may cease to cuckoo for the leadership of the People's Commissariat of Water Transport. . . .[17]

This sharp personal criticism characterizes much of the criticism of this convocation; it is clearly a reflection of the purge atmosphere pervading the entire polity. Its sharpness is unique to this convocation.

Only the early sessions were remarkable for such incidents; the remainder followed the general pattern outlined previously for all sessions, except for the inordinate glorification of Stalin. Two other distinctive events in Supreme Soviet history occurred at the first convocation: the only non-unanimous votes, and the only real interpellation.

The non-unanimous votes actually recorded in the stenographic reports of the Supreme Soviet did not involve policy and did not involve both chambers. The votes were on procedural questions which concerned the internal organization of the chamber.

All three votes occurred at the first sitting of the Council of Nationalities.[18] On the first, the chairman of the chamber was forced to vote on the standing orders as a whole instead of point-by-point. This was probably due to inexperience. On the second, a majority rejected a motion to require the Council of Nationalities to sit at the same time as its counterpart, the argument being that night sessions for the nationalities was discrimination. The sensitivity of the non-Russian nationalities to even the slightest infringement upon their alleged equality is evident here. The Council of Nationalities has always been their chief forum. They are only too aware that what may appear as a slight procedural distinction may mushroom into a legal rationalization for curbing their real influence. The quarrel over the meeting time of the Council of Nationalities is evidence of this sensitivity. It is further an indication of how the nationalities themselves will seize on any procedural or institutional handle to enhance their position. This is exactly what they did with the Economic Commission of the Council of Nationalities from 1956 until its extinction in 1966. This temporary lapse in the unanimity of the Supreme Soviet undoubtedly served as a warning to the acutely aware Stalin of the double edge to that institution, the Council of Nationalities, which he had created for manipulative purposes. In any case the decision was overruled in 1950, when it was agreed that each chamber should meet on alternate days in the morning in the Great Hall of the Kremlin Palace.[19] Joint sessions are held in the larger and more modern Palace of Congresses.

It will be recalled that the power to interpellate the government has always constituted the backbone of the classic British parliamentary model, and that its use led to the downfall of the Duma. It was also used frequently in the early days of the Central Executive Committee whose bicameral structure the Supreme Soviet imitated. There was only one clear interpellation in this convocation, the Zhdanov inquiry of Litvinov.[20] The line between the verbal critical question and the verbal critical declaration is admittedly fine. This case was a clear question. The right of interpellation is implied in the audit and investigation clause of the Constitution, but has not been used. As we shall see, the new commission system bases its written interrogatories to the ministries on this power, as well as the law expanding the commission system.

THE SECOND CONVOCATION

While the first convocation was perhaps the most exceptional, the second convocation was the most unexceptional. It followed the general pattern almost completely. In the budget speech of the first convocation, the adulatory tone which pervaded all sessions until Stalin's death was set by praising Stalin 25 times in a 26-page report.[21] Adulation and glorification escalated to virtual deification in and out of sessions. There was also a strong blend of exhortation to work harder to increase productivity in both press reports of the sessions and the election speeches. The dominant themes were mobilization for industrialization and glorification of Stalin.

THE THIRD CONVOCATION: RECONNOITERING AND REGROUPING

The third convocation is variegated indeed. There were only five sessions. The 59-minute fourth session of 1953 placed the stamp of legitimacy on the new post-Stalin government, thus ratifying a triple decree of the Party Central Committee, the Presidium of the Supreme Soviet, and the Council of Ministers. This amounted to an approval of the new regime by the organs of legitimacy, legality and administration, which was designed to prevent panic and disarray, as Malenkov put it.

The fits and starts of the convocation probably reflected the succession struggle from Stalin's death to Khrushchev's ascent to power. The entire polity as well was for many years adjusting to the disappearance of its key figure.

This convocation revealed several new departures. Foreign policy speeches for propaganda purposes became part of the repertoire of festivities and remained a rather dominant feature until the economic reforms in 1965.

It was in this convocation that Malenkov foreshadowed those reforms with his oft-quoted suggestion that substantial emphasis be placed on consumer goods expenditures at the implied expense of heavy industry. This pointed to a major shift from Stalinist economic policy. The Soviet press further illuminated this new departure with close to thirty editorials on the subject, many of them taking off from Supreme Soviet speechmaking.

Since no other organ seems to have publicized this new line, one must assume that the Supreme Soviet and not some Party or government body was chosen for the announcement. A precedent was set for future succession crises. It is an available forum for any coalition daring and powerful enough to utilize it.

THE FOURTH CONVOCATION: CRITICIZING THE INSTITUTION

Perhaps the most significant theme surrounding discussion of the Supreme Soviet from 1954 to 1958 was criticism of the institution. Fear of its potential power discussed above probably caused some criticism while the democratizing tendencies unleashed by the Malenkov interregnum may have caused more. In any case, such criticism of the Supreme Soviet in this period reflects a duality, as if a schism prevented the leadership from determining whether to cripple or galvanize the institution. This schism is reflected in Malenkov's resignation from his chairmanship of the Council of Ministers at the second session of this convocation of February 8, 1955.

While Khrushchev revealed a somewhat ambiguous attitude toward the Supreme Soviet, other voices were expressing constructive criticism along a whole range of issues, some of which have been implemented, others of which are still being debated. The first broadside came in the guise of criticism of an attack by three deputies on the functionings of Union Republic supreme soviets.[22] As we shall see, controversial debates concerning the Supreme Soviet are usually first broached to the public as criticisms of the supreme soviets of the Union Republic. This was the first article to appear along these lines; in this case, the Union Republic under fire was the Kazakh SSR. The deputies called for more time to study the budget, for a broader range of reports affecting all aspects of the culture and economy, for activation of the right of "kontrol" over the whole legal system—the courts, Ministry of Justice, and Procuracy—and for increased deputy reporting to constituents.

Shortly after this newspaper article appeared, the first article criticizing the Supreme Soviet itself appeared in *Sovetskoye gosudarstvo i pravo*. This organ of the Soviet Institute of Law and Government has gradually been transformed from a crude instrument of propaganda into a semi-sophisticated journal of Soviet jurisprudence, still liberally sprinkled with ideological rhetoric. This article was the first of a long line suggesting reform, or at least activation, of Supreme Soviet institutional structures.[23] In fact, this piece was an editorial; as such it was a veritable catalogue of stillborn institutional structures. It complained that the customary one session per year violated the constitutional requirement for at least two per year. The authors further argued that this mooted the "kontrol" function and converted the legislative process into mere ratification. Since the sessions were only two or three days long when they did meet, and since many of the deputies did not even prepare their own speeches, the whole institution—the authors implied—was reduced to a festival, not a governing organ.[24]

Another point, still debated today, complained that Presidium ukazes take effect as behavior-regulating norms when issued, thus in effect creating a law without the sanction of a popularly elected body. The normative impact of ukazes prior to their ratification, as we shall see, is still being disputed.[25] Another article in the same journal at about the same time leveled a now-familiar additional criticism of the legislative function of the Presidium of the Supreme Soviet. M. I. Pisotkin argued that interim ukazes violated the exclusive power of the Supreme Soviet to legislate as expressly granted in Article 32 of the Constitution.[26] Pisotkin also asserted that the Supreme Soviet could not exercise its review of the budget unless it also passed on the plan. He suggested that the normative character of the plan in effect rendered it a law, and important legislation at the very least came within the exclusive jurisdiction of the Supreme Soviet. He also pointed out that in a sense the constitutional right to audit and investigate "kontrol" was violated by the Supreme Soviet's inability to consider the plan. He further called for longer sessions.[27]

Apparently, the critics had political support, because changes were made. Prior to the criticism, the Supreme Soviet held three sessions for the first time since 1939—that is, in 1955. Also in that year, the budget was passed for the next year[28]—the first time that a budget had been passed prior to the beginning of a fiscal year. In 1957 yearly plans were included on the agenda along with the budget, satisfying one of Pisotkin's complaints. In February 1956, as we shall see later on, the Economic Commission of the Council of Nationalities was created, ostensibly to assure proper allocation of resources to various federal areas. Some authority over the budget was also devolved to the Republic supreme soviets. In effect, the Supreme Soviet took first steps toward greater involvement in the budgetary process. It is not insignificant that these steps followed only a few years upon Malenkov's first suggestion in the Supreme Soviet that some economic reform might be advantageous. It is also perhaps not without significance that the Supreme Soviet began to discuss important laws more extensively.

THE FIFTH CONVOCATION: DEMARCHE

At the Twentieth Party Congress in 1955, Khrushchev indicated ambivalence toward the Supreme Soviet. He called for more sessions and for the creation of the Economic Commission of the Council of Nationalities, but otherwise continued to remain somewhat noncommittal even when the critics were calling for specific reforms.[29] The speech by Voroshilov, then Chairman of the Presidium of the Supreme Soviet, suggested only one specific reform—a law on the recall of deputies, which was not passed until 1959.[30] This ambivalence may have stemmed from a multitude of overlapping and interlocking motives, not the least of which might have been the regime's fear of this forum being used to call for controversial reforms as in the case of Malenkov's consumer-goods speech.

It is clear that the prospect of institutional reform conjured up radical proposals that might have threatened the very fabric of the polity. The most well-known proposal was a report by the *New York Times* that it had uncovered evidence of proposals for multi-candidate elections such as those in Yugoslavia in 1954.[31] The dual potential of the soviets as a device for manipulation, on the one hand, and, on the other, as an institutional lever for reformers had been clear to Stalin. Multi-candidate elections potentially might unleash a Pandora's box of reform that would threaten the grip of the Party apparatus. The quarrel over the meeting hours of the nationalities had revealed how a slight procedural rule might be seized upon by dissident groups. Multi-candidate elections were not so serious as a multi-party parliament suggested by dissidents in the 1960s, but they were an indication that moderate institutional reforms often lead to demands for more radical reforms threatening the very character of the regime. The leadership reacted quickly to retard the momentum.

The first clear expression of official displeasure came just before the fifth convocation and after Khrushchev's victory over the "anti-Party group." The head of the Institute of Law and Government criticized the recent spate of articles on the Supreme Soviet as follows:

> A number of articles devoted to various phases of activity of the USSR Supreme Soviet and the supreme soviets of the Autonomous Republics (Nos. 3, 7, 9) present a fundamentally one-sided picture of the work of these organs, ineptly pointing out their significant role in the areas of domestic and foreign policy of the Soviet state.[32]

With this, the evolution of the Supreme Soviet ground to a halt while the leadership debated the respective roles of the soviets and the mass organizations. Apparently, Khrushchev feared the potential of the system of soviets. His reform program de-emphasized them. The Twenty-first Party Congress hedged on the development of the soviets. Eventually, Khrushchev accepted the soviets as full partners with the mass organs in building communism. His successors apparently see them as more than partners—they view them as the coordinators of the multiplicity of mass organs whose activities seem to have eluded consistent Party supervision.

THE SIXTH CONVOCATION: REFORMING THE INSTITUTION

The 1961 Party Programme established specific institutional reform and rejuvenation of the state as Party policy. The sixth convocation set about implementing these reforms. Special attention focused on improving the legislative process and activating the "kontrol" function of the Supreme Soviet.

In a sense, the Party Programme reflected the demands of the moderate reformers during the fourth convocation. It called for an extension of jurisdiction of the soviets over a broader spectrum of legislation. At all turns, it emphasized the accountability of the government apparatus to the system of soviets. It stressed the activation of the commission system in the "kontrol" function. It expressed concern for the proper utilization of resources and implied that the soviet system might provide a mechanism for improving the government's management of state affairs.[33]

The essentially new element here is the implicit coupling of institutional reform with the fundamental dilemma of the polity, economic reform. Both subjects had been broached before, but not in conjunction with each other in a fundamental Party document.

Except for the now-standard use of the Supreme Soviet as a forum for propagating foreign policy, this convocation differed little from the standard pattern. The major distinction was the activation of the legislative process and the debates surrounding the proposed expansion of the commission system. Both of these are analyzed and described in detail in the following chapter.

THE SEVENTH CONVOCATION: ECONOMIC REFORM AND "KONTROL"

The dominant themes in this convocation were expansion of the commission system and economic reform—which are recognized as being related: "Not fortuitously at all, it seems, did the institution of the standing commissions coincide in time with the reorganization of planning, the improvement in management and the economic reform."[34]

At the first session of this convocation, N. V. Podgorny reported on the creation of the new system of standing commissions which pursuant to the Party Programme of 1961 had apparently been discussed throughout the entire sixth convocation. The evolution of the commission system is discussed in detail in the next chapter.[35]

Both the seventh and eighth convocations seem to reflect a focus on the struggle to achieve a balance between reform and "kontrol." However, their emphasis is different. Reading through the stenographic reports and the literature, one senses a shift in emphasis from reform in the seventh convocation, to "kontrol" in the eighth convocation, although the two themes are always intertwined and overlapping.

As resistance to the economic reforms of 1965 mounted, the leadership seems to have fallen back on the traditional Soviet approach to economics—enhancing institutional efficiency. The entire system of soviets and especially the new commissions were apparently designed to facilitate more efficient functioning of the government apparatus. However, the regime's reliance on these efficiency-inducing mechanisms appears to have been growing steadily throughout the seventh and into the eighth convocation as reliance on fundamental reorganization of the economy has waned.

The resistance to the reform is clear in the "debates" of the seventh session, which contained a plethora of criticisms of the economic reform. It was in effect a low-key public debate of the reform. Not all the criticisms were destructive; some were constructive, but on balance one feels the weight of the polity shifting away from genuine reform. This interpretation of the "debates" is supported by Soviet commentary.

In discussing the seventh session, the organ of Gosplan (the State Planning Commission), *Planovoye khozyaistvo,* expresses doubt that mere "kontrol" and legislation will resolve economic dilemmas. It, however, cites ministry opposition to the reorganizing and computerizing of the enterprises as the chief barrier.[36] Thus, it joins Academician N. Fedorenko, Director of the Central Institute of Economics and Mathematics of the Academy of Sciences, in his criticism of the ministries.[37] Fedorenko reveals no enthusiasm for the apparent compromise of the leadership—greater efficiency and more reliance on "kontrol" to effect it.

THE EIGHTH CONVOCATION: "KONTROL" AND ECONOMIC REFORM

The first few sessions of the eighth convocation give no evidence of significant departures from the policy expressed by Brezhnev at the Twenty-fourth Party Congress. At the seventh session of the seventh convocation, scattered references to the December 1969 Central Committee meeting and Party Congress reports indicate reform is at an impasse. In the meantime, "kontrol," legislation, and the efficiency they should facilitate form a significant part of the leadership's policy, as excerpts from Brezhnev's report to the Twenty-fourth Party Congress indicate:

(Kontrol)

The USSR Supreme Soviet and the Union Republic supreme soviets have intensified their kontrol over the work of ministries and departments and over the state of affairs in the basic sectors of economic and cultural construction. The increased number of standing commissions and the more systematic organization of their activity enable the deputies to display more initiative, to delve more deeply into the work of executive agencies, and take a more active part in draft laws.

(Legislation)

The Party attaches great importance to *the improvement of Soviet legislation* [emphasis in text]. In the period under review (coinciding with the seventh convocation almost exactly), attention was concentrated on the legislative regulation* of such questions as improving the people's health protection, strengthening the family, further improvement of labor relations, ensuring conservation of natural resources.

(Efficiency)

The successful accomplishment of the tasks confronting us presupposes the precise and well-coordinated work of the *state apparatus* [emphasis in text]. Hence the increased demands on the administrative apparatus. The introduction of up-to-date ways and means of managerial activity, which has begun in the past few years, is creating conditions for the more rational organization of the administrative apparatus, for cutting its cost and reducing its size. Measures along these lines have already been carried out, and they will be continued.

SUMMARY

This attempt to characterize the tenor and themes of each Supreme Soviet convocation has focused on both internal sessional and external events and writings relevant to the evolution of the Supreme Soviet in order to discern some trends, patterns or tendencies.

It is significant that the Supreme Soviet appears to stand in the center with respect to factional and policy disputes. It seems to have developed an image of moderate reform. While it is not tenable to argue that the Supreme Soviet is an arena, it might be argued that it is increasingly emerging as a forum where moderate reforms may be aired. It does not appear to be a bastion of reactionaries or radicals. The discussion of the economic reforms at the seventh session of the seventh convocation reflects this. There was no vitriolic, vendetta-like criticism similar to that which characterized the first convocation. Picayune local requests were minimized. The tone was one of moderately constructive and destructive criticism of the 1965 reforms. One might draw a straight line from Malenkov's suggestions in 1953 to this session. The issue was the same. The tone was restrained. But, most significantly, the forum was the same.

The Party apparatus has always been sensitive to the potential of the Supreme Soviet as a device for radical reform. The lack of unanimity in the early sessions of the first convocation provided the first warning. Proposals for multi-candidate elections in 1956 provided another, and more recently some dissidents have suggested a multi-party Supreme Soviet. The apparat seems to have harnessed this tendency, while retaining the institution to serve its purposes. This is not to say that certain combinations of variables could not resurrect the radicals' proposals.

THE NATURE OF THE SUPREME SOVIET:
LEGISLATIVE OR ADMINISTRATIVE ASSEMBLY?

This analysis focuses on *potential* as well as practice. It is an effort to assess the dynamic potential of present trends, while remaining conscious of the high probability in the Soviet polity that institutional evolution might be arrested at any point.

The Soviet constitution created several institutional systems juridically which have flourished since 1936. It nominally placed the Supreme Soviet at the head of each of these systems, although in differing constitutional positions with respect to each system. The process by which the Supreme Soviet has gradually extended its authority—from both a juridical and a political viewpoint—over each of these systems is also outlined. The analysis is designed to further assess the political potential of the Supreme Soviet's institutional evolution, especially with respect to other institutions in the political system.

The potential of the Supreme Soviet has usually been analyzed with reference to its viability as a legislature. While this will not be ignored, the time is ripe for an analysis of the potential of the Supreme Soviet as the administrative apex of five political institutions. The degree, extent, nature, and form of the Supreme Soviet's influence over each of these institutions varies, but there appears to be a trend toward extending this influence over them all.

The idea that an assembly might act both as executive and legislature is an old one in Russia; the Zemsky Sobor and many major nineteenth-century reforms embodied and advocated this idea. The

Bolsheviks adopted the idea as an antibourgeois device, rejecting both parliamentarism and the separation of powers. Democratic centralism excluded any notion of checks and balances and substituted the concept of separate spheres of competence guided by the same class toward a unified purpose. Thus the Bolshevik notion of union of executive and legislative functions is as old as Russia. The idea of the Supreme Soviet sitting as an assembly at the apex of five systems of administration is natural in the Soviet political culture.

THE CONCEPT OF "KONTROL"

The core of the Supreme Soviet's administrative authority over the five institutional systems is the juridical concept of "kontrol."[1] "Kontrol" in the Russian language is not the equivalent of "control" in English. It is rather more akin to the word "monitor." It also connotes restraint. It carries a less coercive connotation, which conforms to the post-Stalin de-emphasis of coercion in favor of persuasion, especially in legal theory. It is more negative than positive in nature.

"Kontrol" is a restraining, monitoring function. The constitutional power to monitor is derived from Article 51:

> The Supreme Soviet of the USSR, when it deems necessary, appoints commissions of investigation and audit on any matter. It is the duty of all institutions and officials to comply with the demands of such commissions and to submit to them all necessary materials and documents.

Investigation, audit, and publicity are important aspects of the restraining-monitoring functions which are the essence of "kontrol."

Soviet authorities increasingly distinguish between mere supervision of implementation of policy and laws carried out by the ministries and the procuracy, and "kontrol" exercised by the Supreme Soviet. The "kontrol" exercised by the Supreme Soviet is said to be supreme control, which carries two connotations.[2]

The first is that supreme control embodies monitoring by an elective-representative body, which lends it a greater legitimating authority. The second is that supreme control vindicates the Supreme Soviet's right to act in the administrative sphere, exercising "kontrol" over the government.

"Kontrol" pertains to monitoring the effective as well as faithful execution of policy as embodied in legislation, and involves the power to judge whether the laws, policies, and execution should be arrested, reversed, expanded, and modified, while ministries and procuracies are merely charged with seeing that laws are enforced and faithfully carried out; they do not pass judgment on the desirability of the law or policy.

The primary vehicle of "kontrol" for the Supreme Soviet is the Supreme Soviet Commission System, described in much detail further on. As *Izvestia* has put it[3] :

> The commissions are also given broad powers: They must become the eyes, the antennas, of the supreme body of authority [i.e., the Supreme Soviet]; they must become instruments of supreme control.

"Kontrol" is not the only mechanism of Supreme Soviet authority over the five institutional systems, but it has substantially increased in importance, acquiring juridical and organizational flesh. This fleshing out of "kontrol" is a major reason for analysis of the potential of the Supreme Soviet as an administrative arm of the regime. A formerly hollow concept is now buttressed by twenty-six commissions and a plethora of subcommissions.

What follows is an analysis not of the five institutional systems over which the Supreme Soviet has authority, but rather of the potential of existing mechanisms available to the Supreme Soviet for exercising this authority. The focus is on the nexus between the Supreme Soviet and the five political institutions which it nominally heads. One must constantly recall that behind each pyramid and the Supreme Soviet itself stands the CPSU. The evolution of the Supreme Soviet's relationship to each institutional pyramid reflects much about the evolving relationship of the Supreme Soviet and the Party, as well as the changing nature of each respective institution, both of which are examined specifically in a subsequent chapter.

THE SUPREME SOVIET'S AUTHORITY
OVER THE ORGANS OF STATE POWER

The organs of state power are the soviets at all levels. Each soviet, except the local soviets, has a presidium and a system of commissions as well as an apparatus to assist it. The local soviets may appoint commissions, and they have an executive committee which is theoretically distinct from a presidium.

The actual authority of the Supreme Soviet over each level of soviet is not easy to discern with precision. There seems to be an effort to simultaneously expand the activity at each level while systematically and increasingly integrating the whole system into a hierarchy with the Supreme Soviet and its auxiliary bodies at the apex.[4] The number of persons involved in the system is shown in Table 5.1.

The Supreme Soviet exercises its influence and authority over the subordinate organs of state power through five major mechanisms: (1) law; (2) overlapping personnel; (3) "kontrol"; (4) publicity; and (5) circulation of materials.

As discussed previously, the constitution requires the legal acts of subordinate soviets to conform to those of the Supreme Soviet. The proliferation of All-Union Fundamentals of Legislation has brought most major areas of law into conformity with Supreme Soviet zakons. In effect the Fundamentals are concurrent legislation with republic supreme soviets.[5] The ukaz of the Presidium of the Supreme Soviet is also a powerful weapon over lower soviets.[6]

Key officials of lower soviets always sit in the Supreme Soviet as deputies and thus according to democratic centralism serve to represent the central body back to the local one.[7] Overlapping personnel is a pervasive central technique in the Soviet polity, vindicated in

TABLE 5.1
PARTICIPATION IN ORGANS OF STATE POWER

Name of soviet	Number in USSR	Number of deputies
Supreme Soviet of the USSR[a]	1	1,548
Supreme soviets of union republics	15	5,830
Supreme soviets of autonomous republics[b]	20	2,925
Local soviets of working people's deputies[c] including:	48,770	2,045,419
territory, regional, area	129	25,747
district	2,858	223,220
urban	1,868	238,250
urban district	416	86,642
rural	40,174	1,287,826
township	3,325	183,734

a. 1966 election.

b. 1967 election.

c. 1967 election.

Source: V. M. Chkikvadze, Sovetskoye gosudarstvo i pravo (Moscow: Progress Publishers, 1968), p. 121.

theory by the theoretical oneness of a society without class conflict. In the Seventh Supreme Soviet, all fifteen presidents of the supreme soviets of the union republics sat in the Supreme Soviet, and thirty-nine of the chairmen of the executive committees of local soviets occupied seats in the Supreme Soviet.[8]

"Kontrol" involves investigating and auditing at all levels of soviets by the commissions and the Presidium of the Supreme Soviet. These bodies issue recommendations and ukazes which are legally binding, to ensure compliance of lower soviets with the implementation of legal and administrative norms. The expansion of the commission system from eight to twenty-six commissions renders it a formidable weapon of "kontrol" over the soviet pyramid.[9]

> In all this complicated and diversified work of accumulating the experience of the masses of working people in our bodies of power, an important role belongs to the standing commissions of the soviets—from the local soviets to the USSR Supreme Soviet. In the spirit of the decisions of the 23rd CPSU Congress, the system of the standing commissions of the chambers of the USSR Supreme Soviet has been developed. Whereas up to 1966 there were eight commissions in the USSR Supreme Soviet, there are now twenty-six commissions in the two chambers of the Supreme Soviet.[10]

Publicity is also a formidable weapon. The very prospect of commissions discovering and exposing unacceptable practices by lower soviets enhances the Supreme Soviet's authority over them. Such practices may be exposed in public commission discussions, in the debates of the Supreme Soviet itself, and in newspaper reports of such discussions and debates. In a closed polity, publicity of this sort may prove as effective as the old forms of coercion.[11]

Finally, to provide guidance for their operations the Supreme Soviet and its auxiliary bodies circulate vast amounts of literature to the lower soviets.

> The improvement in our work is also being furthered by materials on the work of the soviets of the fraternal Union Republics that are being regularly circulated by the Presidium of the USSR Supreme Soviet. These materials help us to assimilate more quickly what is new in the work of other Union Republic soviets and to see our own shortcomings better and eliminate them promptly. We wish that officials of the apparatus of the USSR Supreme Soviet would visit the localities more often. Also, conferences of officials of the apparatuses of the presidiums of the Union Republic supreme soviets should be held regularly in Moscow. Such conferences could be called by economic-geographic areas. In our opinion, separate conferences of the supreme soviets of the Baltic area republics, Transcaucasia and Central Asia would be advisable.[12]

In a polity permeated by the principle of democratic centralism, this practice implicitly is tantamount to a direct order.

WHO CONTROLS THE LOCAL SOVIETS: THE EMBRYO OF A CRUCIAL DEBATE?

All of the major institutions in the Soviet polity exert some authority over the local soviets, and in a sense the fluctuations of these relationships are a barometer of the institutional balance of power at a given time. After 1967, when the Party Central Committee directed an expansion of the powers of the local soviets, a crossfire of debate developed over the ultimate effect of this directive on the relations of the local soviets with the Supreme Soviet, the Party, and the ministries.

Local soviets were further subordinated to the higher soviets by the Stalin Constitution. The Supreme Soviet deputies were elected directly rather than by the next lower level of soviets, as were the Congress of Soviets Deputies under the 1924 Constitution. Local soviets must "adopt decisions and give orders within the limits of the rights granted to them by the laws of the USSR and the Union Republic" (Article 98). Their executive committees are directly accountable to both the local soviet which elected them and the immediately superior soviet of the Union Republic (Article 101). Since the union republic supreme soviets are subjected to the Supreme Soviet and its Presidium (Articles 14 and 15), a centralized pyramid of soviets exists, sanctioned by law, paralleling the Party pyramid and enhancing its control of society and its fund of information about the polity.

On the other hand, according to the Constitution the local soviets are the foundation of the political system. This and their role in the Revolution has always given them a special aura of legitimacy and authority, implying some independence from the Supreme Soviet.

THE PARTY APPARATUS AND THE LOCAL SOVIETS

There is little doubt that the Party apparatus exercises direct and decisive influence over the local soviets through its activists:

> Constantly, at all levels of the bodies of power, from the local soviets to the USSR Supreme Soviet, vigorous work is under way on the problems confronting these bodies: this work is carried on not only by the deputies but also by

a broad public *aktiv,* by specialists, scientists and representatives of labor collectives.[13]

It is also interesting to note that the Party called a conference of the rural and settlement soviet executive committee chairmen—a sort of extra-legal ad hoc body, the variety most easily controlled by the permanent Party machine—to consider the legislation on the local soviets.[14] This somewhat extraordinary assemblage indicates the concern that Party influence in the local soviets should remain supreme.

AUTHORITY OF THE SUPREME SOVIET VS. THE REPUBLIC SUPREME SOVIETS

Since 1959 there has been a much proclaimed effort to expand the activity of the republic and union republic supreme soviets, but it remains unclear whether the effect was to enhance their independence or to strengthen the arm of the USSR Supreme Soviet.[15] There is no doubt that both levels of supreme soviet participated in drafting the statute on the local soviets.[16] In the process of the debate one official noted that 50 percent of the laws affecting the local soviets were passed by the USSR Supreme Soviet.[17] Other published reports reveal that the Legislative Proposals Commissions of the Supreme Soviet have exercised direct "kontrol" over the local soviets.[18] This "kontrol" function combined with the legislative function seems to indicate that the highest organ of state power remains supreme. There is also evidence that the Presidium of the Supreme Soviet drafted the new rules for local soviets which were only perfunctorily discussed at lower republic supreme soviets.[19]

THE COUNCIL OF MINISTERS AND THE LOCAL SOVIETS

Since the local soviets are both organs of state power and state administration, they partake of both the executive and legislative function and are accountable to both the Supreme Soviet and the Council of Ministers.[20] With the expansion of the "kontrol" function of the Supreme Soviet and the soviet pyramid in general, there seems to be an effort afoot to curb the influence of the ministries over the local soviets in favor of the supreme soviets at all levels.[21] The precise nature of the emerging institutional balance is difficult to identify at any time, but there can be little doubt that a struggle is ensuing.[22]

THE SUPREME SOVIET'S AUTHORITY
OVER THE ORGANS OF STATE ADMINISTRATION

The expansion of the activities of the Supreme Soviet and its auxiliary bodies has been and was intended to be primarily at the expense of the organs of state administration headed by the Council of Ministers. As Brezhnev put it at the Twenty-fourth Party Congress:

> The USSR Supreme Soviet and the Union Republic supreme soviets have intensified their control over the work of ministries and departments and over the state of affairs in the basic sectors of economic and cultural construction. The increased number of standing commissions and the more systematic organization of their activity enable the deputies to display more initiative, and to delve more deeply into the work of executive agencies, and to take a more active part in the preparation of draft laws.[23]

Even though the Supreme Soviet possesses the constitutional power to appoint the Council of Ministers, it has been generally recognized since Stalin's day that it merely ratifies the regime's nominations.

The core of the Supreme Soviet's expanded authority over the organs of state administration is "kontrol" through the new system of permanent commissions, which is described in detail further on. A recent *Izvestia* article is illustrative:

> The creation of the new commissions has not only facilitated an improvement in the legislative work of the country's supreme body of power but has also strengthened its function of control over the administrative agencies. *During the activity of the Seventh USSR Supreme Soviet (1966–70), the standing commissions held 170 sessions,* the bulk of which dealt with kontrol over the implementation of the laws and decisions of the USSR Supreme Soviet by the ministries, departments, and other executive agencies. In studying the state of affairs in various branches of the national economy, the commissions do not limit themselves to the criticism of shortcomings but seek ways and means of overcoming them, and they also work out important recommendations for the administrative agencies.[24]

The organs of state administration are headed by the All-Union Council of Ministers and Ministries which find their subordinate counterparts at the Union and autonomous republic levels. At the lowest level are the local soviets which combine the functions of organs of state power and organs of state administration.

Nominally, the Council of Ministers is completely subordinate to the Supreme Soviet. Article 65 of the Constitution makes it "responsible and accountable" to the Supreme Soviet, and between sessions to the Presidium of the Supreme Soviet. In theory also the Supreme Soviet appoints the Council of Ministers (Article 56); however, the Party leadership selects the Council of Ministers just as it did the Sovnarkom.[25]

Unlike its predecessor, the Council of Ministers was not regarded as a legislative authority but merely as the highest executive and administrative organ of state power (Article 64).[26] In theory, Soviet administrative law allows no administrative discretion in applying zakons or postanovlenia.[27] Article 73 of the Constitution reflects this by requiring ministry orders to be issued "on the basis and in pursuance of the laws."

Nevertheless, "decrees and orders of the Council of Ministers of the USSR are binding throughout the territory of the USSR" (Article 67). In fact, the operation of the Council of Ministers differs little from its predecessor, the Sovnarkom, which wrestled with the Central Executive Committee for legislative authority. At the same time that Vyshinsky was stressing the absence of any legislative role residing in the Council of Ministers, it was enacting a vast quantity of activity-guiding norms in contrast to the Supreme Soviet.[28] Thus, like the Presidium of the Supreme Soviet, the much-proclaimed non-legislative role of the Council of Ministers was a fiction.

INTERPELLATION AND INVESTIGATION

The Constitution grants two powers to the Supreme Soviet which in theory could be instruments for restraining arbitrary exercise of the administrative powers of the Council of Ministers.

A Supreme Soviet deputy may address a question to the Council of Ministers or an individual minister regarding some aspect of administration, and a reply must be forthcoming within three days, according to Article 71 of the Constitution. As we have seen, this power of interpellation was exercised very seldom in Stalin's day. [29] The job of prodding any high government official during the purges or the war was an extremely delicate matter.

The power of questioning government officials constitutes a major bulwark of the English Parliament. It also proved a potent weapon for the Second Duma, thus accelerating its demise (see Chapter 1).

The procedure for exercising the power of interpellation under the old Congress of Soviets had been more elaborate and less vague, reflecting, perhaps, the real power of the CEC in early revolutionary days.

In short, in the Stalin era the power of interpellation represented a mere trapping of a parliamentary system, a form without content, but nevertheless one which could take on substance under proper circumstances. The power of interpellation encroached very little on the powers of the Council of Ministers in fact.[30]

Another theoretically formidable power vested in the Supreme Soviet by the Constitution is that of appointing commissions of investigation and audit (Article 51). All institutions are required to submit any documents requested by these commissions. Since few commissions were appointed and those that were comprised a small number of amateur deputies, this power also encroached very little on the prerogatives of the Council of Ministers. However, under the authority of Article 51, the Supreme Soviet created permanent commissions ostensibly to draft legislation as well as carry out audits and investigations.[31]

The permanent commissions, created at the first session of the first Supreme Soviet, did not really draft legislation. They served primarily as a final board of review, checking the language and adding some details to bills drafted by the Council of Ministers. They were a sort of administrative conduit putting bills in final form before submission to the Supreme Soviet for ratification. As such they encroached little on the de facto legislative authority of the Council of Ministers.[32] There was some evidence of more detailed scrutiny of budgetary bills.[33] However, the small size of the commissions, their lack of experience, and the war prevented their performing much more than mild revisions in preparation for ratification by the plenum of the Supreme Soviet. The actual draft bills emanated from the Council of Ministers.

In fact, the Supreme Soviet has never exercised substantial influence over the organs of state administration; however, there has been a trend since Stalin's death in that direction through four of the mechanisms described before: law, overlapping personnel, "kontrol," and publicity.

In law, of course, the Council of Ministers, as described above, is accountable to the Supreme Soviet according to the Constitution. The organs of state administration according to principles of socialist legality implement the fundamental laws of the Supreme Soviet at all levels.

The republic-level ministries have traditionally guided the work of the local soviets; however, there is evidence of attempts to transfer some of these powers to the higher soviets and the Party to reduce the government's authority.

High officials of state administration sit in the Supreme Soviet, although they are not permitted to sit in the Presidium of the Supreme Soviet or its commissions (unless co-opted as non-voting members). Thus, overlapping membership is a weak element of "kontrol."

Since Stalin's era, "kontrol" appears to be the major mechanism in theory, law, and fact by which the Supreme Soviet exercises its influence over the organs of state administration. Investigations and audits at all levels of state administration by the corresponding organs of state power provide a vast system of checking up on the administration and implementation of law and policy. The expansion of the commission system at all levels provides an apparatus, staffed by experts, to facilitate this "kontrol" or monitoring and restraining of the organs of state administration. The details of the commission system's functioning are discussed further on. The Supreme Soviet's role in the budgetary process illuminates the potential of "kontrol" at many stages of a rather crucial process for the polity.

The Supreme Soviet participates in the drafting of both the plan and the budget. It discusses the budget reports of its commissions at relatively considerable length at its sessions; it then unanimously ratifies them. Then most of its commissions monitor the government's implementation of the budget.

The budget has the force of law, cutting across federal lines to centralize the polity. There is little doubt that the expansion of the Supreme Soviet's law-making and "kontrol" functions through the expansion of size, powers, and activities of its auxiliary bodies greatly extends its real influence over the system of organs of state administration, especially through the budget process.

THE SUPREME SOVIET'S AUTHORITY OVER THE JUDICIAL SYSTEM

The USSR Supreme Court stands at the top of the Soviet judicial system and is nominally accountable to the Supreme Soviet in theory, law, and to some extent, apparently, in fact.

To begin with, since all state organs are theoretically subordinate to the highest organ of state power, the Supreme Court is accountable to the Supreme Soviet. This general power is reinforced by the constitutional power (Article 105) of the Supreme Soviet to elect the Supreme Court for a five-year term. The power of election is, of course, somewhat circumscribed by the requirement that the Court include the chairmen of the supreme courts of the union republics ex officio.

The real power of the Supreme Soviet over the judicial system evidently stems from the powers of its Presidium. The Presidium may exercise its influence over the Supreme Court through its two constitutional powers to issue ukazes and to interpret the laws (Article 49: b, c). The evidence that these powers have been utilized is fragmentary and scarce.

Also, since the Supreme Court, like all state organs, must conform to the law, it is naturally subject to the two legislative devices of the Supreme Soviet, the zakon of the plenum and the ukaz of the Presidium.

An example of the use of zakon is the Fundamentals of Court Organization, regulating all of the Court's activities, which was passed by the Supreme Soviet in December 1958, after apparently long deliberation in secret by jurists and other specialists in the subcommissions of the Legislative Proposals Commissions of the Supreme Soviet.[34]

Since Soviet courts do not interpret the law but merely apply it (in theory), the entire judicial pyramid is subject to the constitutional power of the Presidium to interpret the law. This has apparently been exercised sparingly, probably because the judicial system has ample opportunities to evaluate the position of the regime before a case reaches the Presidium of the Supreme Soviet.

A recent article in the Soviet law journal stated that Supreme Court judges could not sit on the commissions of the Supreme Soviet because this would mitigate the "kontrol" function. The article implies that there is substantial support for an extension of the "kontrol" function of the Supreme Soviet—through its vastly expanded commission system—over the judicial system.[35]

Calls for increased supervision over and monitoring of the judicial system are not new in the polity. The reformer critics of the Supreme Soviet recommended such at the time of the Twentieth Party Congress.[36]

It is not possible to determine precisely from available evidence how much the Supreme Soviet supervises the judicial system. However, two facts are relevant. First, in a recent session of the Presidium when "kontrol" over such diverse organs as the procuracy, the ministries, and the USSR People's Control Commission was evident, there is not the slightest mention of the judicial system. This is, of course, far from conclusive evidence of anything, but it does indicate that the Presidium is not preoccupied with monitoring the judicial system.[37]

The power of the ukaz was evident recently when the Presidium of the Supreme Soviet in effect downgraded the importance of the judicial system by granting chiefs of militia the power to impose fines for hooliganism.[38]

Another example of the exercise of the general power to review activities of the Supreme Court, implicit in both the interpretation and decree powers of the Presidium of the Supreme Soviet, is the establishment of a special commission to draft a law based on proposals of the Supreme Court and the Procuracy with respect to criminal parole and recidivism.[39]

Second, and most important, A. F. Gorkin, Chairman of the Supreme Court, appears to be a living symbol of Party and Supreme Soviet Presidium supervision of the judicial system. Gorkin joined the Party in 1916. He served his early career as a Party professional, including a short term with the Central Committee apparatus in Moscow in 1930. In 1937 he became Secretary of the USSR Central Executive Committee. The next year he became Secretary of the Presidium of the Supreme Soviet, a post which he held for fifteen years, approximately, until his appointment as Chairman of the Supreme Court in February 1957. Here is clear evidence of the overlapping and interlocking of these two state organs, the Presidium of the Supreme Soviet and the Supreme Court.

THE SUPREME SOVIET'S AUTHORITY OVER THE PROCURACY

The Office of the Procurator exercises the highest supervision over the accurate execution of laws by all ministries and institutions subordinate to them, as well as by individual officials and citizens of the USSR (Article 113). Since the Procurator-General is appointed by the Supreme Soviet for seven years (Article 114), he remains nominally subordinate to it.

The Procuracy is an extra-departmental organ, independent of the executive power of the ministries. In theory, it exercises supervision over the proper implementation of laws by the Council of Ministers. Its office is highly centralized, controlling all lower-level procurators.

If the Supreme Soviet were to acquire effectual supervision over the Procuracy, its real power, especially vis-à-vis the Council of Ministers, would expand significantly. In addition to its legal watchdog function, the Procuracy acts as prosecutor for the government much like the United States Attorney-General.

In fact, the Supreme Soviet's control over the powerful pyramid which comprises the Procuracy is only potential, however much lip service is paid to it in theory and law. Nevertheless, the forms might conceivably take on substance and therefore deserve description in this study.

To begin with, the Supreme Soviet has the constitutional power to appoint the Procurator-General. Also, since the Procuracy is an organ of the Soviet state and since the Supreme Soviet is the highest organ of state power, the former is nominally subordinate to the latter.

As the guardian of socialist legality, the Procuracy acts as the state's prosecutor and as a sort of ombudsman. In the ultimate sense its prosecutions are subject to the power of the Presidium of the Supreme Soviet to interpret the law, which is seldom exercised, as we have seen, and thus is moot.[40] Also, in the sense that the Procuracy must obey the law which is theoretically made by the Supreme Soviet, it is subordinate to that highest representative organ.

The Procurator-General usually sits in the Supreme Soviet as a deputy, which is obviously not a sign of its influence over the Procuracy. For example, R. A. Rudenko, Procurator-General and a member of the Central Committee of the CPSU since 1956, sat in the seventh convocation.

There is some evidence of an effort to extend the "kontrol" function of the Supreme Soviet over the Procuracy. Published reports of sessions of the Presidium of the Supreme Soviet reveal instances of its hearing reports from commissions of the Supreme Soviet with regard to the activities of the Procuracy. At the same sessions the Presidium is said to have ordered the Procuracy to intensify its efforts to carry out its ombudsman function, in this particular instance by enforcing a ukaz providing a procedure for citizens' complaints.[41]

In a relatively recent article in the Soviet law journal, a scholar argued that Procuracy officials cannot sit on Supreme Soviet commissions because commissions must supervise the Procuracy. He lamented that this was not specifically written into legislation governing the commissions of the lesser soviets. His tone implied a yearning for greater "kontrol" over the Procuracy by Soviet organs.[42] There is no hard evidence of substantial exercise of this kind of "kontrol," although it would fit the pattern of the Party's attempts to centralize its control over all organs.

Calls for increased "kontrol" over the Procuracy by the Supreme Soviet are not new; they were sprinkled throughout the criticism of the Supreme Soviet at the time of the Twentieth Party Congress. These critics portrayed a picture of total neglect of monitoring the Procuracy.[43] The modern critics seem to be seeking a more formal procedure exercised more frequently with some sanctions.

THE SUPREME SOVIET'S AUTHORITY
OVER THE MASS ORGANS

Any generalization concerning the vast, complex, and above all shifting relationships between the soviet pyramid and the mass organs must remain subject to innumerable qualifications which deserve more detailed consideration in another study. However, some effort at illuminating salient trends is pertinent to this study of the evolution and potential of the Supreme Soviet, since it stands at the apex of the soviet pyramid.

The consideration of these interrelations should begin with two fundamental considerations. The first is that both mass organs and soviets are considered "schools of administration," in theory to prepare the populace for the utopian self-administrating state of pure communism. Their central role in this much-acclaimed, but increasingly long-range, goal constitutes a major reason for the vast proliferation of literature on the subject.[44]

The second fundamental consideration is that there are at least three general categories of mass organizations, each with varying relationships to the soviet pyramid. These three generic categories are (1) volunteer mass organizations; (2) independent pyramids; and (3) arms of Party apparatus.

It should be noted that the soviets are frequently identified as having a mass character, which refers to the popular participation in them. However, they are distinguished from the mass organs because the soviets possess the power of coercion through law. Mass organs are said to be persuasive in nature; state bodies are said to have a dual nature which is both coercive and persuasive, although the coercive has been specifically down-played since de-Stalinization.[45]

The evidence indicates that Khrushchev initially intended to rely on the mass organs as the schools of administration. This ideological axiom gradually became intertwined with the economic reform as well as the obvious political reform set in motion by de-Stalinization.

It now appears clear that Khrushchev met opposition to what appeared as a down-grading of the soviets. The 1961 Party Programme appears to reinstate them ideologically and practically.[46]

As the decade of the sixties wore on it became clear that the mass organs were increasingly difficult to control, thus launching a move to strengthen the soviet pyramid not merely as a partner of the mass organs in the reform process, but as the coordinator and perhaps even the director of their activities. This process of strengthening the influence of the soviets over the mass organs appears to be continuing and permeating the entire polity.[47] The permeation is of a different kind, character, and degree with respect to each category of mass organ, which we shall briefly consider.

VOLUNTEER MASS ORGANIZATIONS

These once ad hoc bodies, which in some cases have taken on permanent status, were elevated to legitimate status by Khrushchev and have proliferated to perform a vast array of functions.[48]

It is here, among the volunteer agencies, more than any other area that evidence exists of the intent to expand the coordinating and, perhaps, directing influence of the soviet pyramid over these bodies. This coordinating and directing function is usually said to reside in the local soviets. Thus, here again, we discern an area where extension of the Supreme Soviet influence vis-à-vis the Party apparatus could be quite significant. The enhanced role of the soviets is exemplified in the following:

> The active section of the population grouped around the soviets is ten times greater than the number of deputies and now runs to more than 23 million.

> There are now a great many mass organizations of working people grouped around the soviets, such as block and neighborhood committees, volunteer people's patrols, comrades' courts, parent-and-teacher committees at schools, women's councils, deputy groups, sanitary teams, councils for assistance to departments of executive committees, commissions of public control over the operation of commercial enterprises and catering establishments, etc. Through mass organizations and standing commissions, the Soviets of Working People's Deputies attract millions of people to active participation in their work.[49]

Soviet literature on the subject is voluminous and has appeared in the form of bibliographies on the subject published in the press.[50]

INDEPENDENT PYRAMIDS

The major example of this kind of mass organization is the trade union pyramid, which although termed a mass organization in theory, in practice is a fundamentally different institution when compared to the volunteer organizations. It is a long-standing institution whose leadership has almost continually included powerful Party officials. It is also a pyramid extending to all levels of the polity, not an ad hoc single-level institution. Clearly, any extension of soviet influence over it would encounter political resistance at the highest levels.[51]

There is no substantial evidence of the extension of the "kontrol" function of the Supreme Soviet to the trade unions, but there is some evidence. For example, a recent session of the Presidium of the Supreme Soviet published in both *Pravda* and *Izvestia* reported the following[52] :

> With a view to intensifying kontrol over the observance of the labor laws at enterprises of several all-Union ministries, the Presidium of the USSR Supreme Soviet resolved to forward a note with recommendations from the Legislative Proposals Commissions to the presidiums of union republic supreme soviets and to USSR ministries and departments.

On the other hand, power over certain aspects of labor legislation has been delegated to the trade unions—in effect a delegation of a small increment of legislative power.[53] Since the above quote does not specifically mention the trade unions, it is not clear whether it represents an extension of the soviet pyramid's influence over the trade unions, or whether it is evidence of the two working in tandem on behalf of the Party apparatus.

This example reflects a central query surrounding the expansion of the whole Supreme Soviet system: To what extent is the institution emerging as an independent structure vis-à-vis the Party apparatus?

ARMS OF THE PARTY APPARATUS

Although all organizations in the Soviet Union might arguably be termed arms of the Party apparatus, some, such as the People's Control Commissions and the Komsomol (Young Communist League), traditionally appear to respond more immediately to the authority of the Party apparatus.

There is evidence of efforts to extend the authority of the soviet pryamid over the People's Control Commissions, but the record concerning the Komsomol is barren, probably because of its traditionally direct subordination to the Party.

The People's Control Commissions at all levels are nominally under the supervision of the People's Control Commission of the Council of Ministers; however, it was created by the Presidium of the Supreme Soviet with joint Party and Council of Ministers' approval to check and supervise the fulfillment of policy norms and has always worked closely with the Party.[54]

A recent session of the Presidium of the Supreme Soviet heard reports from the USSR People's Control Commission.[55] Also, a recent article in the Soviet law journal called for coordination between the soviets at all levels on the one hand, and the Control Commissions on the other, even going so far as to suggest that the latter open its files to the soviets.[56]

Here again the evidence is scant, the relationships complex and overlapping. It is not clear how far the above indicates an augmentation of the independent power of the soviet pyramid in contradistinction to a mere activation of that pyramid as an arm of the Party apparatus.[57]

CONCLUSION

In concluding this analysis of the evolutionary development of the Supreme Soviet as an administrative assembly at the apex of many institutional pyramids, several brief summary comments seem appropriate. The first is that the foregoing represents an analysis of an ongoing process, the direction and tempo of which change continually. The effort here was to highlight the salient trends immediately relevant to the Supreme Soviet.

The second is that the precise delineation of the institutional and political relationships between the Supreme Soviet and other bodies in terms of their relative power is a monumental and impossible task. What should emerge from the selective foregoing treatment is an appreciation of the growing activity of the Supreme Soviet at the legal-administrative apex of a series of institutional pyramids, the effect of which is to increase the importance of that institution in the polity. Finally, this descriptive analysis was designed to highlight potential as much as practice.

Chapter 6

THE EVOLUTION, ORGANIZATION, AND FUNCTIONING
OF THE COMMISSION SYSTEM
OF THE SUPREME SOVIET

The Constitution of the USSR authorizes the Supreme Soviet to create commissions to assist it in its various roles and functions, and the Supreme Soviet has utilized this authority to develop over time a complex system of twenty-six permanent (standing) commissions, as well as numerous subcommissions and ad hoc commissions[1] (see Figure 1.1, Chap. 1). The commissions help administer the chambers, assist in drafting laws, monitor implementation of laws, serve as a public and publicized forum for the Party leadership, and verify the credentials of the deputies. The details of their organization and functioning, which were once based on internal decrees (posta-novlenie) of the individual chambers, are now spelled out in a major zakon, ratified in 1967. In short, these once relatively dormant bodies have expanded in size, number, and activity, have grown in legal status, and constitute a major instrument of the Party apparatus in governing the polity.

The expansion of the system of permanent commissions opens up a whole new line of control over the state administration for the Party apparatus—this is legal control (*pravo kontrolia*). At the same time, this expansion has probably stimulated the hopes of those who seek at least moderate democratization of the polity. Thus, ironically, the expansion appears to have the support of two generally opposed factions in the polity, the conservative elements of the Party apparatus, who view it as one means to facilitate the legalization of their ideological legitimacy, and the reformers, who view it as potentially a step toward democratization.

The most important functions of the commission system in 1974 are the drafting of zakons and "kontrol"—which is essentially checking up on the implementation of the laws by the administrative apparatus. The fleshing out of the procedures and mechanisms for carrying out these two tasks is the central story in the evolution of the commission system. The two most important commissions (in each chamber) in this evolutionary process are the Legislative Proposals Commissions (LPC), which supervise the drafting process, and the Planning and Budget Commissions (PBC), which supervise the "kontrol" activities of the commissions.[2] Because the evolution of these two functions is quite complex, let us see how these two commissions operated in 1974, before tracing the tortuous route of the legal steps and political conflicts leading to the present system.

THE LEGISLATIVE PROPOSALS COMMISSIONS: COORDINATORS OF THE DRAFTING PROCESS

Jurisdiction over the preparation of the final revision of all draft bills for submission to the Supreme Soviet for ratification rests with the Legislative Proposals Commissions.[3] When a body with legislative initiative presents a draft bill, that is, tables it with the LPC, the LPC has four options: review and put the bill in final form itself; hold public discussions on it; refer it to other commissions; or reject it.[4] If the draft is rejected, another permanent commission may introduce it into the Supreme Soviet itself, but there is no record of this ever having occurred. In the other cases (referral to the public and to other commissions), the LPC ultimately reviews the bill, puts it in final form and submits it either to the Supreme Soviet itself or the Presidium of the Supreme Soviet. This process has evolved over a long period of time and is not spelled out precisely in law, nor is it the undeviating practice, but it appears to be the central pattern for finalizing major laws.

The LPCs also participate in "kontrol" of the implementation of laws by the legal system, which essentially means supervising the Procuracy. Although the zakon creating the new commissions system in 1967 granted the LPCs this authority, there is little evidence that it has been exercised extensively, except for one proposal (predlozhenia) submitted to the Presidium, discussed further on. This aspect of "kontrol" over the Procuracy remains rudimentary, although its potential is obvious when one considers the evolution of the Budget Commissions' "kontrol" over the implementation of the plan and budget. Nevertheless, the primary function of the LPCs is coordinating the drafting of major zakons and perhaps some ukazes and regulating their introduction into the Supreme Soviet for ratification.

THE PLANNING AND BUDGET COMMISSIONS: COORDINATING "KONTROL"

When the Budget Commissions (renamed Planning and Budget Commissions in 1967) were created in 1938, their chief task was to serve as a final board of review for the yearly budget, and perhaps to make a few minor changes based on complaints raised by their members. This function remained relatively dormant until 1957 when they received the power to review the economic plans also. Gradually, this process of review brought in more and more complaints until it began to take on the character of an audit (which is one connotation of the Russian word "kontrol") of the implementation of the plan and budget. The 1967 zakon on the commission system implicitly gives the new Planning and Budget Commissions (PBC) the authority to coordinate fourteen new branch commissions, specially created to audit specific sectors of the economy.[5]

"Kontrol" generally operates in the following fashion: A branch commission, individual deputy, or the Presidium of the Supreme Soviet submits a complaint (oral or written) about the implementation of the plan or budget to the Planning and Budget Commission, which then investigates the complaint itself or requests a branch commission to do so, and then recommends necessary changes on the basis of its (or the branch's) findings.

Let us look a little more closely at the procedure for exercising the "kontrol" function as outlined in the 1967 zakon on the permanent commissions. Essentially, there are three stages: the complaint stage, the investigatory stage, and the remedial stage. Complaints arise out of budget and plan reviews or out of specific complaints lodged by the members of the PBCs or the branch commissions or the Presidium of the Supreme Soviet.

The investigation is carried out under three articles of the zakon.[6] An inquiry may be sent to the Council of Ministers or an individual minister (Article 24), which would take the form of a proposal or predlozhenia but is not apparently legally binding on the recipient. Or, an official of the responsible ministry or organization may be summoned to appear, again by predlozhenia, before the PBC or branch commission investigating. Such a summons is obligatory by law (Article 21). Thirdly, the investigating commissions may require the responsible ministry or organization to submit an explanation of a particular matter. This request is also legally binding (Article 22).

There is no clear statement that any of these measures is binding on the Council of Ministers. Nothing is said about an inquiry being legally binding on the Council of Ministers, and the Council itself is not mentioned in the articles dealing with the summons to appear and the request for an explanation.

After the complaint and investigatory stages, the investigating commissions may reject the complaint as ill-founded or adopt one of three available remedies under the commission zakon.[7] It may forward a recommendation (*recomendatsia*) to the responsible organ, which is legally bound to conduct its own investigation and issue a report to the commission within two months (Article 23). Secondly, it may submit a predlozhenia to the Council of Ministers, but the zakon does not require a reply (Article 24). Finally, it may draw up a predlozhenia and submit it to the Presidium of the Supreme Soviet which may convert it into a ukaz, which is legally binding throughout the land (Article 20). Only the last step provides a legal sanction for "kontrol" which binds the Council of Ministers as well as the ministries.

All of this complex procedure evolved slowly through trial and error and political conflict from 1938 to 1967 (as discussed further on), and is, of course, not yet clearly crystallized into accepted practices. Its impact on the relative authority and influence of various political institutions still remains unclear.

OTHER COMMISSIONS

Other than the LPC and the PBC, the commission system includes the branch or sectoral commissions for each chamber (industry, construction, agriculture, public health and social security, public education, science and culture, trade and everyday services, transportation and communication), all of which assist in the "kontrol" function. It also includes the Credentials Commission which perfunctorily verifies deputies' election credentials, and the recently created Youth Affairs Commission and Protection of Nature Commission.

The Seventh Supreme Soviet had the following number of deputies on the commissions of each respective chamber[8] :

Legislative Proposals Commission: 35
Planning and Budget Commission: 51
Foreign Affairs Commission: 32
Youth Affairs Commission: 31
Industry Commission: 41
Transportation and Communication Commission: 33
Construction and Building Materials Commission: 33
Public Health and Social Security Commission: 31
Trade, Everyday Services and Communal Economy Commission: 31
Credentials Commission: 31

Thus, participation on commissions has risen from 89 (8 per cent of the Supreme Soviet membership) at the first convocation to 144 at

TABLE 6.1

GROWTH OF SUPREME SOVIET COMMISSION MEMBERSHIP BY CHAMBER

| | Convocation | | | | | | | | | | | |
| | 1 | | 2 | | 3 | | 4 | | 5 | | 6 | |
Commission	SU[a]	SN[b]	SU	SN	SU	SN	SU	SN	SU	SN	SU	SN
Credentials	11	11	15	15	17	17	17	17	21	21	21	21
Legislative proposals	10	10	19	19	19	19	19	19	31	31	31	31
Budgetary (or planning and budgetary	13	13	27	27	27	27	26	26	39	39	39	39
Foreign relations	11	10	11	11	11	11	11	11	23	23	23	23
Economic (of the Soviet of Nationalities)	—	—	—	—	—	—	—	31	—	31	—	31
TOTALS	45	44	72	72	72	72	72	103	114	145	114	145

a. SU = Soviet of the Union.
b. SN = Soviet of Nationalities.
Source: M. Saifulin, The Soviet Parliament (Moscow: Progress Publishers, 1967), p. 17.

the second, 175 at the fourth, 259 at the fifth, 760 at the seventh, and 912 at the eighth.

There are also ad hoc and subcommissions. The two are really almost synonymous. Subcommissions are appointed on an ad hoc basis by the permanent commissions to study and investigate specific problems, as well as to draft specific legislation. The LPC appointed many subcommissions to draft all-Union codes, and the old Budget Commissions, as well as the now defunct Economic Commission of the Council of Nationalities, had more or less permanent subcommissions which were the models for the branch commissions.

The number of subcommissions has also been increased as have been the number of ad hoc commissions.[9] For example, to study the state budget for 1969 and the new five-year plan, the Supreme Soviet formed 32 subcommissions comprising over 200 deputies of the Supreme Soviet plus other persons who may be co-opted, each of which held 100 sessions. In addition, there were 27 plenary sessions of the Planning and Budget Commission of each chamber. The number of members of the subcommissions dealing with specific legislation in 1965 was roughly as follows: Basic Principles of Land Use, 31; Fundamentals of Matrimonial Law, 32; Fundamentals of Legislation on Exploitation of Water Resources, 50; Fundamentals of Legislation on Health Protection, 44; Fundamentals of Corrective Labor Legislation, 40; Basic Principles of the Exploitation of Mineral Wealth, 28; Basic Principles of Forest Exploitation, 40; Law on Accounting and Statistics, 44.[10]

DECLINE OF THE LPC?

Upgrading of the former subcommissions of the LPC and the Budget and Economic Commissions by the 1967 zakon, transforming them into full-fledged commissions called Branch or Sectoral Commissions, may have diminished the central co-ordinating role of the LPC, or it may merely signal greater influence and power for the whole commission system in the Soviet polity which would further enhance the role of the LPC. Some Western experts maintain that the latter is the case. In fact, the official line appears to be that the importance of the LPC is just as great as in the past, that it is the key commission in the drafting process but now it receives support from many new full-fledged branch commissions. However, there is some evidence to the contrary, indicating that the LPC's role may be waning, for reasons other than the implicit diminishing role suggested by the creating of the Branch Commissions.

The first two of the Branch Commissions are chaired by chairmen or deputy chairmen of departments of the Central Committee of the CPSU; however, the LPC chairman in the Council of the Union, Solomentsev, is also a department head, and alternate member of the Politburo. Secondly, as we shall see further on, the LPC reports to the Presidium of the Supreme Soviet, according to published reports, and the Presidium appears to be attempting to solidify control over the coordination of the drafting and ratifying of legislation which would enhance the influence of its chairman, Podgorny, who is a full Politburo member. Undoubtedly this apparent uncertainty over the role of the LPC reflects real uncertainty within the leadership. The relative powers of these bodies must be considered fluid at present and somewhat subject to the fortunes of leadership factions and groupings—fortunes which they may also affect.

THE INSTITUTIONAL PRECURSORS
OF THE NEW COMMISSION SYSTEM

From 1956 until 1967 both the Economic Commission of the Council of Nationalities and the Budget Commission developed permanent subcommissions whose jurisdiction extended to various sectors or branches of the economy and whose function was elaboration, especially of the economic plan and the budget. From the practice of these sectoral subcommissions as well as from the practice of a few union republic supreme soviets, came the paradigm for the 1967 legislation which codified the practice, composition, jurisdiction, and function of the permanent commissions of the Supreme Soviet of the USSR.[11]

This legislation strengthened the legal basis of the permanent commissions because their existence henceforth is sanctioned by a zakon representing, in theory, the will of the Soviet people and not just an internal regulation (postanovlenie) of one chamber of the Supreme Soviet, which was the case prior to 1967. While the zakon did little more than codify existing practice, nevertheless its wide discussion and promulgation imputes to the permanent commissions a degree of authority and stability heretofore lacking.[12]

Let us turn now to a more detailed discussion of the political and legal evolution of the commission system, beginning with an analysis

TABLE 6.2
PERMANENT COMMISSIONS OF
THE SUPREME SOVIET

Four original commissions:
  Credentials (1936)[a]
  Planning and Budget (1938)
  Legislative Proposals (1938)
  Foreign Affairs (1938)

Seven sectoral commissions:
  Industry (1966)
  Construction (1966)
  Agriculture (1966)
  Public Health and Social Security (1966)
  Trade and Public Services (1966)
  Public Education, Science and Culture (1966)
  Transport and Communication (1970)

Two new special commissions:
  Nature Conservation (1968)
  Youth Affairs (1968)

a. Dates signify time of creation by the chambers.
Source: Vedomosti Verkhovnogo Soveta SSSR, 1970, No. 29, pp. 401, 424.

of the checkered career of the Economic Commission of the Council of Nationalities.

THE RISE AND DEMISE OF THE ECONOMIC COMMISSION
OF THE COUNCIL OF NATIONALITIES

The Economic Commission of the Council of Nationalities rose and fell in one decade (1957–67), revealing and reflecting in its short life much about the role of the Supreme Soviet in the context of Soviet politics, as well as about the interrelationships of Soviet political institutions. The commission's life provided not only an institutional mirror of some aspects of the Soviet nationality problem, but its emergence also conjured up a continuing debate, still unresolved, over five institutional interrelationships: the Supreme Soviet to the Council of Ministers; the Supreme Soviet commissions to the Council of Ministers; the Presidium of the Supreme Soviet to the Council of Ministers; the Presidium of the Supreme Soviet to the

Supreme Soviet itself; and the Presidium of the Supreme Soviet to the commissions of the Supreme Soviet.

The commission was composed of thirty-one members (two from each union republic) and a chairman. Deputies from autonomous republics and provinces and from national regions were entitled to take part in the commission proceedings when questions arose affecting the interests of their respective areas.[13] The commission was assigned three rather vaguely worded functions by the decree of the Council of Nationalities creating it.[14]

    a. preparation for the Council of Nationalities, on the basis of study and calculation of comparative date, of recommendations on questions of economic and soviet cultural work in the union republics;

    b. preliminary examination of the requests of union republics regarding various measures in economic work,and in public education, public health, improvement of cities and villages;

    c. preparation of conclusions for the Council of Nationalities regarding the conformity of national economic plans submitted for approval of the USSR Supreme Soviet with the tasks of economic and cultural development of the union republics.

To facilitate its work the commission was to "receive" the necessary information from state agencies and to consult appropriate experts. The commission appointed four subcommissions concerned with agriculture and deliveries, trade and culture, public health, and construction of living quarters. Each subcommission had ad hoc working groups for special problems.[15] These sectoral subcommissions with ad hoc working groups were to provide a partial model for the system of specialized branch commissions formally created by statute late in 1967.

Khrushchev called for the creation of the Economic Commission of the Council of Nationalities at the historic Twentieth Party Congress, ostensibly to study the uneven development of the respective union republic economies and especially their disproportional budgetary allocations.[16] Apparently, the innovation was a political sop to nationalities dissatisfied with the gross inequities in budget allocations among the union republics. In all probability, it was also designed to enlist support for the consolidation of Khrushchev's position.[17]

The concession was small. The commission could make only recommendations to the Supreme Soviet or the Council of Ministers. It could "request" the Council of Ministers to prepare a draft law, as could the Legislative Proposals Commissions of each chamber, and it could request but not demand information from the ministries to prepare its conclusions and recommendations.[18] That all was not well with the Economic Commission from its inception appears from the complaints of its chairman in 1962 that:

(1) The membership should be enlarged;
(2) Members should periodically be freed from their work duties;
(3) Influence over the implementation of its resolutions should be increased;
(4) Ties with localities should be increased; and
(5) More regular sessions should be held.[19]

These complaints seemed to reflect a failure of the commission to achieve a meaningful impact on policies and decisions.

From its inception, the intended raison d'etre of the commission appeared to be a clearinghouse for complaints of national minorities about health, education, and other welfare facilities, and about disproportionate budget allocations. In fact, it is not unlikely that the commission gradually began to serve as a focus and arena for debating national minority problems, and perhaps as an institutional lobby for their grievances. This, coupled with the known national unrest, probably provided the real impetus for the commission's abolition, although the official explanation was that the reorganization of the government economic apparatus in 1965 along sectoral lines required reorganization of the Supreme Soviet commissions along the same lines, thus obviating the need for the Economic Commission of the Council of Nationalities.[20]

Whether and to what extent the commission served as an institutional lobby for the minority nationalities is largely conjectural. What is certain is that the vague language of the decree creating it involved it in a controversy over the relation of the permanent commissions of the Supreme Soviet to the Council of Ministers.[21] Since legal language seldom provides the real impetus to controversies in the Soviet polity (as it might in the Anglo-Saxon world), one must speculate that behind this facade of juridical debate lurks a political impulse, e.g., nationality unrest in the instant case.

The early debate over the relationship between the Council of Ministers and the permanent commissions of the Supreme Soviet and the Economic Commission of the Council of Nationalities revolved around three questions raised by the vague statutory language creating it and also by varied practices which evolved:[22]

(1) What are the commission's legal rights to secure information from the ministries?
(2) What is the legal effect of a commission "proposal" submitted to the Council of Ministers?
(3) What is the role of the commission in the drafting process?

Before 1966, when this debate raged, the permanent commissions had little power to monitor (that is, no real power of control over) the work of the Council of Ministers. They could not make legally binding demands for information on the Council of Ministers, except for the Legislative Proposals Commission, and could only "recommend" drafting of legislation.[23] This was especially true of the Economic Commission of the Council of Nationalities. The extent of their present power in fact, as distinguished from law, is discussed further on.

In practice, the relations of the permanent commissions and the Council of Ministers assumed four general forms. First, a whole series of decrees (postanovlenie) issued by the Council of Ministers was adopted which incorporated proposals (predlozhenia) drafted by the Economic Commission.[24] Second, the Economic Commission often actually drafted the decree which carried the imprimatur of the Council of Ministers and was based on the Commission's original proposals. In other words, the Commission submitted proposals, then drafted the final decree which the Council of Ministers enacted as an administrative regulation (postanovlenie). Third, on one occasion only, the Economic Commission examined a draft Council of Ministers decree (postanovlenie) at the request of the Council of Ministers, and submitted recommended suggestions which were then incorporated by the Council of Ministers in its final decree. Here, the Council of Ministers conducted the major drafting work, but allowed its draft decree to be reviewed by the Economic Commission and altered its final decree to conform to some extent to the Commission's wishes. Fourth, pursuant to a 1959 budget law, the Economic Commission occasionally sent recommendations to the Council of Ministers concerning distribution of reserve funds, which had been specifically allocated for distribution among the union republics. The Council of Ministers' final resolutions usually reflected the Commission's suggestions.[25]

These practices constituted the immediate background against which the 1967 zakon on the permanent commissions was drafted. In it, as we shall see, the influence of these institutional paradigms is clear. Critics of these helter-skelter practices argued for clear legal demarcation of the relations between the permanent commissions and the Council of Ministers.[26] The critics suggested, among others, the following guidelines:

(1) Spelling out the right of the permanent commission to address proposals (predlozhenia) regarding the budget allocations to the Council of Ministers when the Supreme Soviet was not in session;
(2) Clarifying the duty of the Council of Ministers to consider commission proposals and inform them of the results within a time limit;
(3) Clarifying the duty of the Council of Ministers to aid the commissions in obtaining information from the ministries.

It is interesting to note that some of these suggestions become law simultaneously with the abolition of the Economic Commission of the Council of Nationalities whose existence played a substantial role in stimulating the debate from which the suggestions originally emerged. Many of the patterns as well as the dilemmas of the commission system today can thus be traced back to the experience of the Economic Commission of the Council of Nationalities. Let us turn now, from this rather specific case, to a more general analysis of the functional evolution of the commission system.

In general, the permanent commissions gradually shifted the functional emphasis of their activity from merely helping to administer the Supreme Soviet to drafting laws and finally to monitoring government activities. A concomitant of the latter two functions is the investigatory function—that is, the function of gathering information, not only as to the state of public opinion but also highly technical information. Since this functional evolution proceeded somewhat chronologically (and naturally with much overlapping), we shall analyze it in that order. The shifting functional emphasis reveals much about legal-institutional evolution in the Soviet Union. It also further illuminates aspects of the evolving interrelationships between the organs of the Supreme Soviet and their relationships with the Council of Ministers.

THE EVOLUTION OF THE LEGISLATIVE FUNCTION: FROM ADMINISTRATION TO DRAFTING

In the Stalin era, the Legislative Proposals Commission served as little more than an administrative conduit funneling zakons to the

Supreme Soviet for ratification. Its only role in the actual authorship of a bill was the addition of a few details. Primarily, it checked the wording of the bills to determine whether they were ready for the rubber stamp—the unanimous vote of the chambers of the Supreme Soviet. In a sense, it was a perfunctory final board of review before ratification. The Budget Commissions of both chambers performed much the same function with respect to laws relating to the budget and the annual plan. The vast bulk of the authorship of all bills resided in the Council of Ministers. The semifinal drafts were then forwarded to the Legislative Proposals or Budget Commissions for final wording. In short, the commissions' activities were limited. The commissions were small, sessions were brief and far between, the number of laws were few, and their very permanence remained in doubt since their existence rested on internal decrees of the respective chambers.[27]

Much has changed since the Party began to activate the Supreme Soviet in 1955, though one must still resist the temptation to exaggerate the extent of the role of the permanent commissions in authoring bills. There is no doubt that detailed policy, on the basis of which bills are drafted, originated in the Party Central Committee or its secretariat. All Soviet authorities agree that policy decision-making is not a function of the commissions. Likewise, most of the actual authoring of the basic bills remains with the Council of Ministers, and most norm-regulating activity still emerges from the Council of Ministers. However, the extent to which the permanent commissions elaborate bills—that is, the number of amendments, rewording, and other details added to these bills—appears to have significantly increased.[28]

The official Soviet version of the drafting of a zakon describes three stages: first, the submission of a bill to the permanent commissions by those bodies possessing legislative initiative; second, discussion and elaboration of the bill by the commissions; and third, ratification of the bill by the Supreme Soviet.[29] The second stage, review or elaboration, is the stage where the commissions have played a more significant role in the post-Stalin era, according to these sources.

To an extent, this enhanced role of the permanent commissions can be inferred from their increased size and activity. Since their creation in 1938 at the first session of the first convocation of the Supreme Soviet, the membership of the Legislative Proposals and Budget Commissions has tripled.[30] In addition, ad hoc subcommissions of the Legislative Proposals Commissions, chaired by a member

of one of those commissions and created for drafting specific legislation, have proliferated. The subcommissions send members out to
the provinces to hold meetings with the populace and with experts,
where amendments are suggested. They correspond with experts on
the substance of the legislation and, most interesting, they actually
co-opt experts from the ministries and academic institutes onto the
subcommissions, rather than holding hearings where experts testify
as is the practice of the United States congressional committees. The
co-opted members have only a consultative vote in commission
decisions.[31] The size of the subcommissions varies according to the
desires of the chairman of the Legislative Proposals or Budget Commissions.[32]

The extraordinary complexity and comprehensiveness of Soviet
legislation in the early sixties required expertise not only at the
drafting but also at the elaborating stage, which in effect greatly
enhanced the role of the permanent commissions and especially the
subcommissions. Most of the major commissions assigned the task of
drafting specific legislation appear to be composed of a majority of
expert-specialists.[33] The technical nature of much legislation requires an information input of a technical nature. Thus, it appears
that the subcommissions are acquiring a more significant role in the
actual authoring of the bill. From mere administrative conduits and
final review boards the commissions are being transformed into
organs for integrating proposals, emanating from various funds of
expertise, into rough draft bills. There can be little doubt that the
experts on the subcommissions contribute to the drafting process
substantially and are not sitting there merely for symbolic purposes.[34] The subcommissions approve draft bills by a majority vote
after much deliberation, which apparently takes place in secret. They
then submit the draft bills for final approval to the parent commission at sessions which are increasingly publicized and where
approval is usually unanimous. This unanimity implies, of course,
that the real deliberation over amendments to the bills takes place in
the subcommissions.[35]

The impact of the permanent commissions, as independent institutions, on the drafting process should not be exaggerated. While the
new law on the commissions forbids the members of the Council of
Ministers to sit on the commissions, it allows representatives of the
ministries to sit on the subcommissions.[36] In some cases, officials of
the ministries even chair the sessions of the subcommissions. Since
much of the real deliberation and debate apparently takes place in

the subcommissions, usually in secret, it is difficult to assess the independent contribution of Supreme Soviet deputies to the drafting process.[37]

THE LEGISLATIVE FUNCTION OF THE SUPREME SOVIET: DECISION-MAKING OR DECISION CONFIRMATION

The Russians have always been extremely sensitive to the criticism of the Supreme Soviet that it is a mere rubber stamp which ratifies, but does not make, decisions and thus, lacking any decision-making role, cannot validly be called a legislature. The best evidence of this, according to critics, is the absence of any real debate or deliberation in the sessions, and, as we have seen, there is indeed very little of that. Instead, it appears that deliberation over Soviet legislation takes place primarily in the higher Party arenas, while the major burden of drafting is carried out by organs subordinate to the Council of Ministers. Of course, most of the normative acts emanate from the Council of Ministers (postanovlenie or rasporizhenia) or the Presidium of the Supreme Soviet (ukaz). Zakons, which are issued only by the Supreme Soviet itself, are few and even then the major drafting is done by the organs of state administration. The activation of the Supreme Soviet since 1965 has increased the number of zakons and with it the role of the Supreme Soviet in drafting zakons has been enhanced. The following analysis describes the legislative process for a zakon in contrast to the pattern before the activation of the Supreme Soviet. Table 6.3 illustrates both patterns for zakons only, since other kinds of laws follow different paths.

It is clear that the decision to enact major legislation such as a zakon has always emanated from the highest level of leadership in the regime, which was of course Stalin in his time and the Party apparatus since. What is new in the legislative process is the role of the commissions in the drafting process, which has gradually reduced the role of the Council of Ministers. At first, it appears that the commissions merely expanded their old function of elaborating bills drafted by the Council of Ministers to include some major revisions. Now, substantial revisions seem almost inherent in the process of deliberation within the commissions and at public discussions.

Since the Party leadership dominates most commissions, it is still very much a part of the deliberation process while, on the other hand, members of the Council of Ministers are excluded by the

TABLE 6.3
**TWO PARADIGMS OF THE LEGISLATIVE PROCESS
FOR ZAKON[a]**

Functional stage	(1) Structural actor (II)	
	Old paradigm (1937–56)	New paradigm (1956–72)
(1) Decision to legislate	Party apparatus	Party apparatus
(2) Drafting	Council of Ministers	Subcommissions
(3) Deliberation	In the above	a. Subcommissions b. Public c. Subcommissions d. Joint commissions
(4) Ratification	Plenum of Supreme Soviet	Plenum of Supreme Soviet

a. The thrust of the analysis is that there is a subtle, incremental evolution within the Soviet polity from the process in column one to the process in column two, even though the former remains predominant on the most urgent and important questions requiring legislation. The official Soviet version of the process is found in Komsomolskaya Pravda, March 18, 1962, p. 2, and December 5, 1967, p. 1.

zakon on the permanent commissions, unless they are co-opted into a subcommission:

> The following persons cannot be elected to standing commissions: the chairmen of the chambers; their vice-chairmen; deputies who are members of the Presidium of the USSR Supreme Soviet, the USSR Council of Ministers, the USSR Supreme Court; and the USSR Prosecutor General.[38]

The power of co-opt remains with the chairman of the parent commission, who is almost always a member of the Party Central Committee.[39] Thus, the Council of Ministers and its subordinate organs can be legally excluded from the legislative process by the Party apparatus at the latter's discretion, except at two points: the Council of Ministers' right to initiate (table) a bill; and the right of an individual deputy to introduce a bill into the plenum of the Supreme Soviet itself.[40]

THE DISTINCTION BETWEEN INITIATING AND INTRODUCING A ZAKON

Initiating a zakon means placing a draft bill before a commission of the Supreme Soviet for deliberation; introducing a bill means presenting that bill to the Supreme Soviet plenum for ratification. Soviet authorities tend to blur this distinction because it is crucial to legal and practical control of the legislative process. Both the right to introduce a bill into the commissions of the Supreme Soviet (initiative), and the right to introduce the bill into the Supreme Soviet for final ratification are controlled by the Party apparatus through the personnel selection process, but potentially there are holes in its legal control if it should lose control over the selection of personnel for the Supreme Soviet.

A leading Soviet authority provides the standard Soviet description of legislative initiative and introduction in the quote below. He identifies the organs which may table a draft bill, and indicates that a representative of the organ tabling the bill usually introduces it into the Supreme Soviet itself. What is less clear is what happens between the tabling (initiative) and the introduction of the bill. The last paragraph of this extended quotation suggests the answer, which is that the commissions, under the supervision of the Legislative Proposals Commission, determine whether a tabled bill can be introduced.

Legislative initiative is taken to mean the right of specified organs and persons in office to table bills for debate by the Supreme Soviet, which for its part is duty bound to examine the bill. In respect of all-Union legislation, legislative initiative is vested in both Chambers of the Supreme Soviet of the USSR—the Soviet of the Union and the Soviet of Nationalities—the Presidium of the Supreme Soviet of the USSR, Deputies of the Supreme Soviet of the USSR and their groups, the Council of Ministers of the USSR, the Supreme Court of the USSR, and the Union Republics in the person of their Supreme Soviets.

The institution of legislative initiative does not at all mean that no other body or person may table proposals for adopting a new law or amending an old one. On the contrary, constitutional practice shows that the most diverse organs, mass organisations, and even citizens are in a position to propose the promulgation of laws. These proposals are given a preliminary study in organs vested with legislative initiative and are then tabled in the Supreme Soviet of the USSR, in the case of all-Union legislation, or for debate by the Supreme Soviet of the Republic, in case of Republican legislation.

Bills are debated in the Supreme Soviet of the USSR either at a joint sitting of both Chambers or in each Chamber separately. The debate usually opens with a report by a representative of the body tabling the bill. On many bills, the Supreme Soviet also hears co-reports by its Standing Commissions. In the course of the debate, deputies state their views on the merits or demerits of the bill before them. Whenever a bill does not evoke any remarks or amendments, the debate is short, and the Supreme Soviet of the USSR goes on to adopt the statute without opening a debate.

Before being debated by the Supreme Soviet, bills are subjected to careful scrutiny by the Commissions for Legislative Proposals of the Soviet of the

Union and the Soviet of Nationalities, or by other Standing Commissions of the Supreme Soviet. Large groups of scientists and government experts take part in drawing up the conclusions of the Commission for Legislative Proposals.[41]

Thus, many bodies may initiate a zakon, but this draft bill must be reviewed by the Supreme Soviet commissions. Although Chkikvadze is not precise on this point, it appears that the commissions legally determine whether a bill may be reported to the Supreme Soviet. This control over the introduction of bills can be inferred from the zakon on permanent commissions.

> Art. 1. The standing commissions of the Council of the Union and the Council of Nationalities are subsidiary bodies of the chambers, formed for the preliminary examination and preparation of questions under the jurisdiction of the USSR Supreme Soviet and for rendering active assistance in implementing the decisions of the USSR Supreme Soviet.
>
> Art. 2. The chief tasks of the standing commissions of the Council of the Union and the Council of nationalities are:
>> elaboration of proposals for examination by the appropriate chamber or by the Presidium of the USSR Supreme Soviet;
>> preparation of conclusions on questions submitted for examination by the USSR Supreme Soviet and its Presidium.[42]

Since zakons are exclusively under the jurisdiction of the Supreme Soviet under Article 32 of the constitution of the USSR, the commissions appear to have the implicit right to review them when they are tabled. According to the zakon on the permanent commissions, the Legislative Proposals Commission implicitly controls non-economic legislation and can determine whether other commissions should review it.[43]

The Planning and Budget Commission implicitly controls the economic legislation and can determine what other commissions should review it. Apparently, the primary function of the branch commissions for various sectors of the economy is "kontrol," not review and drafting legislation.[44]

Legally, the implied control of the Legislative Proposals and Budget Commissions over legislation is not exclusive and can be circumvented. According to Article 26 of the zakon on commissions, a deputy may introduce a bill directly into the Supreme Soviet if he does not agree with his commission's conclusions, but it can only be introduced during the discussion of the issue with which the deputy disagrees. If that issue is not raised then, of course, he cannot introduce his proposal.[45] Also, a commission may submit a bill directly if it disagrees with another commission:[46]

> If a standing commission thinks a question referred to it for examination is also within the jurisdiction of another standing commission, or if it deems it necessary to express its opinion on a question under examination by another commission, it has the right to submit a proposal on this to the chamber or to the Presidium of the USSR Supreme Soviet.

Should the Party apparatus' control over the selection of personnel ever relax, both of these devices provide a mechanism for bypassing the Legislative Proposals Commission and Planning and Budget Commission and introducing a bill directly into the Supreme Soviet itself.

THE LEGISLATIVE INITIATIVE

Legislative initiative is a legal right vested in both chambers of the Supreme Soviet individually, the Presidium of the Supreme Soviet, individual deputies to the Supreme Soviet, groups of deputies, the Supreme Court, and the supreme soviets of union republics.[47] Other bodies may exercise legislative initiative, but it is not "legal" initiative, which means a draft bill submitted by a mass organization, for example, must first be examined by auxiliary bodies of the Supreme Soviet. In practice, there may be little distinction between "legal" and "direct" mass initiative, but the distinction is made by Soviet jurists.[48] They also imply that there is a third category of legislative initiative, ostensibly a subcategory of Party initiative, which is exercised through detailed Party directives only in the most important questions.[49]

The gradual evolution of the concept of legislative initiative reflects an attempt to rationalize the legislative process. The concept of "legal" initiative, which is relatively new, appears to be an attempt to channel legislating activity through the mechanism of the Supreme Soviet. The first clear evidence of this appeared in the Soviet law journal in 1964. Table 6.4 illustrates the confusion that reigned before.[50]

Table 6.4 gives some clue to the role and importance of different bodies in the legislative process. The Council of Ministers exercised the lion's share of initiation, with the Council of Elders and the Presidium of the Supreme Soviet almost tied for a not very close second. The role of the Party apparatus is unclear, but there are two clues. First, the Party apparatus acts through the previously mentioned exercise of "non-legal" initiative, which means through submission of detailed directives on the most important issues.[51] Another source suggests the second clue, that the Party, that is, the apparatus, determines whether an issue is ripe for legislation—

TABLE 6.4

INITIATION OF QUESTIONS FOR THE SUPREME SOVIET OF THE USSR, 1938–60

Convocation	Number	Leader-ship of one chamber	Supreme Soviet Commissions	Individual Deputies	Council of Elders	Supreme Soviet Presidium	Council of Ministers	Central Committee	Union Republics
1 (1938–46)	41	—	2	3	7	5	19	—	5
2 (1946–50)	22	—	3	—	8	6	5	—	—
3 (1950–54)	16	1	—	1	2	3	4	5	—
4 (1954–58)	33	1	5	—	6	7	12	1	1
5 (partial)[a]	21	—	5	—	6	6	9	3	1
TOTAL	141	2	15	4	29	27	49	9	7

a. Lepeshkin indicates that this does not include all bills tabled, since he was writing near the end of the convocation.

Source: A. II Lepeshkin et al., Kurs Sovetskogo Gosudarstvennogo Prava, Vol. 2 (Moscow, 1962) pp. 418, 429..

whether it should be tabled at all and finally introduced. Thus, the suggestion is that no matter can be initiated without the Party's review and approval. The determination of ripeness goes to the core of legislative initiative.[52] One also strongly suspects that the Council of Elders and the Presidium of the Supreme Soviet exercise their initiative on behalf of the Party apparatus.

SECRET SUBCOMMISSIONS

There is evidence that a significant amount of the drafting of and deliberation over legislation takes place in the subcommissions and ad hoc commissions of the Supreme Soviet.[53] The acquisition of this power has been a gradual process since Stalin's death and may reflect the apparent attempt of the Party apparatus to downgrade the state apparatus and to adapt itself to the emerging post-industrial society.

The subcommissions provide an alternative organ for drafting and deliberating on the details of legislation which implements general Party directives. The All-Union Scientific Research Institute of Soviet Legislation (VNIISZ) is an arm of the Juridical Commission of the Council of Ministers, which has apparently drafted most of the bills which the Council of Ministers has initiated. Its assigned function has been to draft bills incorporating opinions of specialists and the public into Party directives.[54] According to its director and deputy director:

> The government has placed the following major tasks before VNIISZ: study and synthesis of proposals to amend and supplement normative acts now on the books, and participation in the drafting of laws; coordination of the work of research institutions engaged in the improvement of legislation; scientific research into codification and systemization of Soviet legislation; study of and the drawing of conclusions from legislation of foreign countries.[55]

The subcommissions may be viewed as competitors in this area. From 1958 to 1962 over 400 sessions of the subcommissions of the Commission on Legislative Proposals were held. In 1963 about 450 legal scholars were brought onto the subcommissions, and 350 others were invited to consult with the subcommissions on drafting.[56] Special ad hoc commissions were created to deliberate on and draft particular bills. The following Soviet source describes the deliberative process in a subcommission:[57]

> Take a sitting of the subcommission drafting the fundamentals of the Public Health Law. Its Chairman, N. N. Blokhin, is a prominent surgeon and scholar,

and no newcomer to the Supreme Soviet, having been a Deputy in its two previous terms. Invited to its sitting by the commission were economists, trade unionists, jurists, financial experts and medical men. Every line of the projected law was closely scrutinized. Purely stylistic alterations were made, then a few substantive ones. An argument broke out: may a patient be operated on without his consent or that of his close relatives?

"How are we to get the required consent if, say, the patient is in a state of shock? The relatives may be away or their whereabouts unknown. The doctor simply has no time."

"I know of no country where legislation allows for forcible operations."

"Take an intestinal perforation. You may not get the patient's consent until its too late. To save life the surgeon should be allowed to operate. . . . "

"I disagree. During the war some wounded refused to be amputated. And though not all, many did get well. Don't you understand that I cannot saw off a man's leg without his consent?"

"There are all kinds of cases. You cannot prescribe for all of them."

"That should be legislatively formalized, lest we tie the hands of our doctors in emergencies. When an operation is urgent, the surgeon should not have to search for relatives or guardians."

They put that down: a doctor may, is obligated even, to decide for himself, but this in "exceptional cases" only, when delay "imperils the patient's life" and when "obtaining consent appears impossible." This, eventually, was the formula that became law. And needless to say, many people's lives depend on it.

Admittedly, the issue at hand was not a monumental one for the polity but, of course, such a question would be handled in secret.

EMBRYONIC FUNCTIONS: DECISION-MAKING, PARLIAMENTARISM, PARTICIPATION

It is interesting to note that 46 of the 55 articles of the Public Health Law discussed above were reportedly altered in the subcommissions.[58] Table 6.5 indicates the composition of some of these special arms of the Supreme Soviet.[59]

It appears that deliberation in the subcommissions is acquiring a formalized style reminiscent of the much maligned "bourgeois parliamentarism." Lenin would perhaps look askance were he to read the following comment of a Soviet scholar:

The Supreme Soviet has many commissions, subcommissions and working groups, and each finds its own specific approach. The approaches are many. At working sessions, usually attended by 30 or 40 people, prepared speeches are rare. The custom is to speak off the cuff, which, incidentally, contributes

TABLE 6.5
OCCUPATIONAL COMPOSITION OF SELECTED DRAFTING SUBCOMMISSIONS OF THE LEGISLATIVE PROPOSALS COMMISSION[a]

Zakon	Total no. of members	Specialists and manual workers	Scientific workers	Representatives of mass organizations	Heads of ministries and departments	Managers of enterprises, organizations, and establishments
Basic principles of land use	31	10	8	3	5	5
Fundamentals of matrimonial law	32	11	9	4	5	3
Fundamentals of legislation on exploitation of water resources	50	19	10	6	9	6
Fundamentals of legislation on health protection	44	17	12	6	5	4
Fundamentals of corrective labor legislation	40	9	14	5	8	4
Basic principles of the exploitation of mineral wealth	28	11	8	3	3	3
Basic principles of forest exploitation	40	12	15	3	5	5
Law on accounting and statistics	44	17	12	3	7	5

a. There is no indication how many deputies sat on these commissions.
Source: M. Saifulin, The Soviet Parliament (Moscow, 1967), p. 134.

to the *art of oratory, the art of quick reaction and response, the art of finding the apt word, the joke that drives the point home.* The search for the best decision creates a tense but by no means grim or strained atmosphere.[60]

In 1958 subcommissions drafted the very important Fundamental Principles of Criminal Law, and Fundamental Principles of Criminal Organization. Each of these subcommissions was composed of from 25 to 45 persons. A large percentage of them were lawyers, who often acted as secretaries and chairmen of the subcommissions.[61]

The subcommissions have two advantages. Their meetings are generally secret, while the standing commissions increasingly hold public meetings which facilitate their primary function—"kontrol."[62] Also, they may co-opt specialists in whatever area they are working, as shown in Table 6.5. This gives the Party apparatus another source of expertise in addition to its own experts and those of the government.[63]

A practice of circulating drafts of key laws seems to be evolving. [64] These drafts are circulated to academics and jurists of the institutes and their comments are collated by the subcommissions. After a draft bill has been tabled and examined by the subcommissions, they farm it out, then collate the feedback. A Soviet correspondent describes (and embellishes) the process below[65]:

> The long life of a law depends largely on how well it is drawn up. The best way to avoid amendments is to put them in before the law is adopted. That is why a ready draft, which, presumably, its makers consider faultless (why else would they let it out of their hands?) is sent out for verification to all concerned: research institutions, and the like, the list of which is a long one. In the case of the Fundamentals of Water Law it contained 130 addresses.

> One ministry is responsible for the purity of water reservoirs. Another does its worst polluting them. One occupies itself with afforestation. Another with felling timber. A controversy erupts suddenly over timber floating. Ichthyologists protest: the rivers are congested, and fish die. The timbermen retort heatedly: for the present they cannot give up floating. The State Planning Committee, the Central Council of Trade Unions, the Academy of Sciences, the Health and Finance Ministries, are all consulted. Volumes of conclusions are drawn and many columns of figures put down.

> When attitudes are irreconcilable, conferences are called, as in the case of the cadastral surveying. Or else a ministerial conference, with ministers arguing their respective points, as in the case of the timber-floating. Ultimately, it was found that floating could not be completely eliminated, for no other way was yet available for getting the timber out of remote places like the taiga, where roads are non-existent. But provisions were made protecting spawning grounds, recreation areas and navigable rivers, where the ban would be unconditional.

Again notes and objections are collated, studied by the deputies, and sten-
cilled: seventeen amendments to Article 1, fourteen to Article 2, twenty-five
to Article 3, etc. Following fresh debate, a new variant of the bill emerges and
is sent to different parts of the country—the Presidiums of the Supreme
Soviets of all fifteen of the constituent republics, because the future law must
be measured against the traditions, climate and development of each. The
people in the Baltic states, for example, think that the marriage age should be
raised to 21 whereas some of the southern republics think 18 is too high.

In effect, it is at this collating stage that the subcommissions seem to
be edging out the VNIISZ of the Council of Ministers. One should
temper this conclusion by pointing out that members of the Council
of Ministers sit on the subcommissions, some of whom are doubtless
from VNIISZ. The new emphasis on publicizing most, but not all,
laws in an effort not only to socialize the populace but also to seek
further comments has the effect of magnifying the collating function. Collation of comments derived from public discussion of draft
bills is the job of the subcommissions, not the Council of Ministers.

PUBLICITY AND PUBLIC PARTICIPATION IN DRAFTING

The publicity surrounding these activities of the Supreme Soviet is
intended to enhance its image as a meaningful body in whose
activities one should participate. This image may develop some
credibility and encourage the masses to participate in the system as a
whole. Even if the deputies themselves are already socialized to
participate to a large extent, the populace may perceive the Supreme
Soviet as a meaningful institution which could encourage their participation in its activities as well as the activities of the lower soviets.
Both the plenary sessions and sessions of the commissions have
received increasing publicity in the press and other media. The
mandate for this is contained in the 1961 Party Programme[66] : "It is
necessary to ensure in full . . . publicity and the free and full discussion of all important questions of government and of economic and
cultural development at meetings of soviets." Some measure of the
extent of the publicity campaign surrounding the increasing activities
of the Supreme Soviet is indicated by the following comment from a
Soviet work on the Supreme Soviet[67] :

In addition to the publication of main bills in the central press, another
widespread practice is to publish those of a less general nature in special
magazines and bulletins. The purpose is to invite a more thorough and
efficient discussion, to draw into it the scientists and experts concerned, and
to enable them to exchange their views on the pages of those magazines.

Published in February–March 1958 were drafts of such important legislative acts as the Fundamentals of Criminal Legislation and the Fundamentals of Criminal Procedure of the USSR and the Union Republics; in July–August 1960–the draft Fundamentals of Civil Legislation and the Fundamentals of Civil Procedure of the USSR and the Union Republics; Fundamentals of Labour Legislation and the Bill on Enhancing the Role of the Community in Combating Violations of Soviet Legality and the Rules of Socialist Community Life. Some publications were made in the magazines *Sovety Deputatov Trudyashchikhsya, Sovetskoye Gosudarstvo i Pravo, Sovetskaya Yustitsia, Sotsialistichoskaya Zakonnest, Sovetskiye Profsoyuzy, Sotsialistichesky Trud, Voprosy Ekonomiki* and the bulletin *Byulleten Verkhovnogo Soveta SSSR* as well as in some other periodicals. The total circulation of those magazines exceeds half a million copies.

There is some evidence that the Soviet populace is beginning to respond to the appeal to participate in such activities of the Supreme Soviet as public discussions of bills as well as in submitting written suggestions for amending draft bills. For example, the same source reports a meeting of 400 women at a textile mill in Riga to discuss divorce simplification procedures and of 250 women in Daghestan in 1965 to discuss alimony with regard to a draft bill on marriage. Members of the Commission on Legislative Proposals and subcommission members arrived from Moscow to conduct the meetings.[68] Soviet sources like to create the impression that these public discussions result in massive amendments to the law, an allegation which is difficult to prove either way. One report claimed that 2,000 amendments resulted from discussions of the Fundamentals of Civil Legislation. If public involvement actually did have such an impact, participation would certainly increase. It is doubtful that such was the case. What is clear is that the regime would like the populace to think they had such substantial influence. This is, of course, manipulation, which the Soviet citizen can probably readily identify and thus tends to diminish the efforts of the regime to socialize the populace to participate.

Another aspect of public participation in the drafting of Supreme Soviet zakons is the large number of letters from citizens expressing views on various bills, which allegedly pour into the offices of individual deputies and commissions and subcommissions. The Legislative Proposals Commission allegedly received 12,000 letters commenting on the draft bill on state pensions in 1956.[69] The permanent commissions reportedly received 7,000 suggested amendments to the draft marriage law of 1968, and 3,000 suggested changes to the health protection law of 1969.[70]

THE EVOLUTION OF THE "KONTROL" FUNCTION

In theory, the Supreme Soviet performs both legislative and executive functions, since Soviet sources continually stress its role in implementing the legislation which it has enacted through "kontrol." This means ensuring that the government bureaucracy carries out the laws and the policies behind them. It is checking on the implementation of those juridical norms embodying Party policy which have been ratified by the Supreme Soviet or its Presidium. It is a watchdog function which, in theory, the Supreme Soviet has delegated to its permanent commissions.

The 1961 CPSU Programme makes three separate references to increased "kontrol" over the ministries by the soviets as essential to the perfection of socialist democracy.[71] Though "kontrol" was not an explicit function of the Legislative Proposals Commission according to the 1947 regulations creating them, in 1962 the chairman of that commission identified "kontrol" as a key new function of the permanent commissions.[72]

Leading legal scholars took up the cudgel, asserting that the creation of sector commissions (that is, subcommissions with jurisdiction over specific branches of the economy), modeled on those previously created by the Economic Commission of the Council of Nationalities, would enhance the effectiveness of "kontrol." They urged union republic supreme soviets to create sector commissions as well, and called for more qualified deputies to sit on the commissions and for more released time for deputies to work on them.[73] Then followed Khrushchev's ouster, the announcement of the economic reform, and the Twenty-third CPSU Congress where Brezhnev reiterated the need to intensify the "kontrol" function and suggested new permanent commissions to facilitate it. Taking their cue, legal scholars called for extension of "kontrol" (that is, supervision or monitoring) over not only the ministries, but also the Procuracy—that huge, highly centralized guardian of legality.[74] They further sought a precise legal definition of the status of the permanent commissions.[75]

In August 1966 each chamber created six new commissions by postanovlenie and in October 1967 a zakon outlined the structures and functions of the commissions. It appeared that the immediate concern of its drafters was to facilitate the economic reform. In place of the nine old commissions, the new zakon created twenty, of which fourteen were concerned primarily with the economy. Twelve commissions were assigned jurisdiction over various branches of the economy following the paradigm of sectoral subcommissions under the Economic Commission of the Council of Nationalities and the Budget Commissions. Their assigned role was in-depth analysis of their respective branches of the economy, and exercise of "kontrol" over the government bureaus administering them.

In December 1968 a Youth Affairs Commission was created in each chamber, and in 1969 the Transportation and Communication Commissions in each chamber were split—thus, twenty-six commissions had replaced the eight created in 1938. The former Budget Commissions were renamed the Planning and Budget Commissions with responsibility not only for elaborating drafts of the plan and budget, but also for "kontrol" over the implementation of them. The new commissions involved 912 deputies, over one-half of the Supreme Soviet, a large proportion of which were assigned to commissions charged with "kontrol" over, or monitoring, the economic bureaucracy.[76]

In short, a major shift in emphasis with respect to the functional role of the permanent commissions had been finally juridically institutionalized. Let us now turn to an examination of the precise institutional mechanisms by which "kontrol" is exercised in order to assess its potential effectiveness in reality.

THE LEGAL SANCTIONS FOR "KONTROL"

That the responsibilities and powers of the commissions with respect to "kontrol" (affecting primarily their relations with the Council of Ministers and the ministries) are spelled out in a widely discussed and promulgated zakon emphasizes the increasing importance of the monitoring function.[77] One need only recall the multifarious practices which developed in the relations between the ministries and the Economic Commission of the Council of Nationalities to realize that the precise definition of the monitoring function strengthens it.

When the commissions wish to address the Council of Ministers in order to facilitate the implementation of a law which they have discovered is being ignored or improperly administered, the legal form is a proposal (predlozhenia).[78] When addressing the ministries directly, for the same purposes, the legal form is a recommendation (recomendatsia).[79] While the ministries must examine the recommendations (Article 23), nothing is said as to whether the Council of

Ministers must also examine proposals. In any event, apparently proposals and recommendations are just that—mere recommendations, mere suggestions. There is no legal sanction to force the Council of Ministers or the ministries to adopt resolutions which would implement proposals or recommendations directed to them by the permanent commissions.[80]

One authority, nevertheless, argues that requiring ministries (Article 23) to at least examine the recommendations is a significant step, since they were previously often ignored altogether.[81] However, most Soviet sources report glowingly of the ministries and Council of Ministers adopting resolutions implementing proposals and recommendations of the permanent commissions.[82] Clearly, the only real pressure on them to do so is publicity, which in a tightly controlled society such as the Soviet Union could be a significant sanction. Promulgation of recommendations and proposals is authorized but not required by the law creating the commission system.[83]

Of course, the proposals and recommendations could be submitted to the Supreme Soviet or its Presidium for conversion into law, thus further publicizing them and lending whatever increment of authority legal instruments possess in the Soviet Union to persuade the government to redress the practices cited in the proposal; however, ratification by either body, especially the plenum of the Supreme Soviet, is quite cumbersome and ill-suited to continual monitoring. The increasing activity of the Presidium of the Supreme Soviet in conjunction with the commissions is discussed in detail further on.

Although the commissions may now legally address the government, which must consider the communications, and although the commissions may now, in effect, sit in permanent session through their subcommissions, it is debatable how much the relationship of the Supreme Soviet to the government has changed. Immediately prior to the publication of the 1967 zakon on permanent commissions, one legal scholar argued that in effect the relationship was one of "co-operation and inter-action" with no real "kontrol" by the Supreme Soviet. But, having argued that "kontrol" was a hollow shell, he called for breathing life into it.[84] In rebuttal, another legal scholar retorted that such accountability already existed and was guaranteed by Article 65 of the Constitution.[85] The first article had appeared in *Sovetskoye gosudarstvo i pravo,* the leading legal journal; the rebuttal appeared on the third page of *Izvestia.*

The vehemence of the rebuttal and the publicity given both points of view suggest a debate within the political leadership over the changing relationship of the legislature to the administrative and executive arms of the government, which was implicit in the prospective legislation on the permanent commissions announced soon after the publicity by N. V. Podgorny. The increasing size and potential viability of the commissions as political institutions encroaching on the executive authority conjured up resistance to the proposed changes in the commission system. That this resistance was partially successful is evidenced by the emasculated nature of the "kontrol" function in the final draft creating the new commission system.

To these legal limitations on the "kontrol" function one must add the political limitations, previously described in connection with the drafting function—that ministry representatives, though forbidden on permanent commissions, may sit on the real working bodies, the subcommissions, and in fact sometimes even chair their sessions. However, the chairmen of the permanent commissions have the sole power to form the subcommissions; thus, by implication they may exclude ministry representatives. Clearly, the "kontrol" function represents a threat to the ministries, thus its extent and limits remain in a state of flux.

VERTICAL AND HORIZONTAL EXTENSION OF THE "KONTROL" FUNCTION

Nominally, the entire pyramidal structure of soviets remains under the supervision of the Supreme Soviet.[86] Since deputies at local levels do not elect deputies at higher levels in the pre-1936 fashion, the mechanism of supervision is more implicit than explicit. In the early 1960s, the union republics modeled their legislation on that of the Supreme Soviet.[87] This, plus the constitutional authority of the Supreme Soviet over union republic supreme soviets and over the local soviets, provided the most visible framework of supervision until 1967 when the new permanent commission system legislation was enacted. Even before that it became increasingly clear that the Soviet leadership was determined to enlist the union republic supreme soviets in the economic reform drive for increased efficiency.[88]

Since 1967 almost all of the union republic supreme soviets have enacted legislation modeled on the 1967 zakon, creating the twenty permanent commissions, thus endowing the permanent commissions of the union republic supreme soviets with monitoring functions. The permanent commissions of the Supreme Soviet can, of course, address recommendations to these permanent commissions of the union republic supreme soviets. The Supreme Soviet and its Presidium could also convert these recommendations into law. Replies from the bodies addressed must be forthcoming within two months.[89] This vastly increases the size of the apparatus nominally headed by the Supreme Soviet and its commissions and thus its potential as a monitor of government economic activity at all levels.

In addition to this apparent extension of "kontrol" vertically down the soviet pyramid, the Supreme Soviet appears to be extending its supervision horizontally over the courts and the Procuracy. The monitoring of the Procuracy is less stringent than that of the courts. In general, the all-Union zakon creating the permanent commissions and the union republic zakons modeled on it exclude the Supreme Court judges and Procuracy officials at any level from sitting on the commissions, thus symbolizing, if not ensuring, their independence to perform the monitoring function. In some union republic zakons on the permanent commissions, the procurator of the republic is not excluded from membership on the commissions.[90] Also, neither the union republic nor the all-Union zakons make the procurator directly responsible to the commissions. That there is support for increasing the supervision over the Procuracy and especially the courts by the permanent commissions of supreme soviets at all levels is apparent from the discussion of gradual extension of the "kontrol" function by legal scholars.[91]

However feeble or embryonic, these discussions and legislation constitute a significant attempt to flesh out the provisions of the constitution which imply accountability of the judicial system and Procuracy to the Supreme Soviet. It is at least a symbolic step toward strengthening the real power of the Supreme Soviet over the legal system. It is also an extension of the monitoring function from the burgeoning realm of economics to the burgeoning realm of law. In a sense, it is a tacit institutional recognition of the intimate relationship between the two spheres in a modernized society.

In summary, the drive for economic efficiency in the sixties which conjured up the economic reform also produced a monitoring function which took its place alongside, if not somewhat superior to, the drafting function of the permanent commissions of the Supreme Soviet. It was the midwife of a zakon creating many new permanent commissions with significantly, if not substantially, increased powers. Precisely how much this altered the relationship of the Soviet executive authority to the Supreme Soviet remains relatively obscure. However, one may at least infer from the public debate preceding the creation of new commissions that significant but still quite limited additional powers have accrued to the legislature. Perhaps the possibility of a small breach in the dike provided the real impetus for the debate. To some extent, that possibility had been realized with the extension of the "kontrol" function vertically to the union republic supreme soviet permanent commissions, and horizontally to the judicial and Procuracy pyramids.

Chapter 7

THE FUNCTIONS OF THE SUPREME SOVIET
IN THE SOVIET POLITICAL SYSTEM

Broadly speaking, the Supreme Soviet (and its auxiliary bodies) serve two major functions in the Soviet polity. First, it is an organ of legitimation, and second, it is an organ of efficiency seeking to grease the wheels of government in a highly complex, multinational modernizing state. It is not a decision-making organ, although there is evidence that, through the evolution of the functions and mechanisms described herein, it may gradually and incrementally be acquiring elements of decision-making.

This analysis will focus on specific subfunctions of the two broader categories. Legitimation includes the symbolic, representational, ombudsman, socializational, and participatory functions, and some aspects of the legislative, "kontrol," and foreign policy functions. The efficiency function focuses primarily on "kontrol," which is emerging from obscurity as a most important function.

Because of the overlapping and intertwining of functions, the multiplicity of organs in the Supreme Soviet system, and their rapid evolution, it is not particularly fruitful to draw rigid structural-functional paradigms. The representational function is described in the section on the composition of the Supreme Soviet. The evolution of the "kontrol" and legislative functions is analyzed in detail as they affect the relationships of state bodies further on.

The effort here is to provide an outline of the essential nature and evolution of the most important functions, focusing specifically on details of institutional development only where such developments appear to be germane.

THE SYMBOLIC-LEGITIMATING FUNCTION

The Supreme Soviet's evolution since Stalin's death evidences a propensity to endow this somewhat hollow shell with content, to transform a mere vehicle of propaganda into a political institution of significant utility for the regime in many respects. Historically, the Supreme Soviet emerged immediately prior to two enormous crises of the Soviet polity—the "great" purges in which Stalin secured total control over the polity, and World War II, which nearly decimated that polity. Thus, like the Zemsky Sobor, the Imperial State Duma, and the Central Executive Committee, the Supreme Soviet was weaned, if not conceived, in disorder and crisis. Also like its predecessors, it proved unwieldy and of little utility in resolving upheavals of such magnitude. As a result, its development remained arrested, and its significance largely symbolic until the postwar period.

While the purges marked Stalin's triumph over the Party, the 1936 Constitution signified a major step in the legalization of the Party's control over other political institutions. Unlike the previous constitutions, this one mentions the Party in Article 126: " ... the CPSU ... is the vanguard of the working people in their struggle to build a communist society and is the leading core of all organizations of the working people, both public and private."[1] In effect, the 1936 Constitution formalizes and sanctifies in a juridical instrument the pattern evolving since 1917, in which the Party emerged as the "leading core" and fountain of orthodoxy within the Soviet polity.

Concomitantly, the Constitution is a juridical expression of the notion that socialism is built, that the period of transition from capitalism to socialism is complete, and that no classes remain except the peasants and workers and a "stratum," the intelligentsia.[2] It further signified the need for a state apparatus in the coming transition from socialism to communism, because of the international situation which found the Soviet Union surrounded by capitalist powers. Stalin argued that this capitalist encirclement vindicated the necessity for organs of state power such as the Supreme Soviet.[3]

While the Constitution portrayed the Supreme Soviet as a central organ in this new transition process, Stalin apparently pictured it as a mere transmission belt, subservient to the Party.[4] The Stalin Constitution was the first Soviet constitution to claim that it embodied the "sovereign will of the people" as a whole.[5] Thus, in theory, it marked the conversion of the populace en masse to a proletarian mentality.[6] The Supreme Soviet, in theory, is a symbol of this "popular sovereignty": " . . . personified in the highest organs of state authority, the will of the people—of the masses of missions of workers, peasants and intellectuals—finds expression."[7]

Thus appears a subtle distinction between the will of the Party and the will of the masses, with the Supreme Soviet representing the latter. This conjures up a notion of residual legitimacy reminiscent of the Zemsky Sobor.[8] Like the Tsar, the Party has never recognized a "residual legitimacy" resting in the populace, but continues to stress the unity of Party and people.

THE SUPREME SOVIET AS INSTITUTIONAL SYMBOL OF SOCIALIST DEMOCRACY

The Supreme Soviet institutionalizes and reflects the concept of Socialist Democracy. The first element of that concept is "sovereignty of the people," which resides in the Supreme Soviet and its auxiliary bodies. The second element is direct democracy as symbolized by the amateur deputy who, in theory, is not a professional parliamentarian deliberating and debating, but an actual worker or peasant, a man of action. The deputy leaves his work and locality, comes to Moscow, votes for legislation, and then returns to mobilize support for it.[9] The third concept of Socialist Democracy symbolized by the Supreme Soviet is non-separation of powers—that is, the union of executive and legislative functions.[10] Following Marx and Lenin, Stalin renounced separation of powers as a device to maintain that domination by the bourgeoisie which the 1936 Constitution declared extinct.

The fourth element of Socialist Democracy incorporated into the Supreme Soviet in theory is the equality of nationalities.[11] In theory, the Supreme Soviet represents and expresses the united will of all the nationalities of the Soviet Union, each of which theoretically has its independent voice in the Soviet of Nationalities. The last element of Socialist Democracy, institutionalized in the Supreme Soviet, is the system of electing deputies. Universal suffrage, a key revolutionary objective, restricted by the Imperial State Duma and denied by the constitutions of 1918 and 1922 to all but workers and peasants, is formally granted by the 1936 Constitution to all Soviet citizens who, upon the victory of socialism, have in theory achieved or are achieving a proletarian mentality.

In summary, the Supreme Soviet symbolizes three principles of Socialist Democracy through five institutional forms:

(1) *Direct democracy:* Institutionalized in the amateur-deputy and universal suffrage.

(2) *Unity of popular will:* Institutionalized in the union of executive and legislative functions and in the nationality principle of unity in diversity, embodied in the two chambers of the Supreme Soviet—the Soviet of Nationalities, representing diversity, and the Soviet of the Union, unity.

(3) *Sovereignty of "all" the people:* Residing in the Supreme Soviet as the supreme organ of state power.

THE SUPREME SOVIET AS SYMBOL OF SOVIET FEDERALISM AND NATIONALITY POLICY

The Supreme Soviet institutionalizes the Soviet concept of unity within diversity, which is the essence of its concept of federalism and its nationality policy.[12] In theory, the Council of the Union represents the interests of the Soviet state as a whole, while the Council of Nationalities represents the diverse interests of the Soviet nationalities. Both interests are equally considered in theory.

> The presence of the second chamber, the Soviet of Nationalities, in the structure of the Supreme Soviet of the USSR brilliantly expresses Soviet democracy, in which the starting points of all enactments are the specific national (no less than the general) interests of all the USSR toilers. Thereby the mutual faith and collaboration of nations are strengthened, and national peace is guaranteed.[13]

The creation of the Council of Nationalities, at least in theory, fulfills a prime revolutionary goal—that of providing a voice for the nationalities in government, a voice which was denied by the Tsar, even in the Imperial State Duma. Ostensibly, Stalin strongly supported its creation against amendments to the contrary.[14]

The real equality of the Council of Nationalities pales against the background of Party democratic centralism, but it is continually and vociferously proclaimed.[15] The following quotation from Stalin's chief jurist, Andrei Vyshinsky, describes the various constitutional provisions allegedly supporting its equality:

> Both houses of the Supreme Soviet of the USSR, the Soviet of the Union and the Soviet of Nationalities, are elected for four years and at the same time. Consequently, in neither house of the Supreme Soviet in the USSR is there, or can there be, the advantages (associated with the dates of powers and of election) herein before referred to as enjoyed by the second chambers of capitalist countries. Both houses of the USSR Supreme Soviet have equal

rights—genuinely equal rights. In the Soviet system there are no "higher" or "lower" houses, nor can a situation arise in which the second chamber could hold back or put a brake on legislative proposals of the first. The class nature and essence of both chambers of the Supreme Soviet is the same: Both are chosen by all the toilers of the USSR. Each of them has alike a single goal: the strengthening of socialism. Both enjoy a like measure of legislative initiative; a statute is deemed affirmed if adopted by both houses by simple majority vote of each.

Joint sessions of both houses are conducted in turn by the President of the Soviet of the Union and by the President of the Soviet of Nationalities. The Presidents and their two Vice-Presidents are chosen separately by each house. Statutes adopted by the Supreme Soviet of the USSR—that is to say, having passed both houses—are automatically published by the Presidium of the Supreme Soviet of the USSR in the languages of the Union Republics, over the signatures of the President and Secretary of the Presidium of the Supreme Soviet of the USSR. The USSR Constitution of 1936 points out (Art. 47) that in case the houses do not agree, controverted questions are transferred to be decided by a board of conciliation made up of equal representation of both houses. If this board does not arrive at a harmonious decision, or if its decision fails to satisfy one of the chambers, the question is again considered in the chambers. If this time a harmonious decision of two houses is still lacking, the Presidium of the Supreme Soviet dissolves the houses and directs new elections. Controversies between the houses are thus solved by turning to the voters who finally solve the disputed matters. This feature specifically characterizes Soviet democracy and Soviet popular sovereignty.[16]

These elaborate institutional trappings indicate the lengths to which Stalin was prepared to go to maintain the fiction of equality between the Supreme Soviet chambers.

As we have seen in Chapter 2, there are many legal ways to undermine the Council of Nationalities' equality. The fortunes of the Council of Nationalities and its auxiliary bodies in the post-Stalin era will be traced further on. Though its relative power vis-à-vis the other chamber has not been enhanced, it nevertheless remains a major organ through which independent nationality concerns may be aired before the Party leadership.

SOME FUNCTIONS OF STALIN'S SUPREME SOVIET

Stalin's Supreme Soviet served as an institutional symbol of Soviet democracy, designed to mobilize public support for the regime's policies and to appeal to Western public opinion. One leading scholar considered the latter, the foreign policy function, to have been Stalin's major motive.[17] He noted the irony of the purges ensuing upon the promulgation of the Constitution. With Hitler's star ascending and Soviet foreign policy shifting from a coalition with the "outs" of Versailles to a balancing act between Germany and the West, the foreign policy utility of the Constitution as a propaganda device appealing to Western public opinion with its love of legislature and law could not be discounted. The utter cynicism imputed to Stalin perhaps accounted to some extent for the lack of scholarly interest in the real functions of the Supreme Soviet in his time. Whether or not Stalin ever intended to breathe life into the Supreme Soviet, its growth was arrested by the war and it had barely achieved independence at Stalin's death.

However, two major functions had assumed at least rudimentary form, whatever his intent. They were the ratification function and the barometer function. A brief descriptive analysis of these follows, providing background for a more detailed analysis of the functions of the post-Stalin Supreme Soviet.

THE RATIFICATION FUNCTION

Ratification means converting political decisions into normative juridical instruments. It is the juridical legitimation of decision-making outputs called policy. It is to be distinguished from the drafting function which is the conversion of decision-making outputs into detailed activity-regulating norms, which must then be legally sanctified through the ratification process. Legitimation of zakons in the Soviet Union occurs at two stages of the legislative process: first, the Party sanctifies policy, then the Supreme Soviet sanctifies the draft bill creating the statute or zakon designed to implement the Party policy.

Ratification is thus the legitimating step in the legislative process. In the Stalin era, policy emanated from Stalin and his intimates, was converted to a draft bill by the Council of Ministers, and then was submitted to the Supreme Soviet or its Presidium which, in formal session, formally voted, always unanimously, to endow the document with the title of ukaz or zakon, thereby rendering it legally binding. Since the Supreme Soviet represented the will of the people in constitutional theory, and since the zakon was the vehicle embodying this will, the process of ratification lent an extra increment of authority to this detailed reflection of Party policy. Of course, it simultaneously and subtly conjured the notion of dual legitimacy which theorists explained away by asserting that the will of Party and people were one. The ritual of ratification also implies that law in the Western sense of the rule of law possesses an independent influence in the Soviet polity.

THE BAROMETER FUNCTION

The second political-institutional function performed by the Supreme Soviet for Stalin was providing him with a barometer of public opinion.[18] As he described it:

> In our Soviet country we must evolve a system of government that will permit us with certainty to anticipate all changes, to perceive everything that is going on among the peasants, the nationals, the non-Russian nations, and the Russians; the system of supreme organs must possess a number of barometers which will anticipate every change, register and forestall . . . all possible storms and ill-fortune. That is the Soviet system of government.[19]

In other words, in Stalin's view the Supreme Soviet was an information input device. The content of that input was the state of public sentiment among all groups within the Soviet Union. The content was not of a technical nature to aid in the drafting of detailed legislation. The soviets "register" information to enable the decision-makers to "forestall" crises. The inputs were not necessarily received with a view toward heeding public demands, but rather for the purpose of facilitating their manipulation.

The key word in Stalin's comments is "anticipate." Its implication is that information on the state of public opinion among the "peasants, the nationals, the non-Russian nations, and the Russians" is required by the decision-making leadership in order to better direct and control them, rather than to improve their lot by catering to their wants and needs. That Stalin used the soviets as barometers of public opinion does not imply a desire to satisfy it, but rather to manipulate and control it.

The barometric function is closely tied to the doctrines of the amateur-deputy and non-separation of powers. The amateur-deputy in fact is a passive instrument, a virtual individual barometer of public opinion. He is not a decision-maker, he is not an investigator; he is a human register, a human recording. Thus, his amateur status is crucial to the barometric function. He must be an amateur. He cannot be a professional parliamentarian, for then he could not "reflect" public opinion. He could only "interpret" it from the jaundiced eye of a "non-toiler." The amateur-deputy is not only not a professional parliamentarian; he is in theory a "toiler" and thereby is imbued with the proletarian mentality.

The barometric function also illuminates the dichotomy between form and content inhering in the doctrine of the unity of executive and legislative functions embodied in the Supreme Soviet. That human barometer, the amateur-deputy, performs three roles. He is the literal purveyor of information to the supreme organ of state power, which is an executive function. Then, in theory only, he converts public opinion into legislation, thus performing a decision-making legislative function, while in fact he merely ritualistically ratifies policy decisions designed to anticipate and manipulate the information he conveyed to the real decision-makers. And, finally, the amateur-deputy performs a second executive function by returning to his local constituency to mobilize support for the policy embodied in the legislation and to facilitate its implementation. In short, the amateur-deputy performs in fact as a policy input, in theory as a policy decision-maker, and in fact as a policy output—in that order. He affects legislation at three stages of the Soviet legislative process.

THE FUNCTION OF MASS INVOLVEMENT IN THE SUPREME SOVIET: SOCIALIZATION TO PARTICIPATE?

The symbolic role of the Supreme Soviet as the image of Socialist Democracy is clearly designed to enhance the legitimacy of the regime. Likewise, mass involvement in the organs of state power headed by the Supreme Soviet aims at enhancing the democratic image of the regime and encouraging participation in limited aspects of the governmental process. The extent to which the regime has and is succeeding in this goal of encouraging the masses to participate in the soviets is difficult to assess. Mass involvement is not mass participation. Participation in the political processes implies a belief that the involvement is meaningful or that by being involved one can change the system. Without this conviction that involvement is meaningful, active participation is replaced by mere passive involvement. Involvement can, of course, be induced by coercion, which certainly was one of Stalin's chief instruments, and undoubtedly remains as a powerful if not more latent stimulant to involvement today. However, participation cannot be coerced; it is involvement based on a belief that the activity is meaningful.

The Party apparatus' use of all organizations as transmission belts to mobilize and manipulate the populace throughout Soviet history has probably retarded efforts to convert mass involvement in the soviets into active participation. The apparatus itself is the leading core of the soviets and constitutes a higher proportion of the membership as one moves up the pyramid of organs of state power. Thus, not only will those involved fear manipulation, but in fact there will be manipulation, and to the extent that the perception of this manipulation mitigates a sense of meaningful involvement, participation will lag. Nevertheless, the regime can no longer rely so heavily on coercion and must attempt to encourage participation, which is certainly one major reason for expanding the activities of the organs of state power.

The activation of the organs of state power is more closely related to socialization than to mobilization.[20] The activation of the masses through the soviets does not appear to be primarily focused on some set of goals which will facilitate the transition from traditional to modern society. Rather, the main impetus seems to be to employ the soviets as agents of socialization. Mass involvement in them is aimed at inducing acceptance of the political system, not at mobilizing the masses to change it.

The message which these agents of socialization, called soviets, transmit to the masses involved in them can be summarized as follows: "Participate; involvement is meaningful." Of course, the effectiveness of the communication depends on the kind of activity in which the person receiving it is involved. Clearly, drafting a major zakon is more meaningful than passively listening to Party leaders' marathon speeches at sittings of the Supreme Soviet. The meaningfulness of one's involvement in the soviets determines the extent to which the soviets are an effective agent of socialization. Let us examine some of the expanded activities of the Supreme Soviet and its subordinate soviets to arrive at some evaluation of their impact on the persons involved in terms of participation and socialization.

To begin with, since Stalin's death and particularly since the Twentieth Party Congress, more laws have been passed and more sessions held per convocation. From the point of view of socialization, this may not reflect more participation on the part of the deputies, but rather a more efficient rubber stamp. In fact, however, the deputies have been more deeply involved in the drafting process through the commissions and subcommissions. Here again, one must question whether this indicates any significant change from the point of view of socialization and participation. Since most of the key figures in the drafting process and on the commissions are high Party or government officials, one might argue that they were already socialized to participate and thus little new has been added. The increase in laws and sessions per convocation is shown below in Table 7.1.

The number of persons involved in the Supreme Soviet's activities is also increasing quite steadily. In March, 1961, the Presidium of the Supreme Soviet increased the number of deputies from each union republic in the Council of Nationalities from 25 to 32, in order to maintain approximate numerical equality with the Council of the Union. This increased the number of deputies from 1,443 to 1,517. Even before the 1967 zakon on the Supreme Soviet's permanent commissions (which increased the number of commissions), individual commission membership was increasing.

The regime is also encouraging public discussions of bills as well as submission of written suggestions for amending draft bills. For example, the same source reports a meeting of 400 women at a textile mill in Riga to discuss divorce simplification procedures and of 250 women in Daghestan in 1965 to discuss alimony with regard to a draft bill on marriage. Members of the Commission on Legislative Proposals and subcommission members arrived from Moscow to conduct the meetings (see Chapter 6). Soviet sources like to create the impression that these public discussions result in massive amendments to the law, an allegation which is difficult to prove either way. One report claimed that 2,000 amendments resulted from discussions of a "zakon" entitled Fundamentals of Civil Legislation. If public involvement actually did have such an impact, participation would

TABLE 7.1

**NUMBER OF SESSIONS AND ACTS PASSED
BY THE SUPREME SOVIET**

Convocation	Number of sessions	Number of legislative acts
1 (1938–46)	12	97
2 (1946–50)	5	60
3 (1950–54)	5	41
4 (1954–58)	9	121
5 (1958–62)	7	131
6 (1962–66)	7	111

Source: M. Saifulin, The Soviet Parliament (Moscow: Progress Publishers, 1967), pp. 15–17.

certainly increase. It is doubtful that such was the case. What is clear is that the regime would like the populace to think they had such substantial influence. This is, of course, manipulation, which the Soviet citizen can probably readily identify and thus tends to diminish the efforts of the regime to socialize the population to participate.

Another aspect of public participation in the drafting of Supreme Soviet zakons is the large number of letters from citizens expressing views on various bills, which allegedly pour into the offices of individual deputies and commissions and subcommissions. The Legislative Proposals Commission allegedly received 12,000 letters commenting on the draft bill on state pensions in 1956. The permanent commissions reportedly received 7,000 suggested amendments to the draft marriage law of 1968, and 3,000 suggested changes to the health protection law of 1969.

Again, these claims confront the analyst with the impossibility of evaluating their truth, to say nothing of their significance. We are not told how many of the suggestions were accepted or how important the changes were. Thus, we have no way of knowing whether this activity reinforces the impression that this sort of activity is meaningful. In short, we do not know whether this kind of activity encourages or discourages participation. All we know with relative confidence is that the regime would like to enhance its legitimacy by creating the impression that letter-writing and public discussions influence the formulation of legislation.

Nevertheless, the sheer increase of activity throughout the Supreme Soviet system is impressive and when coupled with wide publicity in the press and the media may gradually impress the population with the notion that involvement in the soviets is becoming more meaningful, and thus induce in them a more positive attitude which strengthens the regime's legitimacy.

In summary, the Soviet regime is hoping to facilitate its rule by encouraging the population to limited participation in some of the governmental processes. Since the Supreme Soviet is composed largely of an elite already socialized to participate, socialization, if it takes place at all, takes place indirectly—chiefly through the image of the Supreme Soviet projected to the population which may persuade them to participate in such activities as public meetings to discuss draft bills and letter-writing to recommend amendments to draft bills. The deputies themselves are not socialized to participate, but perhaps the population is, to a very limited extent.

THE LEGISLATIVE FUNCTION:
A SHIFTING FORUM FOR DRAFTING AND DELIBERATION

The Party's increasing emphasis on the formal ratification of laws, the expansion of the commission system, and the need for a wide range of specialist opinion for wide public support have almost imperceptibly shifted a significant amount of the drafting and deliberation process from the Council of Ministers to the Supreme Soviet and its auxiliary bodies, especially the subcommissions. Important legislation still emanates as joint Party-government resolutions, but the traditional pattern of Party issuing general directives, the government converting them to detailed norms, and the Supreme Soviet perfunctorily ratifying them appears to be gradually evolving.

Let us be clear that the dual paradigm of the legislative process described previously (Table 6.3) is not precise; it is illustrative of two general patterns, one evolving into the other. Both have always and still do co-exist, but the emphasis and reliance on the old pattern seems to be waning into favor of the new. There are all sorts of variations of these two paradigms, as the analyses of the Economic Commission of the Council of Nationalities and the evolution of the commission system of the Supreme Soviet reveal.

In summary, the new pattern shows greater reliance on the specially created subcommissions of the Supreme Soviet for both drafting and deliberation on the details of the draft. These meetings are secret; experts can be co-opted onto the subcommissions by the chairman of the parent standing commissions, who is usually a high Party official. The subcommissions can collate suggestions from experts and the public on the circulated draft, then deliberate upon the incorporation of these suggestions without revealing the dirty linen.

The mechanism is a rather effective means of combining public opinion sampling with expertise sampling, and converting substantive suggestions into legal forms which can be ratified in what is gradually emerging as a two-step process—first, submission to a joint meeting of the commissions, and then to the plenum of the Supreme Soviet. The first step recently produced two public objections to a law which had reached this first step of the ratification stage. This is another example of the complexity and ongoing evolution of the Soviet legislative process—the use of the public sessions of the joint commissions for deliberation.[21] It represents an unfinished evolutionary process seeking to adapt the system to the rapidly changing nature of the environment.

THE "KONTROL" FUNCTION:
ORIGINS, MEANING AND INSTRUMENTS

In the history of the Supreme Soviet, the gradual activation of the "kontrol" function constitutes the best example of inert legal forms assuming real power. Implicit in Article 51 of the Constitution, the "kontrol" function remained relatively dormant until the Programme of the Twenty-second Party Congress activated the soviets and called attention to the "kontrol" function.[22] As described previously, "kontrol" does not connote absolute dominance in Russian as it does in English. It is better translated as monitoring or supervising, perhaps even surveillance. It connotes restraining and persuading rather than manipulating and controlling.

The Stalin Constitution provided for the creation of commissions with investigatory powers buttressed by the right to demand access to government documents (Article 51). This is the legal-constitutional basis of "kontrol." By 1951 these powers had been exercised very little, which was clear evidence that for Stalin "kontrol" was the least important function of the Supreme Soviet, even though the Great Encyclopedia contained the following statement:[23]

> The Supreme Soviet possesses an unlimited right of *Kontrol* of the entire state apparatus. It appoints, when it considers necessary, investigating and auditing commissions on any question. All establishments and officials must present to these commissions when so requested the necessary documents and materials. The Supreme Soviet has the right to annul any edict of the Presidium of the Supreme Soviet or any decree of the government. The right of the deputy to question is an important means of *Kontrol.* . . . The government or the ministries to whom a deputy has directed questions must answer his questions within three days.

The evidence that "kontrol" had not been exercised widely emerged from the criticisms of the Supreme Soviet at the time of the Twentieth Party Congress, when legal scholars demanded greater supervision of all state organs.[24] Khrushchev was reluctant to strengthen the Supreme Soviet; however, he altered his position, perhaps under pressure, by the time of the Twenty-second Party Congress, as evidenced in the following extracts from the Party Programme:[25]

> The Party regards the perfection of the principles of socialist democracy and their rigid observance as a most important task. It is necessary to ensure in full . . . regular accountability of executive government bodies to meetings of soviets—from top to bottom; checking the work of these bodies and *Kontrol*

over their activity; systematic discussion by the soviets of questions raised by deputies; criticism of shortcomings in the work of government, economic and other organizations.

... The supreme soviets must systematically *Kontrol* the activities of ministries, departments, and economic councils; they must actively contribute to the implementation of the decisions adopted by the respective supreme soviets. To improve the work of the legislative bodies and increase *Kontrol* over the executive bodies, deputies shall be periodically released from their regular employment for committee work.

The "kontrol" function was to be exercised by all soviets from top to bottom, to improve the functioning of the state apparatus. A major vehicle of implementation was to be the commission system.

What followed was an extensive debate over the precise forms and methods to be used in expanding and activating the Supreme Soviet. It was reminiscent of the less prolific outpourings, which were soon silenced, at the time of the Twentieth Party Congress. This time, however, the debate focused on some tentative experiments which had been going on since the earlier debates.

The ultimate outcome of these debates and experiments was the new zakon on the standing commissions promulgated in 1967.[26] The debates leading to this legislation and the implementation of the zakon itself are analyzed in detail in the previous chapter; however, it is relevant here to present a broad picture of the "kontrol" function's operation throughout the whole Supreme Soviet system.

IMPLEMENTATION OF "KONTROL"–STRUCTURAL INSTRUMENTS AND ACTORS

A multiplicity of institutional structures participate in the "kontrol" function. The most prominent are the permanent commissions of the Supreme Soviet, which according to Soviet sources held 170 sessions in the seventh convocation (1966–70), all primarily devoted to "kontrol." Table 7.2 lists the institutional-structural actors involved in "kontrol" and their major instruments or the vehicles through which they exercise it. While all the institutional instruments listed in Table 7.2 have come to life since the 1967 activation of the commission system, the survey description here provides a broad background for the analysis of the sometimes tortuous evolution.

As discussed in Chapter 6, the full chambers of the Supreme Soviet, either in joint or individual sessions, appear to increasingly allow some measure of criticism of the implementation of government policies, and the effect of this is undoubtedly to restrain the state organs and perhaps to encourage modest reform. However, it is

TABLE 7.2
"KONTROL" THROUGH THE SUPREME
SOVIET SYSTEM

Structural actor	Instrument
Supreme Soviet commissions	Recommendation
	Proposal
Presidium of the Supreme Soviet	Ukaz
	Postanovlenia
Joint meetings of all deputies	
on commissions	Public criticism
Plenum of the Supreme Soviet	Public criticism
Individual deputy	Interpellation
	Conferences

the auxiliary bodies of the Supreme Soviet which exercise "kontrol" most effectively.

About two-thirds of the total membership of the Supreme Soviet (912 deputies) now sit on the commissions of both chambers, and a practice seems to be developing of meeting as a body prior to the full sessions. The meetings are sometimes public and criticism of policy implementation is reported, but here again the effect is to "kontrol" the administrative organs.

As we have seen, the individual commissions of the Supreme Soviet, of which there are now twenty-six, may forward recommendations to a given ministry, which must examine and reply to them within two months indicating how it plans to deal with the complaint.

On its own, or at the behest of the commissions based on information uncovered in their investigations, the Presidium of the Supreme Soviet may issue ukazes or postanovlenie, legally requiring state bodies to act in pursuance thereof.

According to the new zakon on the commission system, a Supreme Soviet deputy on his own initiative may conduct investigations and introduce proposals. Deputies also hold conferences in their constituencies for the purpose of facilitating the implementation of legislation.

In summary, many vehicles for carrying out the once-dormant "kontrol" function have emerged which are, in a sense, the organic outgrowth of one constitutional provision which atrophied in Stalin's day but, given the right conditions and circumstances, appears now to have given rise to many institutional practices in the post-Stalin era.

IMPLEMENTATION OF "KONTROL"–A SURVEY OF ITS UTILITY FOR THE POLITY

In the broadest sense, the activation of "kontrol" can be viewed as a modest progressive institutional reform which provides the Party apparatus with an additional line of supervision of the Council of Ministers and the ministries. It does not involve a fundamental restructuring of the polity or economy. It probably represents a moderate answer to the demands of the more radical economic and political reformers.

"Kontrol" involves negative and positive aspects in that it is ostensibly designed to facilitate the implementation of policy, but at the same time it is fashioned to restrain all political organs at the behest of the Party apparatus. This duality, this internal contradiction, remains unresolved. In the wider sense, these dual purposes of the "kontrol" function of the Supreme Soviet reflect the dilemma of the regime and the polity. "Kontrol" could be potentially an instrument of either transformation or reaction. If fully activated it might prove to be a unique vehicle of transformation in a highly complex, modernizing multi-national state.

THE SUPREME SOVIET DEPUTY AS OMBUDSMAN

Both the symbolic function of the Supreme Soviet and, to a more limited extent, the socialization function impart increments of legitimacy to the Soviet regime. Another important function of the Supreme Soviet deputy appears to be emerging which could also help ameliorate citizen dissatisfaction and facilitate the stability and legitimacy of the polity.

The distinctive function of the Swedish ombudsman is to pursue citizens' grievances against the government bureaucracy. The evidence suggests that this is increasingly a major task of the individual Supreme Soviet deputy. That the Party apparatus should encourage the ombudsman function is natural in a nation where petty bureaucrat is a universal epithet. The purpose is to channel personal grievances relating to bureaucratic ineptitude before they accumulate into dissatisfaction with the political system as a whole. An effective ombudsman system would enhance the stability and legitimacy of the regime. The decline of terror as an instrument of rule provides an opportunity for this function to grow, since there is less likelihood of citizen complaints and deputy inquiries about bureaucratic incompetence being interpreted as political dissent, which could lead to extermination of the complainant.

The Supreme Soviet has always possessed the power to create ad hoc commissions of inquiry.[27] The new zakon on the permanent commissions gives individual deputies the power to conduct on-the-spot studies on their own initiative.[28] A recent ukaz of the Presidium of the Supreme Soviet requires that the ministries reply to a deputy's inquiry within one month and inform the deputy in person as to what action has been taken to remedy the alleged grievance.[29] Another recent ukaz instructs the Procuracy and People's Control Commissions to supervise this grievance procedure.[30]

Both of these bodies appear to be increasingly under the authority of the Presidium of the Supreme Soviet. For example, the Presidium, at a recent session, adopted a resolution ordering the ministries to redouble their efforts to guarantee that citizens' grievances are properly handled. The resolution referred specifically to the elimination of red tape, and to a more thorough consideration of citizens' complaints. In the same session, the Presidium ordered the Procuracy and People's Control Commissions to intensify their surveillance of the grievance procedure.[31]

All recent accounts of the life and duties of deputies stress the red-tape cutting, grievance-procedure role of the deputies. It is generally agreed that this function was insufficiently attended to in the past. It is also generally agreed that the Procuracy, which technically might have pursued this function, has not done so adequately.[32] Recent actions by the Presidium of the Supreme Soviet appear to be aimed at activating the Procuracy in this area as well as facilitating action by individual deputies.

In summary, the extent and efficacy of the ombudsman function of the Supreme Soviet deputy remains difficult to identify precisely. However, the legal instruments are available, increasing lipservice is publicly paid to it, and its functionality for the legitimacy and stability of the system in the post-Stalin era can hardly be doubted.

THE INVESTIGATION FUNCTION

Essential to improving the drafting of complex legislation in a complex society, and to checking up on its fulfillment by a complex bureaucracy, is the need for access to vast amounts of information. Investigation to uncover technical information is a concomitant of the drafting and monitoring functions. Gathering technical information (which we shall call investigation) might arguably be identified as the major function of the Supreme Soviet permanent commissions. While the Supreme Soviet system served Stalin primarily as a barometer of public opinion, the specialized commissions of his successors provide specialized information from the technical community in the Soviet Union.

All the various new legal forms of addressing the ministries and the Council of Ministers, plus the increased size and activity of the commissions, have the practical effect of bringing to light—and to the attention of the Soviet leadership—technical information from other than government sources. Most important is the large number of specialists of one sort or another co-opted onto the subcommissions. These experts from various scientific institutions, enterprises, and mass organizations provide information that might be deliberately withheld by government bureaucrats seeking to protect some vested interest. It is this obscuring of information or its distortion that causes much of the economic inefficiency in the Soviet Union. The presence of experts on the subcommissions with representatives of the ministries further substantiates the inference that the real deliberation on details of legislation takes place in secret sessions of the subcommissions.

In addition, the fact that increasing numbers of Supreme Soviet deputies themselves are technical specialists, and that the deputies assigned to ad hoc submissions to draft specific legislation are specialists, further strengthens the argument that technical information gathering is a primary function of the Supreme Soviet's commissions. The commissions write to institutes seeking information and the institutes frequently volunteer information in the course of public discussion of draft bills in the press or at meetings.

The commissions also have the formal legal right, sanctioned in the new legislation and based on the Constitution, to hear reports from the ministries, to "demand" documents from them, and to require answers to specific inquiries submitted to the ministries. While all these new forms and practices were designed to facilitate drafting and monitoring, they have the practical effect of providing information.

In summary, then, the system of standing commissions of the Supreme Soviet has evolved from an administrative funnel and final review board for legislation to a body with significant capabilities and power to draft legislation and to monitor its implementation. Although these functions remain embryonic, the new forms and practices, which are concomitants of drafting and monitoring, have the practical effect of bringing to light the varying points of view of technical specialists in the multiplicity of institutions throughout the Soviet Union. For the generalist politicians governing this complex polity, this investigatory function may prove extremely valuable.

THE FOREIGN POLICY FUNCTION

Merle Fainsod considered the foreign policy facade of the Supreme Soviet its major raison d'etre.[33] Other leading scholars have viewed the foreign policy function as one of its most important functions.[34] However, no one has seriously argued that it performs a real decision-making role in foreign policy. The foreign policy function is viewed as primarily symbolic, ritualistic, and propagandistic in nature. As long as the other functions of the Supreme Soviet performed the same kind of role, one could hardly quarrel with these assessments of the relative importance of the foreign policy function of the Supreme Soviet, especially if one is analyzing the period from 1955 or thereabouts to 1965 (announcement of the economic reform) which is usually the basis for these evaluations. The burgeoning importance of the legislative and "kontrol" functions, along with the concomitant expansion of the commissions system, may have decreased the *relative* importance of the foreign policy function of the Supreme Soviet, although one must constantly bear in mind the relative ease with which institutional evolution can be arrested in the Soviet polity. One of the reasons for this is the success of its internal propaganda function, as indicated by a press article appearing about the time of the expansion of the commissions system[35] :

> Or let us take the question of publicity in the work of the soviets and local Party, trade unions, and other public organizations. As concrete research shows, the dissemination of information on questions of nationwide concern and on events in international life has been organized most satisfactorily in our country.

The adherence of the Supreme Soviet to the Inter-Parliamentary Union (IPU) in 1955, coinciding with the "Spirit of Geneva," marked the activation of all Supreme Soviet bodies for foreign affairs propaganda purposes. Stalin's "democratic facade" had never been taken very seriously abroad because of the simultaneous spread of the purges. Most of the Supreme Soviet's time prior to that had been devoted to cursory review of the budget.[36] The expanded foreign policy activities dominated it until the Twenty-second Party Congress when the expansion of the legislative and "kontrol" functions were initiated.

A leading analyst of the foreign policy function of the Supreme Soviet lists seven categories of formal institutional authority:[37]

> The formal authority of the Supreme Soviet in foreign policy falls into seven categories: (1) the enactment of basic legislation and constitutional amendments; (2) the confirmation of the decisions and decrees of the Presidium and the Council of Ministers; (3) ratification of selected treaties; (4) declaration of a state of war and peace; (5) confirmation and authorization of territorial changes and of the creation, admission, promotion, demotion, and abolition of new republics; (6) hearing and approving of foreign policy reports delivered by the Premier or the Foreign Minister; and (7) the preliminary examination of treaties prior to ratification by the Presidium. Since Stalin's death, all activities have been accorded greater publicity.

The Supreme Soviet exercises its authority through five institutional vehicles: the plenum of the Supreme Soviet, the Presidium of the Supreme Soviet, the Foreign Affairs Commission of the Supreme Soviet, the Inter-Parliamentary Union delegation, and the election speeches to the constituencies. For example, Deputy Demichev, Party Secretary of the Moscow Oblast, introduced a postanovlenie for ratification on May 6, 1960, which amounted to virtual approval of the Council of Ministers foreign policy in toto. It was unanimously passed with prolonged applause, and without any sort of interpellation or criticism.[38] At another session on January 15, 1960, the Supreme Soviet heard Khrushchev's report on his coexistence and disarmament policies, a major ideological and policy shift, without comment, to say nothing of dissent.[39]

This manner of utilizing the Supreme Soviet began on January 25, 1955, when it proclaimed an end to the state of war with Germany. The pattern began to take on flesh on August 4, 1955, when Bulganin called the Supreme Soviet into special session to hear a report on the Geneva Summit Conference. Such a procedure had not been invoked since Molotov addressed a special session on the Nazi-Soviet Pact in 1939.[40] It was to become a familiar scenario.

The Presidium of the Supreme Soviet acts as a collegial head of state for the Soviet Union in law, although the Chairman of the Presidium generally performs the ceremonial duties in its name. This position had gradually evolved into the third most important post in the polity, partially because of this ceremonial function, but also, as we shall see, because of the expansion of the whole mechanism that is the Supreme Soviet system.

> In accordance with the universally recognized doctrine of international law, the supreme representation of the modern state is vested in the chief of state, whether he be an actual person (monarch, president of the republic) or a collective body (Presidium of the Supreme Soviet of the USSR, Federal Council of Switzerland). . . . As a general rule, the competence of the chief of state includes the declaration of war and conclusion of peace, nomination and reception of diplomatic agents, granting powers for the conclusion of international treaties and agreements of special significance, and the ratification and denunciation of these treaties and accords.[41]

The Presidium's ceremonial duties include conferring diplomatic rank and appointing and recalling the USSR's foreign envoys.[42] Its substantive powers under Article 49 include appointing and removing the high command of the army, and proclaiming a state of war, mobilization, or martial law.[43]

As we have seen, even in law the Presidium's jurisdiction and competence in these areas vis-à-vis the Supreme Soviet is a matter of considerable dispute. In fact, it appears to act much as it pleases with little regard for the plenum of the Supreme Soviet in foreign policy matters. It is an instrument of the apparatus of the Party, as the high proportion of Party apparatchiks on it illustrates. Even the foreign affairs commissions serve as no check on the Presidium, since they also are traditionally dominated by the Party apparatus.

THE FOREIGN AFFAIRS COMMISSIONS

Until recently the foreign affairs commissions appeared to be the most important commissions. They were and are headed by important members of the Party Secretariat and have a large proportion of members who sit on the Party Central Committee. Their formal areas of competence are:

(1) Submittal to the chambers of the Supreme Soviet of conclusions on bills concerned with foreign relations and referred to the Supreme Soviet of the USSR for approval;

(2) Preparation on their own initiative and submittal of bills and other Soviet foreign policy acts to the Supreme Soviet of the USSR or one of its chambers for consideration;

(3) Submittal to the Supreme Soviet of the USSR or its Presidium of conclusions on ratification, denunciation, or annulment of the most important treaties, conventions, and agreements concluded by the Soviet Union with foreign countries.

In general, these commissions seem to serve two purposes. First, they are a final board of review, checking the wording of treaties and laws dealing with foreign affairs before their presentation to the Supreme Soviet for ratification. Second, their joint sessions, addressed by a high official, can serve in lieu of a full plenum as the forum for propagating policy of less importance than that advanced at full joint sessions of the chambers.[44]

Vernon Aspaturian has also noted that the formal powers of the Supreme Soviet and its auxiliary bodies provide certain advantages to Soviet diplomacy. As he puts it:[45]

> The invocation of the formal prerogatives of the Supreme Soviet, however, is no idle exercise . . . (1) It serves to infuse the citizenry with the notion that their representatives participate in the formulation of foreign policy decisions. (2) As a propagandistic maneuver it strives to create the illusion of evolving constitutionalism in the Soviet system. (3) As a purely diplomatic device, it permits the Kremlin to invoke constitutional procedures as a stumbling or delaying mechanism in negotiations and affords a basis for demanding reciprocal action in the ratification of treaties and other diplomatic instruments.

THE SUPREME SOVIET IN THE MIRROR OF THE INTER-PARLIAMENTARY UNION

In 1955 the Supreme Soviet joined the Inter-Parliamentary Union (IPU), which is essentially a discussion club for influential world parliamentarians who may converse and exchange views at its meetings with the relative impunity afforded by non-governmental contacts. The prime Soviet motive for adhering to the Union was undoubtedly to utilize it as a foreign policy propaganda forum, which it has done faithfully at every meeting. For example, at the 1955 conference of the IPU, the Soviet delegation promoted peaceful coexistence; at the 1957 conference, it promoted a resolution on disarmament; at the 1959 conference, it passed a resolution forbidding "the use of literature, films, television, the press and toys encouraging violence and aggression." In 1960 the Soviet delegation denounced colonialism and racial discrimination; in 1965 it denounced NATO and American aggression in Vietnam.[46]

The Inter-Parliamentary Group of the USSR (UPG) consists of all the Supreme Soviet deputies who pay one ruble per month for membership.[47] It sends a delegation of twenty-two members to the IPU, the largest contingent of the eighty member nations. It usually meets concurrently with the Supreme Soviet. The UPG appoints a guiding committee of one chairman, two vice-chairmen, a secretary, and fifty-one members. This body conducts the UPG's activities in the interim, although an even smaller body, the Bureau, composed of a chairman, two vice-chairmen, a secretary, and seven members, conducts daily business and may issue statements on behalf of the entire group. In theory the UPG may make representations to the Council of Ministers or any Supreme Soviet body. The UPG forms standing commissions also, although their size and frequency of meeting is not known. The commissions apparently prepare Soviet positions at each IPU Conference. The five commissions are: political and juridical; disarmament; economic and social; colonial matters; and cultural ties.[48] The formal functions of the UPG are:

(1) Participation in the work of the Inter-Parliamentary Union;
(2) Issuance of statements and appeals on vital questions of international politics;
(3) Exchange of delegations and visits by individual members of parliaments.[49]

The more tantalizing aspect of the IPU connection is the feedback and impact upon the Supreme Soviet perception of itself emanating from contacts with Western parliaments.

Almost every deputy belongs to the IPU, which is his right merely by paying his dues. However, only trusted Party and state officials and intellectuals may leave the Soviet Union to attend the IPU conferences.[50] The UPG publishes its own biennial bulletin, describing its activities in the IPU, which is primarily propagandistic in nature and hardly provides its readers with any insight into the nature of Western parliaments.[51]

However, some of the UPG activities must provide this comparative insight. For example, the IPU soon after Soviet adherence initiated a project comparing various aspects of world parliaments which caused considerable agonizing in Soviet circles. Eventually the UPG supplied its version of the answers to the IPU questionnaire, portraying the Supreme Soviet as the central source of all power in the Soviet polity. The mere exercise of answering the questionnaire must have been somewhat instructive for Soviet parliamentarians.[52]

The extensive visits abroad by delegations of Supreme Soviet deputies from the UPG (obviously carefully selected) with Western parliamentarians must undoubtedly be quite revealing to them. Supreme Soviet delegations visited fifty foreign countries in the thirteen years from 1957 to mid-1967, as shown in Table 7.3.

Likewise, the extensive visits of foreign parliamentary delegations to the Soviet Union, with the UPG as hosts (see Table 7.4), provides further opportunity for the UPG to compare its own trappings with the realities of power in other parliaments.

The UPG has formed two other interesting organizations, unions with both the French and Italian parliaments. This provides contacts with parliamentarians whose assemblies hold large bodies of communists. The Soviet-French Parliamentary Group was formed in 1956 and the Soviet-Italian Parliamentary Group in 1957. These groups might serve also as one among many channels of Soviet diplomacy, although there is little concrete evidence of such. It is tantalizing to imagine French or Italian Communists explaining parliamentary tactics to Supreme Soviet deputies; however, one must not exaggerate the nature, extent, and impact of such contacts upon the UPG. Palmiro Togliatti, long the head of the Italian Communist Party, never subscribed to the need for democratization of Soviet society, although his parliamentary colleague and one-time ally,

TABLE 7.3

FOREIGN COUNTRIES VISITED BY UPG[a]

Year	Countries visited
1954	Finland
1955	Albania, Bulgaria, Czechoslovakia, German Democratic Republic, Hungary, Poland, Yugoslavia
1956	Austria, Belgium, Britain, Luxemburg, Rumania, Sweden, Syria
1957	People's Republic of China, Democratic Republic of Vietnam, Iran, Korean People's Democratic Republic, Mongolian People's Republic
1958	Burma, India, Pakistan, Uruguay
1959	Indonesia
1960	Bolivia, Denmark, Guinea, Iceland, Mexico, Norway, Poland
1961	Afghanistan, Chile, Czechoslovakia, Hungary
1962	Bolivia, Rumania
1963	Bulgaria, Ghana, Democratic Republic of Vietnam, Mali, Yugoslavia
1964	Greece, India, Indonesia, France, Japan, Mexico, Mongolian People's Republic, Nigeria, Somalia, United Arab Republic
1965	Congo (Brazzaville), Hungary, Sierra Leone, Turkey
1966	Britain, Cambodia, Canada, Chile, Ethiopia, Libya, Pakistan, Czechoslovakia, Lebanon, Mali, Zambia

a. Supreme Soviet delegations made two official visits to Bolivia, Britain, Bulgaria, Chile, the Democratic Republic of Vietnam, India, Indonesia, Mali, Mexico, the Mongolian People's Republic, Pakistan, Poland, Rumania and Yugoslavia; and three visits to Czechoslovakia and Hungary.

Source: Allan Kornberg, Democratic Participation and Institutions for Nation-Building: Report on the Feasibility of an International Program of Legislative Studies, prepared for AID, January 1971, under Contract no. csd-2607, pp. 127–28.

TABLE 7.4

FOREIGN PARLIAMENTARY DELEGATIONS VISITING USSR[a]

Year	Visiting delegation
1955	Albania, Austria, Belgium, France, India, Iran, Japan, Luxemburg, Poland, Sweden, Syria, Yugoslavia
1956	Brazil, Bulgaria, People's Republic of China, Czechoslovakia, Democratic Republic of Vietnam, Denmark, German Democratic Republic, Greece, Hungary, Indonesia, Korean People's Democratic Republic, Norway, Pakistan, Rumania, Uruguay
1957	Burma
1958	Cambodia, Iceland, Mongolian People's Republic, Sudan, Thailand
1959	Afghanistan, Guinea
1960	Bolivia, Chile, Costa Rica, Ghana, Mexico, Nepal
1961	Bolivia, Brazil, Cyprus, Japan, Libya, Peru, United Arab Republic, Venezuela
1962	Afghanistan, Ceylon, Czechoslovakia, Hungary, India, Kenya, Mali, Poland, Togo, Yugoslavia
1963	Brazil, Bulgaria, Colombia, Congo (Kinshasa), Costa Rica, Indonesia, Mexico, Nigeria, Rumania, Sierra Leone, Somalia, Tunisia, Turkey
1964	Burundi, Congo (Brazzaville), Japan, Mongolian People's Republic, Pakistan
1965	Canada, Chile, Costa Rica, Dahomey, Democratic Republic of Vietnam, Lebanon, Somalia
1966	Austria, German Democratic Republic, Hungary, Iran, Mali, Nepal, Rumania, Sweden, Turkey, Yugoslavia, Zambia
1967	Ethiopia, United Arab Republic

a. Parliamentary delegations from Afghanistan, Austria, Bolivia, Bulgaria, Chile, Czechoslovakia, Democratic Republic of Vietnam, German Democratic Republic, India, Indonesia, Iran, Mali, Mexico, Mongolian People's Republic, Nepal, Pakistan, Poland, Somalia, Sweden, Turkey, and United Arab Republic came to the Soviet Union twice; delegations from Brazil, Costa Rica, Hungary, Japan, Rumania, and Yugoslavia came three times.
Source: Kornberg (Table 7.4), pp. 125–126.

Pietro Nenni of the Italian Left-Wing Socialists, believed it to be necessary.

There is no way of measuring precisely the impact of such contacts on the evolution of the Supreme Soviet. Certainly one must, at the very least, include these contacts with the many catalysts potentially facilitating the gradual evolution of the Soviet "Parliament" from a purely ceremonial body into a rule-making institution. However, one must remember that only one-third of the countries visited had genuine parliamentary systems, and that the Soviet delegations were very carefully selected for their loyalty to the system.

Chapter 8

THE PRESIDIUM OF THE SUPREME SOVIET:
EXECUTIVE-LEGISLATIVE CONFLICT IN THE SOVIET SYSTEM

The Presidium of the Supreme Soviet, which is elected by the Supreme Soviet from among its own deputies and which, along with the Supreme Soviet, is one of the higher organs of state power, exercises a wide range of ceremonial and substantive powers which are legislative, executive, judicial, diplomatic, and military in character. According to the Party principle of collective leadership, it constitutes a collegial or plural head of state, although its chairman in fact acts as the ceremonial chief of the Soviet state on most occasions.

The Presidium is now composed of thirty-seven members: a chairman, fifteen vice-chairmen, a secretary, and twenty regular members. By law since 1958 each republic has received a vice-chairman, and by custom this is normally the chairman of the presidium of the republic supreme soviet. Among the other members of the Presidium are other important figures such as high officials of the republic Party organization, several full or candidate members of the Politburo, and high-ranking military officers. The interrelationship of the membership of the Presidium with state and Party organs is shown in Figure 8.1 and Table 8.1, with the one rule throughout being that no member of the organs of state administration—that is, the Council of Ministers and the ministries—may sit simultaneously on the Presidium.

Clearly, the overlapping of the personnel in higher Party bodies with the membership of the Presidium of the Supreme Soviet, and

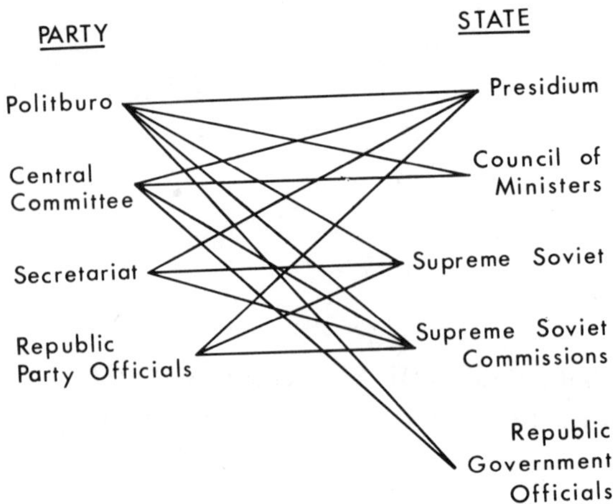

Figure 8.1: SOURCES OF MEMBERSHIP OF PARTY AND STATE ORGANS[a]
   a. Note that the membership of the Council of Ministers and the Presidium of
   the Supreme Soviet do not overlap.

the absence of any personnel overlap between the organs of state administration and the Presidium of the Supreme Soviet facilitates its use by the Party leadership as an instrument of "kontrol" over the state administrative apparatus. Thus, the Presidium is to be distinguished from the Supreme Soviet where officials of the administrative apparatus (the Council of Ministers and the ministries) hold seats, as well as from the Supreme Soviet's commission system to a lesser extent, since although the administrative apparatus is excluded from the commissions by law, it is not excluded from the working subcommissions.

Usually, the Party General Secretary, when he does not occupy an administrative or executive position in the government, is elected as an ordinary member of the Presidium, as were, for example, Stalin and Khrushchev when they held no other government office, and Brezhnev after Khrushchev's fall. One effect of this is to provide the General Secretary with a high state office justifying his presence where protocol might exclude a Party official.

Since the chairman of the Presidium normally performs state ceremonial functions as the de facto "president," he is the most conspicuous but not necessarily the most powerful member of the Presidium. Although as titular head of state he presides over sessions of the Supreme Soviet, signs ukazes and postanovlenia, dispatches ambassadors, receives credentials of foreign emissaries, and issues acts

TABLE 8.1
SOURCES OF MEMBERS OF PARTY AND
STATE BODIES

Politburo	**Presidium of the Supreme Soviet**[a]
Central Committee	Politburo
Secretariat	Secretariat
Council of Ministers	Central Committee
Republic Government officials	Supreme Soviet deputies
Republic Party officials	Local officials—ex officio
Supreme Soviet commissions	and elected
Presidium of Supreme Soviet	Local Party officials
Secretariat	**Council of Ministers**
Politburo	Politburo
Central Committee	Supreme Soviet deputies
Presidium of Supreme Soviet	Local officials—ex officio
Supreme Soviet commissions	Government committees
	Supreme Soviet Commissions
	Politburo
	Secretariat
	Central Committee
	Local Party officials
	Local government officials
	Supreme Soviet deputies

a. Members of the Council of Ministers do not sit on the Presidium
of the Supreme Soviet and vice-versa.

of pardon, he is in law no greater than ordinary members of the
Presidium and may be much less powerful. Only six individuals have
occupied this position: Mikhail Kalinin, who served from 1919 to
1946; Nicolai Shvernik (1946–53), a relatively low-ranking Party
official; Marshal Voroshilov (1953–60), a popular military hero;
Brezhnev (1960–64); Anastas Mikoyan (1964–65); and the present
chairman, N. V. Podgorny. All except Shvernik served simultaneously on the Politburo, but often in the presence of the powerful
General Secretary.

Most of the legal powers of the Presidium of the Supreme Soviet
are original and enumerated in Article 49 of the USSR Constitution,
and are quite broad although, in practice, the Presidium exercises an
even wider spectrum of powers. As we have seen in Chapter 4, there
is considerable discussion and debate among Soviet jurists over the
legality of the manner in which the Presidium of the Supreme Soviet
acts pursuant to the enumerated powers in Article 49, and, as this
chapter will illustrate, there is considerable controversy over the
legality of delegated and derived powers exercised by the Presidium

of the Supreme Soviet. Although in theory and law the powers of the Supreme Soviet are much broader than those of its Presidium, in fact the relationship is reversed because the Presidium actually exercises more power, a situation which, as we shall see, has been attacked for political as well as legal reasons.

As a higher organ of state power, the Presidium of the Supreme Soviet is actually a working legislature, exercising the entire spectrum of state powers between Supreme Soviet sessions, which is about 350 days per year. Although its ukazes by law must be ratified by the Supreme Soviet, they have the force of law in the interim. Party policies can almost immediately be converted into law through the Presidium's power to issue ukazes, as was Khrushchev's request to be relieved of his duties in October 1964, for example. Since the personnel of the Party Politburo and Secretariat overlap the Presidium's membership, the Presidium is in effect the chief legalizing instrument of the Party.

While the Presidium of the Supreme Soviet in practice shares legislative authority with the Supreme Soviet, it also shares the executive powers in the Soviet polity with the Council of Ministers. Among the Presidium's executive tasks are: convening and dissolving the Supreme Soviet, annuling decisions and orders of the councils of ministers of the USSR and union republics (at least those allegedly not conforming to law), granting awards and decorations, and releasing and appointing ministers of the USSR in the intervals between sessions of the Supreme Soviet on recommendation of the Council of Ministers and subject to the subsequent confirmation of the Supreme Soviet. In its diplomatic and military roles the Presidium can declare a state of war, proclaim martial law, create military and diplomatic titles and ranks, and appoint and remove the high command of the army. All of these powers are original and enumerated, although perhaps not exclusive.[1]

The Presidium of the Supreme Soviet also shares the legislative function with both the Supreme Soviet and the Council of Ministers and, as we have seen, the normative activity of the three bodies is in inverse relation to their legal status as organs of the state. In other words, most legal acts emanate from the Council of Ministers which in law is subordinate to both the Supreme Soviet and its Presidium. Next in normative activity is the Presidium, and last is the "highest organ of state power," the Supreme Soviet. In fact, according to one scholar, there is approximately one zakon of the Supreme Soviet for every 50 edicts (ukazes) of the Presidium of the Supreme Soviet and for every 285 decrees (postanovlenie) of the Council of Ministers.[2]

The apparent emergence of the Presidium as the Party apparat's instrument for coordinating and legalizing the "kontrol" function of the Supreme Soviet commissions over the state administrative apparatus futher complicates the already complex task of defining the precise relationships between Party and state organs. Figure 8.2 illustrates the general lines of legal and actual control, responsibility and accountability, as well as the personnel input into these bodies. It is designed to serve as background to guide the reader through the discussion of the legal debates and factional conflicts surrounding the expansion of the Presidium's activities, described below.

The impact of the evolution of the Presidium of the Supreme Soviet on the relationships of state and Party organs in theory and practice is even more complex than Figure 8.2; therefore, before proceeding to a descriptive analysis of this process, let us briefly review the essential distinctions between the major state organs. The Supreme Soviet is a constitutional-legislative body which is the supreme source of legislative, executive, administrative, judicial, and prosecuting powers. It places the stamp of legality on the acts of and appointments to the state organs. The Presidium is primarily an executive-legislative body, although it is authorized to "interpret" the laws, which is a judicial function utilized very seldom. Its paramount roles are the executive functions of a chief of state and the function of issuing ukazes; however, its coordination of the

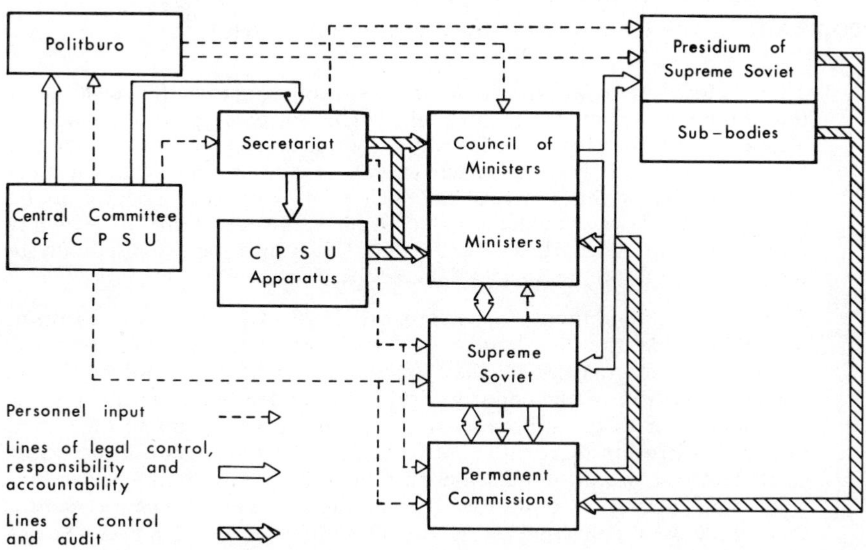

Figure 8.2: **LINES OF CONTROL AND ACCOUNTABILITY AMONG PARTY AND STATE ORGANS**

monitoring functions of the permanent commissions of the Supreme Soviet may be increasing and will therefore be analyzed in detail further on. The chief role of the Council of Ministers, which heads the organs of state administration, is "administration" with special stress on administration of the economy. However, the high level of its norm-creating activity raises the question of which body in fact is the chief legislator in the Soviet polity. The courts, of course, adjudicate and the Procuracy supervises the legal system as prosecutor. With this survey in mind, let us proceed to a more detailed analysis of the expansion of the activities of the Presidium of the Supreme Soviet and the impact of this on these roles and relationships.

THE REPRESENTATIVE IMAGE OF THE PRESIDIUM
OF THE SUPREME SOVIET

Stalin ostensibly created the Presidium of the Supreme Soviet as an executive committee to administer and coordinate the activities of the Supreme Soviet, but not to serve as an independent legislative and executive body; thus, he rejected an amendment to his new constitution which would specifically have granted it independent legislative authority. He also rejected a proposal to elect it directly, which would have implied independent powers derived from the people and not delegated to it by the Supreme Soviet:

> Then follows an addendum to Article 49, proposing that the Presidium of the Supreme Soviet be granted the right to pass provisional acts of legislation. I think that this addendum is wrong and should not be adopted by the Congress. It is time we put an end to a situation in which not one but a number of bodies legislate. Such a situation runs counter to the principle that laws should be stable. And we need stability of laws now more than ever. Legislative power in the USSR must be exercised only by one body, the Supreme Soviet of the USSR.

> Further, an addendum is proposed to Article 48 of the Draft Constitution, demanding that the President of the Presidium of the Supreme Soviet of the USSR be elected not by the Supreme Soviet of the USSR but by the whole population of the country. I think this addendum is wrong, because it runs counter to the spirit of our Constitution. According to the system of our Constitution there must not be an individual president in the USSR, elected by the whole population on a par with the Supreme Soviet, and able to put himself in opposition to the Supreme Soviet. The president in the USSR is a collegium, it is the Presidium of the Supreme Soviet, elected, not by the whole population, but by the Supreme Soviet, and accountable to the Supreme Soviet. Historical experience shows that such

> a structure of the supreme bodies is the most democratic, and safeguards
> the country against undesirable contingencies.[3]

Although Stalin had indicated his intent that the Presidium serve primarily as an executive committee for the Supreme Soviet, it soon acquired many of the powers of the old Presidium of the Central Executive Committee. By 1956 it had encroached substantially on the Supreme Soviet's prerogatives, as one of its reformist critics stated in 1956:

> After many years' experience, it is clear that in practice the Presidium of the
> USSR Supreme Soviet, and on occasion the Council of Ministers, have also
> performed legislative functions. It suffices to note that the Presidium of the
> USSR Supreme Soviet has also issued a number of edicts introducing changes
> in criminal law, criminal procedural, labor, and other legislation. Some edicts
> were actually amendments of the USSR Constitution. When the basic law of
> the state is violated, and in such an important area, this obviously cannot be
> considered a normal situation.[4]

The exercise of substantial legislative functions through the issuance of ukazes has been a primary activity of the Presidium almost from the day Stalin uttered his intent that he preferred it otherwise. More recently, an effort has been made to portray the Presidium as an independent body possessing its own authority by publishing some accounts of its sessions and extolling its representative and elective character.

Until 1968 there was considerable doubt as to whether the Presidium of the Supreme Soviet ever met, even though *Vedomosti Verkhovnogo Soveta SSSR* reported that it met twice in 1966, four times in 1967, and five times in 1968, while never identifying who was present or what was discussed at length. However, in 1968 *Pravda* and *Izvestia* provided a rather detailed account of a session of the Presidium and, in 1967, another source indicated that it meets at least once in every two months. It is clear that one aspect of this reporting was to enhance the democratic image of the Presidium. In the frequent debates over the Presidium's power (discussed below), the crux of its opponents' argument was the non-democratic nature of the Presidium compared to that of the Supreme Soviet. As a result, the Presidium's defenders began to stress its representative-elective character; the following is illustrative:

> In addition to prominent government and Party leaders people engaged in
> production, representatives of the Soviet Armed Forces and workers of
> culture actively participate in the work of the Presidium.

Deputies representing all sections of the country's population are elected to the Presidium of the Supreme Soviet. Thus elected to the Presidium of the Seventh Supreme Soviet of the USSR are: V. I. Bolshukin (chief foreman of the Sredne-Uralsk Copper Works), Z. P. Pukhova (weaver of the Ivanovo Textile Mill), V. M. Kavun and A. I. Kasatkina (collective-farm chairman and chairwoman), A. D. Nutetegryneh (chairwoman of the Chukotsk Area Soviet), M. Jalalov (tractor team leader from Uzbekistan), S. M. Budyonny (Marshal of the Soviet Union) and Academician I. G. Petrovsky (Rector of Moscow University).

At the same time the Presidium of the Supreme Soviet is a body in which all the Union Republics are directly represented. According to Article 48 of the Constitution, the 15 Vice-Presidents of the Presidium are elected one from each Union Republic. By tradition the Supreme Soviet elects to these posts the Presidents of the Presidium of the Supreme Soviets of the Union Republics. There are representatives of 18 nationalities in the Presidium of the Seventh Supreme Soviet of the USSR.

Thus, by its representative character, its social and national composition, the Presidium is, as it were, a small replica of the Supreme Soviet, a collective capable of discharging the complex functions of the supreme organ of state power.[5]

This description treats the Presidium as a microcosm of the Supreme Soviet, composed of deputies from it representing a social and national cross-section of the Soviet Union, and thus implicitly vindicates the Presidium's acting in the place of its parent body. This image strengthens the legitimacy of its acts as well as the claim of some independent authority for it.

All accounts of sessions of the Presidium of the Supreme Soviet remain silent on the crucial questions of what constitutes a quorum and what number of votes are required to decide any question. Neither do they list the names of those who attend, although they do mention the names of some of the speakers. As a miniature Supreme Soviet, one might expect the Presidium to follow the majority rule of the Supreme Soviet itself in deciding questions. It seems clear that decisions on most matters are resolved by the Party apparatus before the sessions, and that in any case the apparatus controls the sessions, since 88 percent of the members of the seventh convocation Presidium (1966–70) were also members of the CPSU Central Committee or Auditing Commission. High officials of the mass organizations, the chairmen of the chambers and permanent commissions, most of whom also sit on the CPSU Central Committee, are also invited. The secretary and chairman of the Presidium must sign its acts, which is at least a nominal check on any effort to overrule the apparatus since they are high Party officials. The chairman, who is always a high Party official, calls the meetings and thus controls whether they are convoked at all.

The "little Supreme Soviet" image is further reinforced by the description of the meetings which indicates that the power to introduce questions rests with the same bodies as the Supreme Soviet and that the Presidium also appoints its own commissions:

> The meetings of the Presidium are called by its President at least once in two months. The meetings are usually attended by the chairmen of the chambers of the Supreme Soviet; the chairmen of the standing commissions, deputies and representatives of state bodies and mass organizations are invited to the sessions. Since the end of the war the number of meetings of the Presidium has considerably increased and the range of questions considered by it has extended.

> All members of the Presidium take part in preparing questions for its meetings, the necessary materials and documents being sent to them beforehand.

> Questions are submitted to the Presidium of the Supreme Soviet for consideration by the Council of Ministers, the Supreme Court, the Procurator's Office and other state bodies of the USSR, the higher organs of power of the Union Republics, mass organizations, members of the Presidium and deputies of the Supreme Soviet of the USSR.

> When questions are to be prepared for consideration at its sittings, the Presidium forms working committees headed by a Vice-President, the Secretary or one of the members of the Presidium. These committees concern themselves, for example, with problems of socialist legality, and prepare questions of awards, citizenship and pardon. There have been cases when Presidium committees were organized to elaborate certain bills.

> For example, the Presidium formed a committee to prepare a bill on ways of recalling deputies of the Supreme Soviet of the USSR. Since 1938 the Presidium of the Supreme Soviet has set up a total of 18 different committees.

> The meetings of the Presidium of the Supreme Soviet are conducted by the President of the Presidium or one of the Vice-Presidents.[6]

The publication of the proceedings of two sessions in the national press appears to be the culmination of this attempt to dress up the Presidium's democratic image. The first in 1968 was somewhat detailed; the second was quite brief. The content of these accounts of sessions is of interest for several reasons, not the least of which is its confirmation of conclusions reached through an analysis of debates over the Presidium's powers in the law journals.[7]

The report on the session of the Presidium of the Supreme Soviet in April 1968 began with a series of reports on various foreign policy matters, most of which were ceremonial. For example, N. V. Podgorny, the Chairman of the Presidium of the Supreme Soviet, had visited Finland. His activities during the visit were approved. D. A. Kunayev, now a member of the Politburo of the Party, reported on his visit to Iran. A visit by A. N. Kosygin to Iran was also discussed. Concluding its discussion of foreign policy matters, the Presidium reviewed the exchange of parliamentary delegations as part of the USSR's participation in the Inter-Parliamentary Union.

The Presidium then turned to the 1967 CPSU Central Committee resolution on improving the rural and settlement soviets. The report notes that the Presidium had created its own commission headed by one of its vice-chairmen to study the question. After studying proposals received from union republic supreme soviet presidiums, ministries, departments, scientific institutions, and local soviets, the report states that the commission of the Presidium (as distinguished from a standing or ad hoc commission of the plenum) placed a draft before the full Presidium which unanimously adopted it. In this case at least, the entire Presidium was present, which must be exceptional since the vice-presidents of the republics plus the ordinary "toilers" could hardly attend once every two months.

The Presidium then instructed the union republic supreme soviet presidiums to adopt conforming laws. No mention is made of the need for the plenums of the supreme soviets at the all-Union or union republic levels to act on this fundamental legislation reorganizing local soviets. Nor is any mention made of the need to consult the permanent standing commissions of the Supreme Soviet. The implication is that the Presidium of the Supreme Soviet regulates the entire soviet pyramid through forming its own commissions and through directions to presidiums of lower supreme soviets.

The report then mentions that the Council of Ministers had enacted a resolution strengthening the financial base of rural soviets, which raises the question of the independence of the soviet pyramid from the organs of state administration. The Presidium then turned to a consideration of the question of strengthening the city and district soviets, as well as improving their financial base. Here again, a vice-chairman, M. A. Yasnov, a member of the CPSU Central Committee, was appointed a chairman of a specially formed commission of the Presidium of the Supreme Soviet to study the question.

The next item was a report of the Legislative Proposals Commission, the Commissions on Public Health and Security, and the Commissions on Public Education, Science, and Culture (permanent commissions of the plenum of the Supreme Soviet). These standing commissions presented a draft bill on marriage and the family. The Presidium instructed these standing commissions to publish this draft in *Izvestia,* then to collate the public response as well as the discussions of the Presidium in this session and prepare a final version of the draft law for submission to the Supreme Soviet.

This may reflect an evolving pattern in the legislative drafting process—preparation of detailed legislation from a Central Committee directive by several standing commissions and their subcommissions which is presented to the Presidium for review before publication. After publication a final draft is prepared. What the report does not indicate is that a more authoritative body than the standing commissions must certainly review the final draft before submission to the Supreme Soviet. We know that meetings of all 912 members of the standing commissions have performed this function. It is also possible that the Council of Elders, perhaps through its inner core of high officials of the regime, performs this last check of the draft. The only other significant item mentioned was the reports of the Procurator-General and the Chairman of the Supreme Court, symbolic of the Presidium's nominal supervision over these bodies.

The second report of a Presidium session in June 1970 was considerably briefer, but it was also illuminating. It began with the usual description of ceremonial and propagandistic foreign policy visits of Soviet officials and IPU delegations abroad.[8] It then turned to a more interesting item. It sent a note with recommendations to lower supreme soviet presidiums and ministries specifying how to intensify control over observance of labor laws. The details of the recommendations ostensibly came from Legislative Proposals Commissions of the Supreme Soviet. Here again we may discern an evolving pattern in which the standing commissions seek out information, draft recommendations, and present them to the Presidium, which converts them to a legal instruction (postanovlenia) to the subordinate organs of state power and administration.

The next action was similar. The Presidium ordered the ministries, the People's Control Commission, and the Prosecutor-General to intensify their surveillance over the implementation of the new ukaz requiring consideration of citizen's proposals. Here the Presidium reinforced the ombudsman function of the Supreme Soviet, which appears to be growing. Such publicity, of course, enhances the image of the Presidium as a "democratic" organ responsive to the population.

The last item reported in this session involves the exercise of the Presidium's power of concretization, which has been much debated, as we shall see below. The Presidium adopted a postanovlenia on the procedure for implementing the new zakon on public health.

EXPANSION OF THE APPARATUS
OF THE PRESIDIUM OF THE SUPREME SOVIET

While before the Twenty-second Party Congress the apparatus of the Presidium of the Supreme Soviet was composed of five sections—Foreign Relations, Protocol, Legal, Chancellery and Secretariat—there is now evidence that its apparatus is expanding considerably to include two offices, five departments, and seven working groups, as well as the ad hoc commissions appointed for special assignments. The five departments are: Functioning of the Soviets, Legal, Awards, Foreign Policy, and Co-ordinating the Permanent Commissions. The working groups include groups on servicing the permanent commissions, protocol, pardons, citizenship, publishing and translating laws, furnishing information on legislation, and rendering financial and economic services. The two offices are the Secretariat and the Reception Office; the former administers the apparatus and the latter receives citizens' complaints. This staff of specialists is managed by the Secretary of the Presidium, who is the chief administrator for the Presidium and is usually a member of the CPSU Central Committee. The staff provides organizational, technical, and administrative help not only to the Presidium but to the permanent commissions of the Supreme Soviet.[9]

The precise function of these sections is not known, but the very titles offer hints. The department dealing with the functions of the soviets suggests that the importance of the Presidium's legal-theoretical supervision of the organs of state power is increasing. This is confirmed by the legislation on local soviets drafted by special commissions of the Presidium as reported in the published records of Presidium proceedings. In short, the Presidium employs a special staff to supervise the activities of the lower soviets and supreme soviets. It also has a department that helps to coordinate the work of the permanent commissions of the Supreme Soviet and a working group which services the commissions, all of which emphasizes its role in directing these bodies.

Another new section, Financial-Economic Services, might reflect the expansion of the "kontrol" function. Perhaps these economically oriented sections coordinate the activities of the permanent commissions as well as servicing the Presidium. The other working groups seem to perform household chores connected with the ceremonial foreign policy function, and the drafting, collating, recording and publishing of laws, as well as instituting and presenting awards. Because the evidence is so insubstantial, one should not attempt to extrapolate too much from these hints that the Presidium's apparatus is expanding. Suffice it to say that this development constitutes merely one more example of once-hollow legal forms developing significant functions.

THE ENUMERATED POWERS OF ARTICLE 49:
ORIGINAL, DELEGATED, OR DERIVED?

Most of the legal debate over the powers of the Presidium centers around the question of whether the long list of powers enumerated in Article 49 are original or delegated or derived (that is, inherent or implied). In other words, do they vest original independent powers in the Presidium as distinct from the powers of the Supreme Soviet? Or are they merely a list of delegated powers which the Presidium is authorized to receive and exercise? Or are they a list of derived powers inherent in an executive-administrative body such as the Presidium of the Supreme Soviet, or implied from specific clauses of Article 49? Soviet jurists provide many interpretations, but before proceeding to analyze them, let us take an independent look at this central Article 49:[10]

The Presidium of the Supreme Soviet of the USSR:
(a) Convenes the sessions of the Supreme Soviet of the USSR;
(b) Issues decrees (ukaz);
(c) Interprets the laws of the USSR in operation;
(d) Dissolves the Supreme Soviet of the USSR in conformity with Article 47 of the Constitution of the USSR and orders new elections;
(e) Conducts nation-wide polls (referendums) on its own initiative or on the demand of one of the Union Republics;
(f) Annuls decisions and orders of the Council of Ministers of the USSR and of the Councils of Ministers of the Union Republics if they do not conform to law;
(g) In the intervals between sessions of the Supreme Soviet of the USSR, releases and appoints Ministers of the USSR on the recommendation of the Chairman of the Council of Ministers of the USSR, subject to subsequent confirmation by the Supreme Soviet of the USSR;

(h) Institutes decorations (Orders and Medals) and titles of honour of the USSR;

(i) Awards Orders and Medals and confers titles of honour of the USSR;

(j) Exercises the right of pardon;

(k) Institutes military titles, diplomatic ranks and other special titles;

(l) Appoints and removes the high command of the Armed Forces of the USSR;

(m) In the intervals between sessions of the Supreme Soviet of the USSR, proclaims a state of war in the event of military attack on the USSR, or when necessary to fulfill international treaty obligations concerning mutual defense against aggression;

(n) Orders general or partial mobilization;

(o) Ratifies and denounces international treaties of the USSR;

(p) Appoints and recalls plenipotentiary representatives of the USSR to foreign states;

(q) Receives the letters of credence and recall of diplomatic representatives accredited to it by foreign states;

(r) Proclaims martial law in separate localities or throughout the USSR in the interests of the defence of the USSR or of the maintenance of law and order and the security of the state.

Although it is not quite clear which clause modifies which (and this provides Soviet jurists with the food for some of their debate), there seem to be five kinds of powers enumerated in the article. There is the dormant, never exercised power to hold a referendum in section (e), which leaves the question of its legal impact completely unanswered. It is not known what kinds of questions could be submitted, how they would be formulated or who would administer them, to say nothing of whether the results would be legally binding or constitute a mere recommendation. Such a provision has so much potential that it could be hugely manipulated, which is undoubtedly one reason why it has remained dormant.

Secondly, there is the power to issue a ukaz in section (b). This might be interpreted as an independent original power to legislate or a delegated power (from the Supreme Soviet) merely to issue an administrative order elaborating on a zakon. Or it might be viewed as a power to issue an executive order, which is inherent in an executive body like the Presidium. Soviet jurists have pursued each line of argument.[11]

Thirdly, there is the power to "interpret the laws of the USSR in operation," which appears to be an exclusive, original power. This would include the power to override decisions of the Procuracy and the Courts, in the application of the law and the Constitution. In effect, the only superior power is the power of the Supreme Soviet to change the law and to amend the Constitution. However, this power to interpret laws does not seem to be utilized much, and there has been no known conflict between the Supreme Soviet and its Presidium over the interpretation of the laws. A subcategory of this power is the power to annul Council of Ministers postanovlenie and rasporyzhenia "if they do not conform to law" in section (f). This clearly extends the power of interpretation over the organs of state administration.[12]

Although the practice of interpreting a law on appeal from the Procuracy or Council of Ministers has been seldom exercised, in effect the Presidium interprets the law in its legislative activity. Every time it issues ukazes there is an implication that it conforms to the Constitution or zakon in operation. Thus, the Presidium is in the position of interpreting the legality and constitutionality of its own acts. This somewhat obvious and important power has not been subjected to attack by Soviet jurists, which suggests a certain sensitivity on the part of the regime. Much of the utility of the Presidium to the regime depends upon an unfettered power to implicitly interpret laws in the process of legislating. Attacks by jurists on the notion that the Presidium possesses independent powers to legislate may be, to some extent, disguised attempts to curb this implicit power to interpret laws. In any case, the availability of this implicit power helps to explain the relative atrophy of the explicit power in section (c).

The fourth category of powers in Article 49 is in sections (a) and (d) which refer to Articles 46 and 47 of the Constitution, setting out the procedures for convening and dissolving the Supreme Soviet, discussed in Chapter 7. These articles provide that the Supreme Soviet be convened twice a year and that it be dissolved when its chambers cannot agree. The only discretion allowed to the Presidium is that it may convene more than two sessions. In short, these appear to be exclusive, enumerated original powers.

The fifth category of powers in sections (g) through (r) has provided considerable confusion. These are the powers of the Presidium to act on behalf of the Supreme Soviet during the intervals between sessions, which is admittedly most of the year. It appears from the actual wording of Article 49, that sections (g) and (m) are the only ones which delegate power to the Presidium to act in between sessions of the Supreme Soviet. However, frequently Soviet jurists treat sections (h) through (l), and (n) through (r) in the same category, instead of as independent, original enumerated powers. Some jurists even imply that the whole article is a list of enumerated powers in effect delegated by the Supreme Soviet to the Presidium to act in the intervals between sessions. Also, as we have seen in Chapter 5, there is support for the contention that the whole article merely lists the kinds of powers on which the Presidium may act but does not specify the manner in which it may act, which is the prerogative of the Supreme Soviet. In other words, it grants jurisdiction, but does not establish competence. Or, to put it another way, Article 49 authorizes the Presidium to act on the matters enumerated, but in accordance with procedures laid down by legal acts of the Supreme Soviet. In effect, the argument is that the Supreme Soviet alone has the power to establish the legal basis for acting. In this view, Article 49 only enumerates the jurisdiction in which it may act. The underlying assumption of course is that the Presidium is basically an executive body concretizing the legal norms of the Supreme Soviet, which is the exclusive legislative body. Let us turn now from this independent look at the Presidium's powers to review some of the leading Soviet commentaries on the powers of the Presidium.

THE DEBATES OVER THE PRESIDIUM'S POWERS

Although not previously disputed, the alleged exclusive jurisdiction over the enumerated powers in Article 49 has been attacked by Soviet legal scholars who assert that the Presidium possesses only the executive authority to order these functions carried out on the basis of criteria established by the Supreme Soviet.[13] This line of argument contradicts Bespaly's.[14] The thrust of Bespaly's argument was that while all state and government institutions are ultimately accountable to the Supreme Soviet (as supreme organ of state power), this does not necessarily indicate an organic agency relationship between them and the Supreme Soviet. He argued further that the powers of the Presidium were not *delegated* to it by the Supreme Soviet, but vested in it by the Constitution as original powers.

His critics cited the constitutional provisions in Article 49 (g) and (m) to act for the Supreme Soviet between sessions as proof of the organic agency relationship existing between the Supreme Soviet and its Presidium.[15] In short, they argued that the Presidium's powers were delegated, not original. To the contrary, Bespaly had argued that this was not a delegated power evidencing an agency relationship, but a specific constitutional power deriving its authority from the Constitution, not the Supreme Soviet.[16] Although the argument is legalistic and reminiscent of many a Western constitutional debate, its significance lies in the fact that such legal hairsplitting in public over specific constitutional provisions is a relatively new phenomenon in the Soviet Union.

From the distinction between general legislation and administrative regulations implementing that legislation in detail (so familiar to Western lawyers) arises the second disputed source of legislative power increasingly exercised by the Presidium of the Supreme Soviet.[17] Although no specific constitutional provision vests the latter power in the Presidium, it has long been exercised. Its critics do not deny that the power exists. They merely assert that it does not constitute or invest separate jurisdiction. They caution against implementing regulations which exceed the intent of the general law that the regulation is designed to implement. And further, they suggest that if there is a question of ultra vires, the disputed regulation should be submitted to the Supreme Soviet for ratification as a separate piece of legislation.[18] In a system with a constitutional court, the judicial system would resolve such ultra vires disputes, but in the Soviet Union, the power to interpret the laws lies only with the Presidium of the Supreme Soviet in theory, which places it in the position of determining whether its own acts exceed the authority of the zakon on which they are theoretically based.

Another important enumerated power is Article 49 (c) of the Constitution—the power to interpret laws, a right which was vested in the Supreme Court under former constitutions. It specifies that the Presidium of the Supreme Soviet "interprets the law of the USSR in operation." The right is rarely used, but could become significant as a means of resolving conflicts of substantial political importance within the government over the application of economic legislation in particular.

The Presidium of the Supreme Soviet is the final forum of appeal for the courts and the Procuracy.[19] Of course, the initiative in bringing such an appeal lies with the courts and the Procuracy. The Supreme Soviet could overrule the interpretive decisions of the Presidium by issuing a zakon or constitutional amendment, but such an event has never been recorded. There is some suggestion that the Procuracy might be able to appeal the interpretation of the Presidium of the Supreme Soviet to the Supreme Soviet itself without having to resort to the legislative process of issuing a zakon. Walter Gellhorn reports that an official of the Procuracy claimed he could report to the Supreme Soviet on any matter beyond the competence of the Council of Ministers.[20] Whether a similar principle would apply to acts of the Presidium of the Supreme Soviet remains unclear, but certainly the case is weaker for an organ of state power with the original, enumerated power to interpret laws in operation.

This power has not been disputed for several reasons: first, because it is used so sparingly; second, because it is a specific enumerated constitutional provision; and third and most important, because the initiative in invoking it remains with the ministries, Procuracy, and courts who are unlikely to utilize it when to do so might threaten some of their own important institutional powers.

The fourth, most disputed, and most significant legislative power is the independent power to issue ukazes without submitting them to the Supreme Soviet for approval.[21] The effect of this practice is to make the Presidium of the Supreme Soviet a separate and distinct legislature in its own right, in violation of Article 32 of the Constitution vesting "exclusive" legislative power in the Supreme Soviet: "The legislative power of the USSR is exercised exclusively by the Supreme Soviet of the USSR."

Powerful arguments seek to vindicate this separate legislative authority. The most vociferously reiterated one is that some body must legislate in the lengthy interim between the brief plenary sessions of the Supreme Soviet.[22] Article 49 of the Constitution specifically authorized the Presidium to act for the Supreme Soviet between sessions in certain respects. The fact that the Presidium is ultimately accountable to the Supreme Soviet and that it is composed of Supreme Soviet deputies (the previously discussed "agency" argument) allegedly prevents any legislative departures from the united will of the Soviet people.[23] Even Bespaly admits this.

Critics opposing this independent legislative power argue in rebuttal that many Presidium acts involve no urgency, that some edicts are issued right before the Supreme Soviet sessions, and that in any case the Presidium has specific emergency powers—Article 49 (m), (n), (r)—which may be invoked for genuine crises. This clearly vitiates the logical strength of the "urgency" argument used to justify most interim Presidium ukazes.[24]

A second argument advanced by many authorities to buttress the independent legislative power of the Presidium of the Supreme Soviet is that there is no specific prohibition against it. These authorities argue further that the constitutional provisions authorizing the Presidium to appoint and dismiss ministers, convene the Supreme Soviet, and schedule elections—Article 49 (a), (f), (d)—

imply an independent power to act in spite of Article 32. However, they usually acknowledge the need for ratification eventually by the Supreme Soviet.[25] Critics of this line of argument point out in rebuttal that ukazes nevertheless retain their juridical force until ratification, thus constituting an independent legislative authority anyway.[26]

Some legal scholars who argue that the Presidium violates the Constitution in exercising this independent legislative power suggest it be halted and that all ukazes be submitted for ratification by the plenary sessions of the Supreme Soviet.[27] This would effectively curb some of its utility to the Party. For example, the ouster of Khrushchev could not have been fully sanctioned immediately by a Presidium of the Supreme Soviet ukaz as it was in October 1964.

Other scholars suggest that this independent power be legalized by a zakon, since the trend toward utilizing Presidium ukazes persists.[28] Though this might satisfy the demands of a rational-legal system, it would vitiate to an extent the fundamental myth that Soviet law derives from the popular will, since the Presidium is neither directly or truly representative in any real sense. On the maintenance of this fiction rests a considerable increment of the authority and legitimacy of Soviet law. However, the effort to enhance the representative image of the Supreme Soviet might somewhat mitigate this, provided that fiction develops credibility with the Soviet masses.

THE RELATIONSHIP OF THE PRESIDIUM OF THE SUPREME SOVIET TO THE PERMANENT COMMISSIONS

Although the Presidium of the Supreme Soviet possesses a substantial apparatus itself, the possibility that it might acquire control over a greatly expanded and specialized system of permanent commissions and subcommissions has sometimes encountered resistance such as that which culminated in the 1966 debate concerning its authority over the new commission system.[29]

O. Ye. Kutafin, an advocate of the Bespaly thesis (raised to the all-Union level), initiated the attack on Presidium control of the permanent commissions of the Supreme Soviet[30]:

> Making the Permanent Commissions responsible to the Presidium of the Supreme Soviet contradicts the very nature of the Permanent Commissions. The Permanent Commissions are organs of the chambers of the Supreme Soviet and must, therefore, be responsible solely to the Supreme Soviet and its appropriate Chamber.

Kutafin acknowledged that, in fact, the Presidium already directed the activities of the permanent commissions. However, he argued that, in theory, the Presidium should not do so, since legally and organizationally the commissions were the agents of their respective Supreme Soviet chambers, just as the Presidium also is an agent of both chambers, at least in theory.[31]

Apparently, Kutafin's sally represented somewhat of a last-ditch attempt by the opponents of the Presidium's encroaching authority.[32] Their immediate objective was to stem the further erosion of the Supreme Soviet's authority implicit in the extension of the Presidium's de facto control over the newly expanded system of permanent commissions.

Another legal scholar, seeking the same objective but more subtly, stressed the legal inability of the Supreme Soviet to delegate its powers to its Presidium. The argument was couched in a discussion of the establishment of the new sector commissions. It reflected the fear of the monitoring function residing in the Presidium.[33]

Kutafin had argued that the chairmen of the chambers of the Supreme Soviet should direct the work of the commissions, not the Presidium as was the present practice:

> The Permanent Commissions, as organs of the chambers, are subordinate solely to the chairmen of the chambers in the intervals between sessions of the USSR Supreme Soviet. But according to established practice, direction of all work of preparing the sessions of the USSR Supreme Soviet—and in this work a quite prominent place belongs to the Permanent Commissions of the Chambers—is allocated chiefly to the Presidium of the USSR Supreme Soviet as an organ of state power; for the Presidium's work is closely connected with the work of the USSR Supreme Soviet, and the Presidium, unlike the chairmen of the chambers for instance, commands all the possibilities and the apparatus necessary for this purpose. As a result the situation is such that the Presidium actually is required to co-ordinate the work of the Permanent Commissions of the chambers and to direct their preparatory work. Neither this obligation nor the rights appropriate to it have been legally formalized.[34]

Kutafin supported his argument with the theory that the Supreme Soviet chambers, not the Presidium, represent the ultimate will of the people and therefore their chairmen should direct the work of the permanent commissions. At the same time, he concedes that the apparatus of the Presidium of the Supreme Soviet might prove helpful in coordinating commission work, especially between sessions. Admittedly, the problem of coordinating the work of the sector commissions with the Planning and Budget Commissions to insure efficacious work procedures is a real one.[35]

Soon thereafter, a legal scholar attacking Kutafin in *Izvestia* advanced the traditional argument that Article 49 of the Constitution authorized the Presidium to carry on the work of the Supreme Soviet between sessions. Thus, he continued, it is the constitutional right of the Presidium to "direct," not just "coordinate" the work of the permanent commissions.[36] The words "direct" and "coordinate" focus the two sides of the debate. The former represents Presidium control of the commissions; the latter represents shared authority with the chairmen of each chamber of the Supreme Soviet. Those supporting Presidium control usually mention both words; those rejecting it mention only "co-ordination" by the Presidium. The debate is yet unresolved, although the Presidium seems to be winning.

In 1966, in his report to the Supreme Soviet on the creation of the new system of permanent commissions, N. V. Podgorny, Chairman of Presidium of the Supreme Soviet, supported the Presidium's "direction" of commission activities:

> The formation of new Permanent Commissions in the Council of the Union and the Council of Nationalities makes it necessary to intensify work on coordinating the activities of all the commissions. . . . This work, as we know, is carried out by the Presidium of the USSR Supreme Soviet, which *coordinates and directs* the activities of the Permanent Commissions of the two chambers in the intervals between sessions.[37]

In presenting the bill legally creating the new commissions in 1967 to the Supreme Soviet, M. S. Solomentsev, Chairman of the Legislative Proposals Committee of the Council of the Union of the Supreme Soviet, stated that the Presidium of the Supreme Soviet merely "coordinates" activities of the commissions:

> . . . resting on the Supreme Soviet's many years of experience, the draft stresses that in the period between sessions, the work of the Permanent Commissions of the Chambers is coordinated by the Presidium of the Supreme Soviet. The chairman of the Council of the Union and the chairman of the Council of Nationalities, in charge of the chambers procedures, assist in organizing the work of the respective chamber's Permanent Commissions.[38]

A book on the Supreme Soviet published in 1967 uses the words "coordinate and direct":

> The standing commissions are accountable and responsible for all their activities to the chambers which elect them; in between sessions the activities of all commissions are coordinated and directed by the Presidium of the Supreme Soviet.[39]

The wording of the zakon itself fails to provide a precise basis for the resolution of this issue.

THE PRESIDIUM AND THE COUNCIL OF MINISTERS

Coupling the Presidium's new legislative powers with its new monitoring and investigating capabilities creates a potentially formidable institutional weapon—the commission "proposal" converted to a Presidium ukaz. As described previously, the permanent commissions of the Supreme Soviet seek out problems in the economic machinery of the government. They may then draft formal "proposals" suggesting solutions to the problems, which the Presidium of the Supreme Soviet may then convert into legal norms binding on the economic agencies and ministries responsible. Such a mechanism would have great utility to the Party leadership as a means of legalizing its control over the government. Such a mechanism, in effect, represents the culmination of the debates over the legislative authority of the Presidium of the Supreme Soviet and over its authority vis-à-vis the permanent commissions of the Supreme Soviet. Such a mechanism appears to be actually utilized increasingly.[40]

In 1966 N. V. Podgorny, Chairman of the Presidium of the Supreme Soviet, acknowledged the intention of establishing such a mechanism in his report calling for the creation of the new monitoring sectoral commissions:

> The Presidium of the Supreme Soviet will continue in the future to support and develop in every way the initiative of the Permanent Commissions and help them in their practical work. The Presidium will adopt measures to ensure the implementation of recommendations and proposals submitted by the Commissions to ministries and departments.[41]

A more recent (1969) *Izvestia* editorial confirmed the practice of the Presidium adopting commission proposals binding on the Council of Ministers and ministries:

> The chambers' commissions frequently submit proposals and recommendations to the Presidium of the USSR Supreme Soviet for consideration; on the basis of these proposals and recommendations, the Presidium adopts decisions promoting further improvements in the activity of individual ministries and departments.[42]

The editorial, of course, recognized that the commissions may still submit recommendations directly to the Council of Ministers.

This practice is being extended horizontally to the union republic supreme soviets which have adopted specific legislation authorizing their presidiums to issue binding ukazes to union republic ministries based on their study of commission reports.[43] The potential effect is to activate the monitoring of the government at all levels under the central direction of the Presidium of the Supreme Soviet.

Even further, as previously discussed, union republic supreme soviets are beginning to monitor the Procuracy and the courts. They are also enlisting the vast mechanism of the People's Control Commissions in their monitoring.[44]

The potential extension of the new powers of the Presidium of the Supreme Soviet vertically and horizontally is substantial. As yet much of it is not formalized, although patterns of institutional practice appear to be increasingly finding their way into Soviet law. Formal legal sanctification of these patterns enhances their legitimacy, and the increasing legalization of institutional relations may prove to be one of the most significant developments in the Soviet polity in the decade of the sixties. In a sense, it reflects a further maturation and modernization of the Soviet legal-political order.

Chapter 9

THE COMMUNIST PARTY AND THE SUPREME SOVIET

The activation of the entire system of organs of state power clearly derives from its utility to the CPSU apparatus, as the apparatus's increasing rhetorical obeisance to the soviets throughout the decade of the sixties indicates. The CPSU apparatus appears to be increasingly active in various bodies of the Supreme Soviet system. In its quest to maintain its legitimacy, what would be more natural than increasing the activity of the organs of state power and the apparatus's activity in them in order to legalize its control over other organs of the polity such as the organs of state administration, the Procuracy, and the Supreme Court?

Analysis of the interlocking relationships between the higher Party bodies (the Central Committee, the Politburo, and the Secretariat) on the one hand, and the higher officials of the Supreme Soviet and its associated and auxiliary bodies (the Presidium of the Supreme Soviet, the officers of the chambers, the commission chairmen, and the members of the Council of Elders) on the other hand, reveals precisely how the apparatus of the CPSU controls the Supreme Soviet, and especially its auxiliary bodies, through the overlapping membership of its leadership with virtually all key Supreme Soviet officials. Such analysis also illustrates how this burgeoning overlap may enhance the influence and role of the Supreme Soviet in the Soviet political process.

THE SUPREME SOVIET AND THE PARTY IN THEORY

The theoretical distinction between the Supreme Soviet and the Party is that the former represents the masses and the latter the vanguard of the masses.[1] In theory also, the will of the Party and the interests of the people are one. The will of the people can deviate from the will of the Party because people may not be the best judge of their historical interests or destiny. Therefore, there cannot be a question, in theory, of the soviets claiming greater legitimacy emanating from their representation of the people.[2]

Repeated assertions that the jurisdiction of the soviets is not distinct from the Party imply a worry about the greater legitimacy implicit in any organ embodying a notion of popular sovereignty over that of an association representing its vanguard. In a recent article two Soviet scholars put it this way:

> Clear delimitation of the functions of the Party and the soviets constitutes a very complex problem in both theory and practice. . . . the nature of the soviets as agencies of state leadership with complete authority, rule[s] out the possibility of assigning to the soviets completely isolated areas outside the sphere of activity of the Party.[3]

The same scholars assert that soviet authority now extends to political as well as cultural and economic matters, a relatively new admission:

> The soviets not only do not stand aside from political questions, but constantly have recourse to them in their state decisions. This is particularly true of the Supreme Soviets, which have the responsibility of resolving the most important questions in the life of the state.[4]

As the Constitution declares, the Party is the guiding force in Soviet society. Allegedly, the Party exercises this "guidance" over the Supreme Soviet through mere persuasion by Party members within the soviets: "The political leadership given by the CPSU is built exclusively on methods of persuasion."[5]

NOMINATIONS, ELECTIONS, AND TRAINING

One important key to Party control of the soviets is its control over selection of the deputies:

The principal channel for Party influence upon the activity of the soviets in the localities is Party work with personnel and real control over the state of implementation. "Allocation, evaluation, and promotion of personnel," M. I. Kalinin emphasized, "are the direct prerogatives of the Party." Initiative exercised by the Party in nominating the most experienced and competent personnel to leading soviet posts, in accordance with the Leninist principles for selection of cadres, does not nearly exhaust the role of Party bodies in this area. In the first place, in elections to the soviets, the Party works out and effectuates guidelines on such cardinal matters as the basic proportions to be maintained with respect to social origins of deputies, the problem of continuity and renewal in the ranks of deputies, etc. As an example we may cite the provisions of the CPSU Program pertaining to soviet representative institutions. In the second place, the core of the work of Party agencies in the selection of personnel is to orient the soviets toward planned, systematic concern for the creation of a reserve of personnel and for training them. In cases in which the initiative in the nomination of personnel possessing the required qualities comes from the soviet agencies themselves, which then come to agreement on this with the corresponding Party bodies in the localities, the matter of Party guidance to the soviets can only benefit.[6]

As discussed previously, the Party exercises influence over a system of election commissions which are responsible to a Central Election Commission. In theory, they make all the arrangements and count the ballots. No mention is ever made of what mechanism secures their honesty. Although some radical elements have suggested multi-candidate elections, this proposal has apparently never received serious consideration because of the implicit threat to the Party's influence over this key traditional mechanism for controlling the soviets.

As the above comment indicates, the Party exercises considerable influence in the nomination of deputies at their place of work. It also sets guidelines for the proportions of various groups represented in the Supreme Soviet.

In the latter half of the sixties, the Party apparently stepped up its efforts to control the deputies and the higher officials of the state system by indoctrination at special Party schools. In 1967 the Central Committee of the CPSU mapped out a special program entitled "On Measures for Improving Training and Refresher Training of Workers of Soviets of Working People's Deputies."[7] The intent of the training is spelled out in the following manner:

It is proposed to the Union-republic Communist Party Central Committees and the territory, province, city and district Party committees that they pay greater attention to the task of training and refresher training for workers of the Soviets and to raising their ideological and theoretical level and business qualifications; that they make wider use of the practice of holding seminars and conferences for exchanging work experience; and that they elucidate more thoroughly in the press questions of the theory and practice of Soviet construction and the positive work experience of the Soviets in the economy and in culture and in perfecting the forms and methods of mass organizational work.[8]

Here again, the relationship between the Party and the Supreme Soviet is a two-way street. While the above implies a strengthening of Party influence, the comment below reveals the converse:

> It is planned to recruit leading workers of the Presidiums of the Supreme Soviets and Councils of Ministers of the Union and autonomous republics and territory and province Soviet executive committees to give lectures and conduct seminars at the higher Party Schools.[9]

This is simply one example of the process by which the pyramid of soviets seems to be gradually increasing its influence in the political process.

A report on one of these training sessions indicates that one central ingredient of the "refresher" training is instruction of the "soviet apparatus" in exercising "kontrol" over the government apparatus. Here is another aspect of the attempt by the Party structure (social power constituency) to use the soviet pyramid (the legislature) to restrain and supervise the government pyramid (executive-administrative authority). The right of interpellation is especially mentioned.[10] The converse, however, appears again in a discussion of the responsibility of soviets at all levels for responding to the instructions of voters at pre-election meetings. Stressing this emphasizes the soviet pyramid's embodiment of popular sovereignty, which certainly strengthens its image of legitimacy and thus its influence, even though the Party exercises itself considerably to guide and control nominations and pre-election meetings through presenting the key speakers and through its activists.

THE LEGAL STATUS OF THE PARTY

The status of the Party in law is quite nebulous and obviously troublesome to the Party as it attempts to exhaust the legal system as a key mechanism of control. The 1936 Constitution was the first Soviet constitution to mention the Party and thus to invest in it any legal status at all, which is quite natural, since until then law was expected to wither away. However, even here, the legal-functional role is not explicit (Article 126):

> . . . the Communist Party of the Soviet Union, which is the vanguard of the working people in their struggle to build communist society and is the leading core of all organizations of the working people both public and state.

The only official legal role assigned by this article to the Party is a "guiding" one, which does not really define its legal status. For example, there does not appear to be any legal reason why the Supreme Soviet and perhaps even its Presidium could not issue a zakon or ukaz amending the Constitution and radically changing the Party's legal status. That Khrushchev, who was a master at manipulating institutional devices, was undoubtedly aware of this and troubled by it is probably one reason he planned to revise the Constitution to upgrade the Party's legal status. According to a leading Soviet scholar, the guiding role of the CPSU was to form the centerpiece of the whole preamble, and it was also to play a leading role in the sections on social structure and fundamental rights and duties.[11] The soviets were to be renamed, supposedly as recognition that they represented the intelligentsia as well as the workers and peasants (the Czechoslovak Constitution of 1960 had already done this); their status would consequently be raised from a stratum to a class.

The Supreme Soviet created a ninety-six member constitutional preparatory commission on April 25, 1962, chaired first by Khrushchev, then by Brezhnev; it has promulgated nothing. That Khrushchev's proposed reforms were not adopted is significant because they would clearly have strengthened the Party apparat vis-à-vis other interest groups. One can only surmise that the increasing importance of law in the Soviet polity has rendered the process of constitutional reform exceedingly difficult, because the wording of that document must be taken more seriously.

A recent comment by a well-known Soviet jurist reflects the Party's ambivalent attitude toward law and the soviets:

> It is impermissible to confuse the functions of Party bodies with those of state bodies, i.e., with those of the Soviets. . . . The Party must secure the adoption of decisions through the Soviets *within the framework of the Soviet Constitution;* the Party seeks to *direct* the activity of Soviets and not to supplant them.[12]

The Party only "seeks to direct," but it must secure its will within the Constitution. Such verbalisms cannot be voiced with as much impunity as in the post-Stalin era, since lip service to the Constitution tends to give life to it.

THE PARTY AND LEGISLATION

Before the 1958 elections, the chairman of the Council of the Union of the Supreme Soviet described the controlling role of the Party over the Supreme Soviet with respect to establishment of the basic policies which are given the force of law by the Supreme Soviet.

> Legislation, as all activity of the highest organ of state power of the USSR is carried out under the guidance of the Communist party. . . . On the basis of party directives, Soviet laws establish concrete means by which to achieve the goals which the party sets for the Soviet people. One example of this was the submission to the Seventh Session [May 1957] of the USSR Supreme Soviet for its examination, by the Central Committee of the CPSU and the USSR Council of Ministers, of a draft law for further improving the organization of the administration of industry and construction.[13]

This comment reflects the old legislative process where joint resolutions by the CPSU Central Committee and Council of Ministers were submitted to the Supreme Soviet which perfunctorily ratified them. Often these resolutions were not even submitted for ratification. Even more recently major legislation, such as that delegating greater powers to Republic supreme soviets, took effect as a joint resolution without Supreme Soviet ratification.[14] However, the frequency of this process had diminished, while the number of Supreme Soviet zakons has proliferated.

The role of the CPSU in lawmaking appears to have two general aspects now: first, eliminating those subjects which are not ripe for legislation;[15] and second, supervising the drafting of laws at each stage through the activists without gross interference.[16] As described previously, the Party is only one among many bodies which exercise legislative initiative—the legal right to propose a bill which the Supreme Soviet commissions convert into a final detailed draft for ratification.[17] Legislative initiative is the right to present a bill to the permanent commissions of the Supreme Soviet with jurisdiction over it. The right to introduce a bill into the plenum resides in each deputy, but only when the matter is already being discussed by the

Supreme Soviet, which in effect gives the chamber chairman the power to rule it out of order.

There is evidence that Party directives are considered more important legally than other initiatives. Party directives usually initiate the most important legislation, according to one source.[18] Party initiative has increased, as have initiatives from other bodies, especially in the soviet pyramid.[19] These latter may represent Party initiatives in disguise. What is clear is that the organs of state power and the Party seem to be initiating more bills while the Council of Ministers seems to be initiating fewer.[20]

THE LOCUS OF PARTY CONTROL IN THE SUPREME SOVIET

Since the Bolshevik Revolution, over 70 percent of the membership of the Soviet legislative assemblies has been comprised of members of the CPSU. However, this percentage dropped from 97.4 in 1922 to 71.7 in 1935 in the Central Executive Committee. In the Congress of Soviets it fell from 94.1 in 1922 to 72 in 1936. Both trends reflect the gradual consolidation of power by the Bolsheviks (see Table 9.1).

The proportion of Communists in the first convocation of the Supreme Soviet in 1938 differed little from the proportion in the CEC—it was 76 percent. However, after the war Stalin increased the Party share of membership in the Supreme Soviet to as high as 85.5

TABLE 9.1

PARTY MEMBERSHIP IN CONGRESS OF SOVIETS AND CENTRAL EXECUTIVE COMMITTEE OF THE USSR, 1922–36

Year	% Party members Congress of Soviets	% Party members Central Executive Committee
1922	94.1	97.4
1924	90.0	91.0
1925	78.1	84.1
1927	72.7	69.7
1929	72.6	71.8
1931	75.3	—
1935	79.0	71.7
1936	72.0	—

Source: Pravda and Izvestia.

percent in the Council of the Union of the third convocation in 1950. Since then, the Party membership has declined steadily, as shown in Table 9.2.

The Party membership in the eighth convocation elected in 1970 is 72.3 percent, almost exactly that of the last Congress of Soviets in 1936, which was 72 percent.[21] Again, this steadiness may represent the growing confidence of the Party in the effectiveness of its control over the soviets following a period of some minor institutional turmoil, as well as the desire to enhance its representative image. Thus, Party membership in lesser soviets (union republic, district, and local) is smaller, reflecting the high percentage of non-Party members in society at large.[22] For example, in 1966 non-Party membership in the Supreme Soviet was 24.8 percent, in union republic soviets 31.5 percent, and in local soviets 53.8 percent.[23]

PARTY AND GOVERNMENT OFFICIALS
IN THE SUPREME SOVIET—THE INNER CORE

The Party and government officials over time have represented roughly one-third of the Supreme Soviet membership, a sort of continuing leading core, in accordance with which the CPSU program requires a two-thirds turnover at every convocation.[24] (See Table 9.3.)

In the fifth, sixth, seventh, and eighth convocations Party, govern-

TABLE 9.2

PARTY MEMBERSHIP IN THE SUPREME SOVIET OF THE USSR, 1937–66: PERCENT WHO ARE COMMUNISTS

Year elected	Soviet of the Union	Soviet of Nationalities
1937	81.0	71.0
1946	84.4	77.6
1950	85.5	81.3
1954	79.8	75.9
1958	76.3	75.8
1962	75.2	76.4
1966	74.7	75.7

Source: Pravda and Izvestia.

TABLE 9.3

PERCENTAGE OF PARTY-STATE OFFICIALS IN THE SUPREME SOVIET

Convocation	Party	State	Combined total
5	19.0	16.0	35.0
6	19.0	16.0	35.0
7	18.0	15.1	33.1
8	17.2	14.3	31.5

Source: Pravda and Izvestia.

ment, trade union, and Komsomol officials together represented approximately 35 percent of all deputies, which is more than eighty times their relative proportion of the occupied population.

The 35 percent figure is down somewhat from previous convocations where full-time Party functionaries and administrative officials always comprised more than 40 percent of the deputies. The non-Party government officials proportion of the Supreme Soviet has also declined, as shown in Table 9.4. Non-Party government officials include military officers, academicians, professionals, and artists who are not officials of the state or Party apparatus.

The decline in officialdom's proportion of seats in the Supreme Soviet in favor of workers and peasants does not reflect a loss of control, since officials occupy all of the seats in the commission system where most Supreme Soviet decision-making apparently takes place. In short, to improve the democratic image of the Supreme Soviet, the regime has decreased the number of officials in the

TABLE 9.4

NON-PARTY STATE OFFICIALS IN THE SUPREME SOVIET

Convocation	% of Supreme Soviet
5	28.0
6	28.0
7	26.0
8	23.5

Source: Pravda and Izvestia.

plenum of the Supreme Soviet while, as we shall see, retaining control of the most important auxiliary bodies of the Supreme Soviet. Over one-half of this ex officio group are Party secretaries, thus evidencing a hard core of Party career *apparatchiks* in the Supreme Soviet—the guiding core.[25]

THE CENTRAL COMMITTEE OF THE CPSU
AS INNER CAUCUS AND LEADING CORE

We turn now to identify the location of key Party officials in the key organs of the Supreme Soviet and its auxiliary bodies. According to one Soviet source:

> The Supreme Soviet functions under the guidance of the Central Committee of the CPSU, which is the leading and directing force of Soviet society. The Central Committee of the Party submits to the Supreme Soviet legislative proposals on the most important issues of state, economic, social, and cultural development.
>
> The Party and its Central Committee direct the activity of the Supreme Soviet itself, through Communists, primarily members of the Party's Central Committee and also the Party Group in the highest legislative organ of the country.[26]

One Western student of Soviet politics adds this further observation:

> Thus the Supreme Soviet, in some respects, represents a selected audience of citizens before which the decisions of the Central Committee are transmuted into legal acts of state, and before which some of the differences in the Central Committee are given a public and esoteric airing.[27]

In support of this contention he points out that although there are similarities in the composition of the Central Committee and the Supreme Soviet, the Central Committee is generally older (70 percent in 1966 were over 50 years of age), has fewer women (5 percent in 1966 as compared with the Supreme Soviet's 25 percent), and has only 2.8 percent workers and peasants, as opposed to about 40 percent in the Supreme Soviet.[28]

The Presidium of the Supreme Soviet, the chairmen of the Supreme Soviet commissions, and the Council of Ministers are filled with members of the Central Committee Group (full and alternate members, and members of the Central Auditing Commission), as shown in Table 9.5. It is this overlapping which implies that the

TABLE 9.5

THE CENTRAL COMMITTEE OF THE CPSU IN HIGHER STATE BODIES[a]

	Total no. of officials	No. of Central Committee group members	% of members on the Central Committee
Presidium of Supreme Soviet of USSR	36	30	88.3
Chairmen of USSR Supreme Soviet Commissions	20	12	60.0
Council of Ministers of USSR	84	83	98.8

a. The Central Committee group includes the Central Committee (full and candidate members) and the Central Auditing Commission.
Source: These figures are derived from the Twenty-third Party Congress and the Seventh Convocation of the Supreme Soviet as reported in Pravda, April 9, 1966 and Izvestia, August 4, 5, 1966.

Central Committee is the arena where functional, institutional, and social groups thrash out policy in the Soviet system.

THE PARTY APPARATUS IN THE SUPREME SOVIET

The Party apparatus has always comprised a significant proportion of Supreme Soviet deputies. In the fifth, sixth, and seventh convocations from 1962 to 1970, approximately one-fifth (18 percent) of the Supreme Soviet deputies were Party secretaries at various levels. This figure includes the first secretaries of the Party bureaucracy at the all-Union, regional, and local levels and is a slight drop from previous convocations where Party and Komsomol officials always comprised between one-quarter and one-fifth of the deputies to the Supreme Soviet. Almost all of the Party first secretaries at the regional level (oblast, Krai) sit in the Supreme Soviet as well as in the Central Committee. Consistently, over 90 percent of these heads of the lower levels of the Party sit in the Supreme Soviet, as shown in Table 9.6. Provincial Party secretaries comprised the biggest group of officials in the first (1938), third (1950), and fourth (1954) convocations.[29] The second convocation (1946) data is incomplete. There

TABLE 9.6
FIRST SECRETARIES OF REGIONAL-LOCAL
PARTY COMMITTEES ELECTED TO SUPREME
SOVIET

Election	Regional-local governmental units	Regional-local units electing the first secretary of their respective party committees	% of governmental units with representation of their first secretaries
1958	145	139	95.8
1962	141	129	91.4
1966	144	135	93.0

Source: Pravda, June 15, 1966, and March 29, 1958; Izvestia, March 21, 1962.

were 103 *apparatchiks* in the 1954 gathering, including all the first secretaries of the republic Party central committees.[30]

THE PARTY LEADERSHIP AMONG THE OFFICIALS OF THE SUPREME SOVIET

The following seeks to identify the positions within the Supreme Soviet organs from which the Central Committee, Politburo, and Secretariat of the CPSU address their fellow deputies, in order to trace the pattern of CPSU control over the Supreme Soviet. The key official positions include the officers of the permanent commissions, the officers of the chambers, the Council of Elders, and the Presidium of the Supreme Soviet.

Generally speaking, the apparently growing utility and importance of the Supreme Soviet to the CPSU leadership is reflected in the increasing proportion of Central Committee, Politburo, and Secretariat members who occupy key Supreme Soviet offices from its Presidium to its commission chairmen to its commissions and to the chairmen and vice-chairmen of its chambers.

THE PARTY LEADERSHIP IN THE PRESIDIUM OF THE SUPREME SOVIET

For the last two convocations (seventh and eighth), the Central Committee and its candidate members held a steady majority of 64 percent of the seats on the Presidium of the Supreme Soviet (88.3 percent if you include the Central Auditing Commission).[31] By contrast, only 39 percent of the seats in the Presidium of the Supreme Soviet, elected by the fourth convocation (1954), were held by Central Committee members elected at the Twentieth Party Congress. Table 9.7 illustrates the rising influence of the Central Committee on the Presidium of the Supreme Soviet in the post-Stalin era. The increased authority of the Presidium of the Supreme Soviet in the sixties apparently requires that an absolute majority of the seats be held by Central Committee members and candidate members.

The number and percentage of Politburo members who sit on the Presidium of the Supreme Soviet have also steadily increased in the post-Stalin era, as shown in Table 9.8.

In 1970 there were almost twice as many Politburo members (full and candidate) sitting on the Presidium of the Supreme Soviet as in 1962, again apparently reflecting the rising importance and utility of that body to the Party leadership. Membership in the Presidium of the Supreme Soviet can now be regarded as a significant credential for climbing the career ladder to the Party summit. The present General Secretary, Leonid Brezhnev, of course, served as chairman of the Supreme Soviet Presidium. Another powerful Politburo figure, N. V. Podgorny, whose star appears to be rising vis-à-vis the Chairman of the Council of Ministers Alexi Kosygin, is now Chairman of the Presidium of the Supreme Soviet.[32] This enhancing of Podgorny's

TABLE 9.7

**PROPORTION OF PRESIDIUM OF SUPREME SOVIET ON
PARTY CENTRAL COMMITTEE**

Convocation	CPSU Congress	Total Presidium membership	No. of Presidium members on C.C.[a]			% of Presidium on C.C.
			f[b]	c[c]		
4 (1954–58)	20th	33	9	4	= 13	39
6 (1962–66)	22nd	33	14	5	= 19	58
7 (1966–70)	23rd	36	18	5	= 23	64
8 (1970–74)	24th	36	17	6	= 23	64

a. C.C. = Central Committee of CPSU.
b. f = full members.
c. c = candidate members.

TABLE 9.8
PROPORTION OF PRESIDIUM OF
SUPREME SOVIET IN POLITBURO

	No. on Politburo			
Convocation	f[a]	c[b]	total	% on Politburo
6 (1962–66)	3	1	4	12
7 (1966–70)	3	2	5	14
8 (1970–74)	5	2	7	19

a. f = full members.
b. c = candidate members.

personal prestige appears to parallel chronologically the rise of the Presidium of the Supreme Soviet's role as legal and economic watchdog over the government bureaucracy. Nearly 40 percent (nine of twenty-three) of the members of the Politburo elected by the Twenty-third CPSU Congress at some time in their careers have sat on the Presidium of the Supreme Soviet.[33]

THE COMMISSIONS AND THE DEPARTMENTS OF THE SECRETARIAT

The intimate connection between the Supreme Soviet commissions and the departments of the Party Secretariat is quite apparent; the commissions are virtually the legal arm of the Secretariat and practically duplicate it in some respects. Three department heads or deputy heads chair important commissions. The names of some commissions and departments are identical, for example, Agriculture, Construction, Trade and Public Services, Transportation and Communication. The function of "kontrol" assigned to the Secretariat by the Party statutes and to the commissions by the 1967 zakon is one of monitoring, checking up on, or supervising policy implementation by the ministries. The commissions are, of course, confined to supervising policy embodied in formal law, not Party resolutions. The commissions constitute a second line of supervision for the Party apparatus—legal "kontrol" over the organs of state administration.

THE PARTY IN THE PERMANENT COMMISSIONS OF THE SUPREME SOVIET

The Party leadership dominates the chairmanships of the key Supreme Soviet commissions by an overwhelming majority. As we shall see, the number of Central Committee members of Supreme

Soviet commissions, as well as the status of a commission chairman in the Party leadership, indicates the importance attached to that commission by the Party. Conversely, occupancy of key commission chairmanships in some cases may have advanced the careers of several high Party officials. As evidenced below, most, but not all, of the chairmanships of the Supreme Soviet's permanent commissions are held by members of the Party Central Committee (see Table 9.9). The exact proportion of commission chairmanships held by Central Committee members has fluctuated from convocation to convocation, reaching a zenith under Nikita Khrushchev in 1962. It is interesting to note that the Council of the Union always has a higher proportion of its commission chairmen sitting on the Central Committee than the Council of Nationalities, thus offering another illustration of the inequality of allegedly equal chambers.

In one recent convocation of the Supreme Soviet, one-fifth of the membership of the permanent commissions also sat in the Central Committee. The actual percentage declined from 23 in the sixth convocation (1962) to 17 in the seventh convocation (1966).

While the proportion of members of the Supreme Soviet commissions who sat simultaneously on the Party Central Committee declined, the actual numbers of the Central Committee members on the commissions increased from 86 to 134, a 56 percent increase. This is due, of course, partially to the increase in the number of commissions from 10 to 26.

Table 9.10 indicates the number of Central Committee members sitting on each respective commission in the sixth convocation (1962) of the Supreme Soviet prior to the expansion of the commission system in 1967. It clearly reveals the relatively high number of

TABLE 9.9

PERCENTAGE OF PERMANENT COMMISSION CHAIRMEN IN EACH CHAMBER ON PARTY CENTRAL COMMITTEE[a]

Convocation	% in C.U.[b] on Central Committee	% in C.N.[c] on Central Committee	% of both chambers on Central Committee
4 (1954–58)	33	11	22
6 (1962–66)	44	44	44
7 (1966–70)	40	25	33
8 (1970–74)	46	31	38

a. Includes full and candidate members.

b. C.U. = Council of the Union.

c. C.N. = Council of Nationalities.

TABLE 9.10

PERCENTAGE OF CENTRAL COMMITTEE MEMBERS OF PERMANENT COMMISSIONS OF THE SIXTH SUPREME SOVIET CONVOCATION (1962)[a]

Commission	No. of deputies	% in C.U.	% in C.N.	Total % both chambers
Budget	39	46	5	24
Legislative Proposals	31	42	.09	26
Foreign Affairs	23	70	61	63
Credentials	21	57	.09	33
Economic	44	—	14	14

a. Includes full and candidate members.
b. C.U. = Council of the Union.
c. C.N. = Council of Nationalities.

Central Committee members on the commissions of the Council of the Union in contrast to the proportion of Central Committee members on the commissions of the Council of Nationalities. Forty-two percent of the deputies on the permanent commissions of the Council of the Union were full or candidate members of the Central Committee. The figure was only 11 percent in the Council of Nationalities. The highest proportion of Central Committee members sat on the Foreign Affairs Commission of the Council of the Union, which was then chaired by a member of the Politburo and Secretariat, M. A. Suslov.

Also, a majority of the Credentials Commission of the Council of the Union sat simultaneously on the Party Central Committee, as did a high proportion of the deputies in the budget and legislative proposals commissions of the Council of the Union. In contrast, the proportion of deputies sitting both on the Central Committee and on the Council of Nationalities commissions did not even approach a majority, except in the Foreign Affairs Commission. The heavy concentration of Party leaders in the Foreign Affairs Commission of each chamber reflects the high priority given to the internal and external foreign policy propaganda function of these commissions under Khrushchev.

A similar table for the seventh convocation of the Supreme Soviet (1966-1970) in which the commission system was expanded reveals much the same pattern, with the Central Committee holding a higher proportion of commission seats in the Council of the Union than the

Council of Nationalities (see Table 9.11). The Foreign Affairs Commission remains the holder of the highest proportion of Central Committee members. It must be recalled, however, that as a whole the commissions' primary functional concern has shifted toward the economy; thus, a much larger proportion of the Central Committee members on the commissions deal with economic questions in the seventh convocation, as contrasted with the sixth convocation.

As expected, the key commission for coordinating the drafting of laws, the Legislative Proposals Commission, holds a substantial number of Central Committee members, as do the key branch commissions for the economy, industry and agriculture. The Foreign Affairs Commission traditionally holds the largest complement of high Party officials. The Budget Commission has a high percentage because of its coordination of the budget and plan review functions. The Credentials Commission, of course, reviews the election credentials of each deputy.

The Central Committee members usually hold other key commission posts such as vice-chairmanships or secretaryships of the respective permanent commissions. For example, the key LPC of the Council of the Union in the sixth convocation was chaired by

TABLE 9.11

NUMBER OF DEPUTIES IN PERMANENT COMMISSIONS OF THE SUPREME SOVIET HOLDING SEATS IN THE CENTRAL COMMITTEE[a]

Commission	No. members	No. in C.U.[b]	No. in C.N.[c]	Total	% both chambers
Agriculture	41	15	3	18	22
Budget	51	17	4	21	20.5
Construction	31	7	0	7	11.3
Credentials	31	11	3	14	22.5
Education	31	4	3	7	4.3
Foreign Affairs	31	11	8	19	30.7
Health	31	5	1	6	9.7
Industry	41	15	6	21	25.6
Legislative Proposals	31	14	3	17	27.4
Trade	31	3	1	4	6.3
Total		102	32	134	

a. Seventh Convocation, 1966–70. Nearly all eligible Central Committee members in the Supreme Soviet (i.e., not officials of organs of state administration or Procuracy) are members of commissions.
b. C.U. = Council of the Union.
c. C.N. = Council of Nationalities.

Polyansky, a current member of the Politburo; his vice-chairman was a candidate member of the Central Committee; and his secretary a full member. In the seventh convocation (1966–70), this same commission was chaired by Solomentsev, who became a Premier of the RSFSR and a candidate member of the Politburo. In the LPC for the Council of Nationalities of the sixth convocation, the vice-chairman and secretary, but not the chairman of the commission were both members of the Central Committee. Of the four chairmen of the sectoral subcommissions of the old Economic Commission of the Council of Nationalities, three were candidate members of the Central Committee.

The chairman of a special agriculture commission of the Council of the Union in 1966 was none other than L. I. Brezhnev, the Party General Secretary himself, symbolizing the Party's great concern for Soviet agricultural policy. The chairman of the Foreign Affairs Commission of the Council of Nationalities in the eighth convocation (1970) was a Party Secretary and a candidate member of the Politburo, Ponomarev. As mentioned previously, the chairman of the Foreign Affairs Commission of the Council of the Union was Politburo member and Party Secretary M. A. Suslov, who has long headed this commission.

THE PARTY CENTRAL COMMITTEE AMONG THE OFFICIALS OF THE SUPREME SOVIET CHAMBERS

The chairmen and vice-chairmen (one chairman and four vice-chairmen per chamber) of the respective chambers have been predominantly members of the Central Committee (either full or candidate) as shown in Table 9.12.

Opponents of the burgeoning authority of the Presidium of the Supreme Soviet argue that the Constitution implies that direction of the permanent commissions activities between sessions should reside with the chairmen of the respective chambers. The original internal decree creating the LPC had implied that this authority lay with the chairmen of the chambers rather than the Presidium.

The apparent defeat of the advocates of this position is supported by the disappearance of I. V. Spiridonov as Chairman of the Council of the Union. Once a candidate member of the Politburo (after the Twenty-second CPSU Congress), his star appeared on the wane when he lost that post and appeared as chairman of the Council of the Union after the Twenty-third CPSU Congress. At the eighth convocation, he held neither position.

Although one can hardly generalize from this one instance, the

TABLE 9.12
SUPREME SOVIET CHAMBER OFFICIALS IN CENTRAL COMMITTEE

| | Council of the Union | | Council of Nationalities | | | % in |
Convocation	f^a	c^b	f	c	Total	Central Committee
4^c	2	1	1	2	6	60
6^c	1	1	2	1	6	60
7^d	2	–	1	1	4	40
8^e	3	–	2	–	5	50

a. f = full members.
b. c = candidate members.
c. Council of the Union chairman is full; Council of Nationalities chairman is candidate.
d. Council of the Union chairman is full.
e. Both chairmen are full.

implication of it and other recent events suggests that the chairmanship of a chamber of the Supreme Soviet is less influential than the chairmanship of key commissions or membership in the Presidium of the Supreme Soviet. For example, Solomentsev, the chairman of the LPC of the seventh convocation, was a former Party Secretary, and then RSFSR Premier and candidate member of the Politburo. Polyansky, chairman of the LPC in the sixth convocation, sat as a full member of the Politburo during the eighth convocation.

THE CENTRAL COMMITTEE IN THE "DEBATES" OF THE SUPREME SOVIET

In addition to controlling most of the key positions in the Supreme Soviet, the Party Central Committee also dominates a substantial amount of the speechmaking in the plenary sessions of the Supreme Soviet. For example, in the seventh convocation, 44 percent (22 of 55) of the speakers in the most important sessions of the Supreme Soviet, the budget sessions, were Central Committee members. In the eighth convocation budget sessions, 53 percent of the speakers were Central Committee members.

In summary, then, while officially published statistics indicate a decline in the proportion of CPSU members sitting in the plenary Supreme Soviet, high Party officials still occupy the vast majority of the key positions in the Supreme Soviet and its auxiliary bodies. Especially noteworthy is the steady proportional increase of Central

Committee and Politburo members sitting on the Presidium of the Supreme Soviet, thus lending support to the proposition that the latter's role and authority are rising in the context of Soviet politics.

THE COUNCIL OF ELDERS

Each chamber of the Supreme Soviet has a Council of Elders (*Sovet Stareishin*). Its most important function is making arrangements for the plenary session of the Supreme Soviet, especially with respect to nominations for the offices of chamber chairmen and vice-chairmen and for chairmen, vice-chairmen, and secretaries of the permanent commissions. It also apparently sets the agenda order for discussion of draft bills.[34] How much discretion it may exercise independent of the Party leadership in these matters is unknown as is the identity of its membership.

The Council of Elders of the Council of the Union had 157 deputies in 1966; that of the Council of Nationalities had 148. The membership of the former is elected by groups of deputies from specially designated territorial areas, and that of the latter in accordance with the following formula: six per union republic, two per autonomous republic, and one per national area.[35]

Its composition allegedly represents a cross-section of the various occupations in the Soviet Union, as does the plenary Supreme Soviet. However, the Council of Elders does not quite constitute a microcosm of the Supreme Soviet. For example, while close to 30 percent of the Supreme Soviet are non-Party people, only 20 percent of the Council of Elders are non-Party deputies.[36]

The Council of Elders is also charged with preparing the final details for the plenary Supreme Soviet's discussion and ratification of draft bills. It is the final board of review before the Central Committee airs its policies before the full Supreme Soviet and transmutes them into law. Its very name conjures up memories of Moscovy where age and messianic spiritual wisdom were said to reside in "elders" of the church. In a sense, it is one more symbolic link with the Zemsky Sobor, that first representative Russian assembly.[37]

THE SUPREME SOVIET IN THE PARTY: INCREMENTS OF INSTITUTIONAL INFLUENCE AND THE POSSIBILITY OF A SHIFTING CAUCUS

The interlocking and overlapping of Party leadership with the heads of other Soviet political instititions has long been accepted as the primary mechanism of Party control. However, the apparent fracturing of the Party's monolithic image in the post-Stalin era has suggested lines of influence flowing the other way from the political institution to the Party leadership.

While the Party leadership's presence in the Supreme Soviet has been increasing in the sixties, the converse is also true and equally significant—that is, the Supreme Soviet's influence in the Party leadership arenas may also be inferred to be increasing.

Since the Twentieth CPSU Congress, the proportion of Central Committee members who also sit in key positions in the Supreme Soviet and its auxiliary bodies (i.e., the Presidium of the Supreme Soviet, officers of the chambers, officers of the permanent commissions, and commission members) has increased from 24 percent to 41 percent, as shown in Table 9.13.

Such an increase supports the proposition that the Supreme Soviet is increasingly of importance to the Party, but it also enhances the institutional influence of the Supreme Soviet in the Central Committee. Thus, one might argue with some validity that on issues before the Supreme Soviet affecting the institutional interests of the Supreme Soviet, potentially 41 percent of the Central Committee— who are officials and not just ordinary deputies of the Supreme Soviet—might tend to back measures enlarging the Supreme Soviet's authority, provided such measures did not encroach substantially on the Party's supremacy.

A more extreme proposition raises the possibility of a shifting policy-making caucus from the Central Committee to the Supreme Soviet, if the former were ever to be dominated by a united majority

TABLE 9.13
PROPORTION OF CENTRAL COMMITTEE IN KEY SUPREME SOVIET POSITIONS [a]

Convocation	% of C.C.
4 (1954)	24
7 (1966)	34
8 (1970)	41

a. Central Committee members in organs of state administration and Procuracy are ineligible; almost all eligible members hold key posts.

of key Supreme Soviet officials. Such a united majority is highly unlikely and would coalesce only under an extraordinary set of circumstances, the conjunction of which is highly conjectural and which is, in any case, outside the scope of this study. However, when the institutional interests of the Supreme Soviet are before the Central Committee for discussion, it is not difficult to imagine relative unanimity of opinion among those Central Committee members who also hold key Supreme Soviet positions in support of enhanced Supreme Soviet authority. A shifting caucus is unlikely, but the burgeoning overlap of Supreme Soviet officials and Central Committee members augurs for gradual incremental increases of Supreme Soviet influence in Soviet politics.

In summary, then, the increasing interlocking and overlapping of Supreme Soviet leadership and Party leadership can arguably support two propositions: one, that Party control over the Supreme Soviet is increasing; and, two, that conversely the Supreme Soviet's institutional interests will and have found increasing support in higher Party policy-making arenas, thus enhancing the Soviet's political power.

THE SUPREME SOVIET IN THE PERSPECTIVE OF "TENDENCY-ARENA" ANALYSIS

Ever since Vernon Aspaturian suggested that formless clusters must exist within the allegedly monolithic CPSU, scholars have raced to identify these forms as structured interest groups, until recently, when the race seems to have come full circle with tendency analysis.[38] Rather than seeking to demarcate precise and continuing interest groups, based on a function, occupation, social status, or whatever, Franklyn Griffiths (almost echoing Aspaturian more than a decade ago) argued that Soviet society is still relatively atomized, and that clusters take form only as issues arise.[39] In other words, there is a tendency for otherwise formless groups to cluster and pressure as questions affecting their interests arise. Different issues are responded to by different clusters. Having dissected Soviet society from every conceivable angle and discovered its interlocking overlapping complexity, scholars led by Franklyn Griffiths may be shifting toward analysis of the tendency of elements of the polity to cluster around selected policy issues plaguing the polity. The following analysis will suggest that tendencies to resort to various decision-making arenas within the polity may also be emerging.

The central argument is that the clusters conjured up by various issues may find one institutional arena more favorable to debate and decision-making than another. The idea is simple. Groups will always seek the most favorable forum for ideas. If a complex gathering of elites is represented in two bodies, the various coalitions of these groups which emerge on respective issues will maneuver to inject the decision-making into that arena whose formal and informal rules and practices encourage policy decisions which must conform to the respective coalition's interests. The focus in this kind of analysis is on the structured nature of the issues and above all on the institutions rather than the clusters.

Such analysis requires the existence of alternative arenas with somewhat established, distinct, and legitimate institutional practice. These are emerging as the Soviet Union matures. As Griffiths implies, tendency analysis is particularly rewarding and appropriate in this polity which, while it may be gradually congealing, has historically been characterized by a high degree of atomization even in the pre-Soviet era. This study suggests that a "tendency-arena" perspective is particularly appropriate at this stage of the Soviet Union's political institutional development.

This study alone suggests several potential arenas for decision-making in the Soviet polity, the two most obvious being the Central Committee of the CPSU and the Supreme Soviet. It is widely accepted that the Central Committee of the CPSU is the primary policy-making arena, and equally widely accepted is that the Supreme Soviet is a mere ratifying body. The import of some of the analysis herein is that through a very gradual, subtle institutional evolution there may already be some deviation from these axioms. In any case, the underlying argument is that the potential for transformation of the Supreme Soviet is great.

The study suggests two other potential arenas: the Council of Elders and the commissions. Since information on the composition and deliberations of these bodies is almost nonexistent, it is not possible to evaluate their decision-making role or potential in any really meaningful way. The only hard evidence indicates that at the very least the Council of Elders finalizes the contents and order of the Supreme Soviet's agenda, and the commissions play an increasingly active role in "concretizing" general policy norms of the Central Committee. Beyond this, one can only speculate on how these bodies might play an even greater role in the policy decision-making process.

Some groups would possess a greater voice in the Supreme Soviet than in the Central Committee if the Supreme Soviet were an independent body; however, these groups tend to be the weaker groups in the polity. Nevertheless, a brief focus on them is illustrative. Some groups which would probably prefer the Supreme Soviet as a decision-making arena are the non-Slavic nationalities, women, youth, and perhaps enterprise directors, academicians, and state apparatchiki. Table 9.14 illustrates why non-Slavic nationalities (those other than the Russians, Ukrainians, and Belorussians) would prefer the Supreme Soviet to the Central Committee.

Four percent of the Central Committee, elected at the Twenty-third Party Congress, were women; 28 percent of the seventh Supreme Soviet and 30.5 of the eighth Supreme Soviet were women. [40] That same Central Committee had 5 percent of its membership under 40, while 40.6 percent of the seventh Supreme Soviet and 41.5 percent of the eighth Supreme Soviet were under 40.[41] Clearly, women, youth, and non-Slavic nationalities would be better represented in the Supreme Soviet. Table 9.15 illustrates the situation for academicians and enterprise directors, comparing the Seventh Supreme Soviet with the Central Committee elected at the Twenty-third Party Congress. Since these groups are represented six and three plus times better respectively in the Supreme Soviet than in the Central Committee, it is reasonable to assume they would prefer the former as a policy arena.

Although the elitist school belittles efforts to demarcate a precise cleavage between the state and Party apparatchiki at higher levels, let us assume (as tendency analysts would have it) that issues might arise which might convert this functional division into temporarily opposing interest groups. In such a case, the state apparatus might prefer the Supreme Soviet as an arena, while the Party apparatus might prefer the Central Committee; but comparing the ratio of Party to state officials in both the Central Committee of the Twenty-third Party Congress and the seventh Supreme Soviet yields an almost identical ratio—6:5 in the Central Committee and approximately 7:5 in the Supreme Soviet.[42] It would not be more advantageous for state officials to transfer decision-making to the Supreme Soviet, unless they could form alliances with other groups, such as the academicians or enterprise directors.

Barring a coup d'etat by some powerful, dissident coalition of interest groups, it is unlikely that the locus of decision-making in the Soviet Union will shift from the Central Committee to the Su-

TABLE 9.14

TWO ARENAS: A COMPARISON OF NATIONALITY REPRESENTATION IN THE SUPREME SOVIET AND THE CENTRAL COMMITTEE OF THE CPSU[a]

Nationality	USSR Supreme Soviet		Central Committee, CPSU	
	% 1962	% 1966	% 1961	% 1966
Russians	43.48	42.52	58.29	57.95
Ukrainians	14.62	13.18	20.00	18.46
Belorussians	3.74	3.69	3.43	5.13
Uzbeks	2.98	3.43	2.29	1.54
Kazakhs	2.29	2.37	1.14	2.05
Georgians	3.19	3.30	1.14	1.03
Azerbaijanis	3.12	3.10	0.57	0.51
Lithuanians	2.08	2.11	0.57	0.51
Moldavians	1.32	1.45	0.57	0.51
Latvians	1.46	1.85	1.14	1.54
Kirghiz	1.32	1.52	0.57	0.51
Tadzhiks	1.94	2.31	0.57	0.51
Armenians	2.77	3.16	1.71	1.54
Turkmens	1.32	1.78	0.57	0.51
Estonians	1.87	1.91	0.57	0.51
Finns	0.14	0.07	0.57	
Jews	0.35	0.33	0.57	0.51
Poles	0.28	0.33	—	—
Bashkirs	0.83	0.59	0.57	0.51
Buriats	0.55	0.59	—	—
Kabardinians	0.42	0.40	—	—
Kalmyks	0.42	0.40	—	—
Karclians	0.35	0.40	—	—
Komis	0.55	0.59	—	—
Maris	0.42	0.33	—	—
Mordvinians	0.49	0.46	—	—
Ossetians	0.90	0.92	—	—
Tatars	0.97	1.19	0.57	0.51
Tuvinians	0.55	0.53	—	—
Udmurts	0.42	0.40	—	—
Chechens	0.35	0.40	—	—
Chuvashes	0.62	0.53	—	—
Yakuts	0.55	0.33	—	—
Kara-Kalpaks	0.42	0.33	—	—
Abkhazians	0.49	0.46	—	—

a. The Central Committee figures are for full members only.
Source: Yaroslav Bilinsky, "The Ruler and the Ruled," Problems of Communism (1965).

TABLE 9.15

**REPRESENTATION OF ENTERPRISE MANAGERS AND
ACADEMICIANS IN TWO ARENAS**

	Central Committee[a]		Supreme Soviet	
	No.	%	No.	%
Enterprise officials	5	1	91	6
Academicians[b]	11	3	154	10.2

a. Includes full and candidate members. Source: Saifulin, The Soviet
Parliament (Moscow, 1967), p. 158.
b. Includes workers in art and culture.

preme Soviet. What is more probable and has perhaps already begun
is a slow, incremental process whereby the concretizing of general
Party policy norms would become more general as Supreme Soviet
norms become more detailed. Or, to put it another way, the Supreme
Soviet's policy-making function would grow as it assumed greater
control over the details of Central Committee norms, which would
become increasingly more general and vague.

It is not difficult to imagine groups attempting to shift every
aspect of the concretizing process out of the Central Committee to a
more advantageous forum. We have seen the budget sessions serving
to air disagreement over economic reform. We have seen a law
arrested at the moment of its passage and sent back to committee.
Both could be interpreted as tactical maneuvers in which groups
attempt to influence decision-making by raising the issues in a more
favorable arena. Both illustrate a process by which the Supreme
Soviet and its auxiliary bodies seem to be acquiring real influence
from what were once the mere trappings of power. Both illustrate a
process by which the more moderate reformers and disadvantaged
minorities could shift increments of the decision-making process out
of a Central Committee apparently still highly influenced by the old
line ideologues within the Party apparatus.

Chapter 10

PROSPECTUS: FUTURE TRENDS

Barring a major upheaval which is always a possibility, however remote, the Supreme Soviet appears destined to perform as an instrument of moderate reform in the Soviet polity. The comments below represent the moderate and radical views of the Supreme Soviet. Conservatives view it primarily as an instrument for controlling the polity and maintaining the status quo.

> Proceeding from the provisions of the CPSU Program on the development of the Soviet state system, the Congress especially emphasized the need for consistently enhancing the role of the soviets which constitute the broadest and most all-encompassing organization of our people.[1]
>
> N. V. Podgorny

> The Supreme Soviet should be a practical forum, not a mechanism (for securing) unanimity. The electoral system should be founded on the multiparty principle.[2]
>
> Anonymous Dissenter

> . . . the judiciary and the militia must be separated from state and Party and the activities of the state security organs and the army controlled by special commissions of the Supreme Soviet.[3]
>
> Anonymous Dissenter

The history of the evolution of the Supreme Soviet indicates that the regime can usually control and eventually silence calls for radical reform of the Supreme Soviet, such as multiparty or multicandidate proposals. Thus, the samizdat suggestions above could not take root in present soil, although a sudden upheaval or military coup might provide very fertile soil indeed for such a plant.

The alternative is moderate-progressive reform in the Soviet context. Massive participation in bodies designed to legalize decisions may provide the polity with a distinctive Russian answer to the problem of bringing a complex, modernizing, multinational, ideologically-retarded state into the post-industrial age. Against the argument that the process is too slow one must juxtapose the argument that participatory processes that proceed toward reform from the base of the pyramid tend to progress geometrically, while those that start at the apex proceed arithmetically. As the legal head of the pyramid with the largest base, the Supreme Soviet sits in a unique position.

As an institution, the Supreme Soviet potentially performs some of the crucial functions required by a modern polity. It incorporates symbolic, historical-ideological legitimacy into a complex of organs which serve as a barometer of public and expert opinion and funnels this information to the decision-making apex outside stagnant traditional channels. It then takes generalized decisions and further incorporates public and expert opinion through concretization of the broad norms.

IMPACT ON THE SUPREME SOVIET OF
EASTERN EUROPEAN LEGISLATURES

It is perhaps worth noting that many of the assemblies in Eastern European Communist Party-states are seeking greater influence in the polity, although what this portends for the Soviet polity must remain as yet conjectural.

The two states most subservient to the USSR, Bulgaria and the GDR, seem to have the least active legislatures, although even there demands for a greater role, primarily for the "kontrol" function, are evident.[4] Two states relatively more independent of Soviet influence, Hungary and Rumania, have taken concrete steps to enhance the "kontrol" and investigatory functions of their legislatures. The Rumanian legislature passed a law requiring the head of government to submit regular reports to it, and asserted that every government minister is responsible directly to it.[5] In November 1965, the answer of a Hungarian minister to a question of the legislature was rejected by the legislature.[6] In 1966, the Hungarian leadership urged deputies to its legislature to "kontrol" the government by asserting its rights, because it "is the master's voice—the voice of the electorate, that is, the people."[7]

Four states seem to be activating the drafting function, but only two appear to have gone beyond the Soviet model—Poland and Yugoslavia. Rumania is establishing a legislative council, a sort of executive committee to coordinate drafting activity of the parliamentary commissions. Its legislature has also established bodies to study ways of improving the drafting procedure.[8] In Hungary the parliamentary commissions are known to have returned several government bills for improvement; they are also debating the general policy of some bills before receiving the draft bill.[9]

Poland and Yugoslavia are the two states which seem to have clearly surpassed the Soviet legislative model. The Yugoslav Assembly actually originates draft laws, and this practice increased throughout the sixties.[10] Government proposals are increasingly subject to considerable amendment. The 1965 economic plan went through twelve versions under the attack of two of the five chambers of the legislature before it was adopted.[11] The *Rechsstaat* model of Yugoslavia does not appear appropriate for the Supreme Soviet for two reasons. First, the Russian polity historically resists rigid legalism; participatory counciliarism coupled with a moderate advance toward an organic legal system conforms more closely to the propensities of the Russian-Soviet polity. Second, of course, the recent and recurrent crises of Yugoslavia reflect not only the fragility of that model but also the danger of emulating it.

Of the legislatures directly under Soviet hegemony, the Polish Sejm is the most active. It does not appear to originate bills, but it does amend them frequently. Of the 174 laws passed by it from 1957–61, only 34 were not amended. The criminal code was heavily amended and the passport law rejected three times before approval.[12] Some negative votes have also been cast.

The Polish parliamentary committees are also quite active. The evidence indicates that they actively debate pending legislation, question ministers, meet between sessions, are increasingly professional, and propose amendments (one hundred amendments in the 53 meetings on the budget in 1961).[13] The number of committees has been increased from seven to nineteen. As described previously, the Polish have professionalized some of their deputies. The new statute on the standing commissions embarks the Supreme Soviet deputy on the same course. Professionalizing the much touted "amateur-deputy" might provide substantial impetus to the activation of all the potential powers of the Supreme Soviet described herein.

Poland has a multiparty parliament, although of course the non-

Communist parties are closely controlled. Nevertheless, this multi-party aspect of the Polish parliament has potential and deserves close scrutiny in the future. As one Polish commentator expressed it:

> This system may be described as a multi-party one but it would be more exact to call it a system of cooperation encompassing the PUWP and other working people's parties and having nothing in common with a bourgeois multi-party system. All parties adhere to the program of building socialism and recognize the leading role of the working class in society. The PUWP recognizes the autonomy of the other parties in regard to organizing work, internal structure, membership and world outlook. On the political scene, it is only the PUWP that represents the working class. It also speaks for other working people. As to the other parties, they represent various categories of working people outside the working class.
>
> All parties are represented on government bodies. Out of the 460 deputies to the Sejm (parliament), the PUWP accounts for 255, the Peasant Party for 117 and the Democratic Party for 39. Thirteen non-party deputies represent progressive Catholic groups.
>
> Inter-party cooperation has developed in definite forms. Thus, the PUWP elaborates its agrarian program jointly with the Peasant Party. There are central, regional and district committees for inter-party cooperation.
>
> The multi-party system in socialist countries, speakers said, has nothing in common with the revisionist concepts of "pluralist socialism" and "free play of political forces." Whether or not there is a multi-party or one-party system depends on historical conditions in the country concerned, specifically on the attitude of the given non-Communist parties. Where several political parties exist they all cooperate in a popular patriotic front. In the absence of class antagonisms there is no ground for opposition between them.[14]

While Poland is clearly in the avant-garde among assemblies in Communist Party-states under Soviet hegemony, an important distinction here is that Poland, unlike the Soviet Union, possesses a parliamentary tradition.

Several other facts are also relevant to the comparison of communist legislatures with the Supreme Soviet. Multicandidate elections are now held in Hungary, GDR, North Vietnam, Poland, and Yugoslavia, but have only been proposed in the USSR—in 1956 by a legal scholar and more recently by dissidents. Poland's Sejm is a multi-party legislature, but elections to it are highly controlled; nevertheless, these forms bear watching as bellwethers of potential Supreme Soviet evolution. The GDR, like the Soviet Union, selectively employs widespread public discussion of some draft laws, but the more liberal regimes seem to avoid this practice.

Finally, the representative image of these Communist legislatures, especially the high proportion of nonelites, is much touted for internal legitimating purposes and for external propaganda as Table 10.1 and comments under it indicate.

While it is undoubtedly significant that there is some evolution in the direction of parliamentary democracy in most Communist Party-states in Eastern Europe, clearly the scope and nature of these tendencies varies widely, and their potential impact upon the USSR is quite unpredictable. Whether the myriad variables present might effect some spillover on the one hand, or reaction on the other, in the USSR, or perhaps even result in forcible Soviet suppression of these tendencies (as in Czechoslovakia) is worth considerable study.

PROSPECTS FOR THE NEAR FUTURE

Let us turn to a more immediate assessment of its propects in the near future. Increasingly in the decade of the sixties, the Supreme Soviet and its auxiliary bodies evolved into an instrument for legalizing and further centralizing the CPSU leadership's control over other major political institutions of the Soviet Union. The "small" Presidium can legislate almost instantly, which is of great utility to the Party. In addition to its own apparatus, the Presidium exercises

TABLE 10.1
SOCIAL MAKE-UP OF HIGHER REPRESENTATIVE
BODIES IN COMMUNIST PARTY-STATES

	Year	Deputies	Workers	Peasants	Intellectuals, office workers, etc.
Bulgaria	1966	416	50	51[a]	315
GDR	1967	500	287	44	169
Hungary	1967	349	126	52	171
Mongolia	1969	297	69	84	144
Poland	1969	460	79	70	311
Rumania	1969	465	92	76	297
USSR	1970	1,517	481	282	854
Yugoslavia	1969	620	4	1	615

a. Together with forestry workers.

NB: The present U.S. Congress does not include a single worker, small farmer or ordinary white-collar worker.

Although workers make up almost 50% of the employed population of the FRG, only 7% of the present Bundestag, following the 1969 election, are workers.

Source: *World Marxist Review* (Supplement) vol. 13 no. 8, August 1970, p. 11.

substantial control over the permanent commissions, which can increasingly be viewed almost as an arm of the Presidium. These commissions greatly enhance the capability of the Presidium to investigate and monitor government activities (especially the economic apparatus) and to legislate corrective action. Increasingly the Presidium has utilized these commissions to supervise union republic and local soviets. The Presidium also appears to be tentatively groping for more authority over the Procuracy as an instrument for monitoring the legal system.

One must not exaggerate the extent and significance of this apparent institutional evolution for several reasons. First, most of the Presidium's increased authority is de facto and could therefore be curbed without any formal public legal act. Second, and more important, its increased authority appears to be disputed and resisted by powerful elements within the CPSU leadership. Most major officials of the Council of Ministers and their ministries sit in the highest Party organs. Clearly it is not in their interest to foster the growth of a monolithic institutional watchdog over their affairs.

Some might argue that the Presidium's rise merely reflects a temporary shifting of institutional powers, reflecting the alleged Brezhnev-Kosygin struggle for supremacy, or the traditional Party-government apparatus struggle for influence in those high arenas of Party politics, the Central Committee and the Politburo. Undoubtedly, such argument carries weight in a polity historically plagued by a multiplicity of political institutions subject to continual flux according to the fortunes of various factions. Organic institutional stability is not the hallmark of either Russian or Soviet history. Despite the undoubted involvement of the Supreme Soviet in such struggles, however, there exist in the Soviet polity conditions from which one may infer with relative confidence the continued evolutionary growth of the Supreme Soviet and its Presidium.

The role and functions of the Supreme Soviet clearly enhance both the legitimacy of the regime and the stability of the political system. The Supreme Soviet performs significant legitimizing, socializing, codifying, investigating, and monitoring functions. Also, an embryonic ombudsman function appears to be evolving. The continued evolution of these structures and functions could significantly facilitate the Soviet Union's gradual transition to a post-industrial society.

The soviets carry the endorsement of Marx, Lenin, and the Russian Revolutionary tradition. They have been continually endorsed as truly representative of the masses as a whole—the institutional incarnation of popular sovereignty in the Soviet Union. As such, they have conjured up a notion of "dual legitimacy" reminiscent of the concept of "residual legitimacy" inherent in the Slavophiles' idealization of the Zemsky Sobors and sobornost. The notion of direct popular initiative threads through the historical memory of the Vieches, Sobors, the Paris Commune, and the soviets to imbue the Supreme Soviet with a sometimes latent, but significant legitimating influence.

Still further, the increasing lip service paid to codification reflects some concern for the utility of law in the modernization process, thus perhaps incorporating some of the legitimating aura of the Western notion of the rule of law into Soviet law. The emergence of the Supreme Soviet and its auxiliary bodies as major vehicles for the creation of law further enhances their legitimating role.

To sum up, the acts of the Supreme Soviet and its auxiliary bodies, whether they involve converting Party directives into legal norms or monitoring the government apparatus at the Party's behest, add a significant increment of legitimacy to Party policy. This legitimacy is derived from the Supreme Soviet's heritage of:

(1) Marx's co-option of the Paris Commune as the institutional form of proletarian government, which served as the model for the soviets in the 1905 and 1917 Revolutions;

(2) Lenin's adaptation of the soviets first as the instrument of revolution, then of antibureaucratic socialization;

(3) The notion of direct popular initiative and the residual authority of the communal spirit of the Russian people inhering in the Slavophiles' idealization of sobornost as embodied in the zemsky sobors, which is somewhat akin to Marx and Lenin's view of the soviets;

(4) Post-Lenin lipservice to the representativeness of the Supreme Soviet as institutional symbol of socialist democracy;

(5) The osmosis-like filtering into Soviet law of the notion of the rule of law, with its inherent notion of legitimacy.

Thus, the imprimatur of the Supreme Soviet on Party Central Committee directives endows them with a significant increment of authority. This legitimating function inherited by the Supreme Soviet from many sources constitutes a major raison d'etre.

Second, the socializing function of the Supreme Soviet in the election and drafting processes may contribute to public acceptance not only of the regime, but especially of Supreme Soviet legislation itself. The involvement in the creation of laws may strengthen commitment to the specific laws and to the idea of law itself. Thus this socializing function contributes to the stable functioning of the political system.[15] While Western scholars are decrying the demise of the educational function in Western legislatures, the socializing function of the Supreme Soviet is burgeoning.

Third, codification, a major function of the Supreme Soviet and its auxiliary bodies, provides a limited first step toward curbing arbitrary capricious rule—thus potentially further enhancing popular support for the regime and facilitating stability and rationality in the complex interrelationships which characterize postindustrial society. The chimera of codification appears sporadically throughout Russian history. In a sense, the Supreme Soviet and its auxiliary bodies represent the first continually functioning codification commission in Russian history—however rudimentary. Nevertheless, one must not exaggerate their importance, since much norm-creating activity is carried on by the Council of Ministers and is not published—certainly a mitigation of the effect of codification efforts.

Fourth, in theory, the investigating and monitoring functions might facilitate economic efficiency, which is crucial in the long run to the regime's stability and credibility. The modernization process tends to exacerbate still further the monumental problems of bureaucratic inefficiency endemic in Russian and Soviet society. The Supreme Soviet commissions, buttressed by the legal sanction of the Supreme Soviet Presidium, offer some potential for ameliorating these conditions.

Last, the emergence of the Supreme Soviet deputy as an ombudsman of sorts could further enhance support for the regime, providing an instrument for remedying immediate personal grievances resulting from sheer bureaucratic inertia, thereby channeling frustrations which might engender more fundamental complaints which could threaten the regime.

Thus, despite the unavoidable involvement of the Supreme Soviet in factional power struggles, substantial reasons exist for the continued burgeoning of its powers. Its role and functions not only are bulwarks the regime's legitimacy, but also contribute significantly to system maintenance.

More immediately, while at present the Supreme Soviet and its auxiliary bodies may appear to be increasingly used by the Party apparatus as a legal weapon against the government economic apparatus, one should not disregard the prospect of a community of interest developing between monitors and the monitored (a familiar pattern in American administrative tribunals) as each becomes increasingly aware of the other's problems. Since both government and state bodies are increasingly comprised of experts, as distinguished from the ideologues who dominate the Party apparatus, the seeds of a community of interest have been planted. This development would, of course, blunt the watchdog role of the Supreme Soviet and its auxiliaries.

Finally, as a heuristic device for illuminating still further the role of the Supreme Soviet in the context of Soviet politics, and not as an exercise in futurology, let us indulge briefly in conjecture regarding the future development of the Supreme Soviet. Based on the previous analysis, there appear to be five major possibilities.

First, the Supreme Soviet, like the Zemsky Sobor, might become a regressive force, an instrument of a conservative-bureaucratic regime bent on utilizing the monitoring, drafting, and investigating functions to retard creative innovation in the economic or legal bureaucracies of the Soviet polity. This would entail a subtle shift from the present concern for eliminating inefficiency toward mere control.

Second, a coalition of interest groups which executed a coup against the regime might utilize the reservoir of legitimacy residing in the Supreme Soviet to legitimate its action and relegate the increasingly parasitic but influential Party ideologues to a very minor role of rationalizing policy in Marxist-Leninist jargon.

Third, a version of the second scenario might occur through a coalition between Party Central Committee members who sit in the Supreme Soviet and progressive government officials in the Party Central Committee, developing a majority in the Central Committee vis-à-vis Party ideologues, especially with respect to crucial economic and legal problems confronting the Soviet Union. This coalition might actually caucus in the Supreme Soviet or its commissions, thus in effect over a period of time shifting the caucus for policy decisions to the Supreme Soviet.

Fourth, the Supreme Soviet might evolve into a parliament. This is most unlikely. There is no parliamentary tradition in Russian-Soviet history. Russian assemblies tend to emerge as administrative arms of the regime, designed to facilitate the rationalization of administration, pacify the masses with some sort of involvement, and provide the administration with a gauge of public sentiment. The deliberative function finds few roots in Russian-Soviet soil; it bore the brunt of Lenin's repudiation of parliamentarism.

The fifth and most likely possibility is a gradual enhancing of the role of the Supreme Soviet in legitimating moderate reforms in the economic and legal systems through its investigation, monitoring, and drafting functions under the aegis of whatever coalition of interest groups dominates the regime. Its subcommissions, which bring experts and generalists of all kinds together for deliberation, would proliferate and serve to channel some new creative ideas directly to the apex of the regime outside the increasingly stagnant Party and government bureaucracies. Thus, to a certain extent, this would facilitate the slow, creaking progress of the present system and avoid the Scylla of anarchy and the Charybdis of reaction and would culminate in a subtle and gradual transformation, through pragmatic adaptation and adjustment, in contrast to stagnation and even degeneration.

NOTES

INTRODUCTION

1. For another example of legality in the vortex of Soviet politics see Vanneman, Peter (1974) "The Hierarchy of Laws in the Communist Party-State System in the Soviet Union," The International Lawyer, 8, 2 (April), 285–302.

2. Bentley, Arthur F. (1949) The Process of Government (Urbana: University of Illinois Press), p. 178.

3. Kirichenko, M. G. (1950) Vysshie Organy Gosudarstvennoi Vlasti SSSR (Moscow: Izdatel'stvo "Pravda"), p. 20.

4. Kulski, W. W. (1954) The Soviet Regime (Syracuse: Syracuse University Press).

5. Scott, Derek J. R. (1957) Russian Political Institutions (London: Allen & Unwin).

6. Fainsod, Merle (1953) How Russia is Ruled (Cambridge: Harvard University Press), pp. 314–315; Hazard, John N. (1953) Law and Social Change in the USSR (Toronto: Carswell).

7. Webb, Sidney and Webb, Beatrice (1937) Soviet Communism: A New Civilization? Vols. I and II, 2nd ed. (London: Longmans, Green).

8. Carson, George (1955) Electoral Practices in the USSR (New York: Praeger).

9. Towster, Julian (1948) Political Power in the USSR, 1914–1947 (New York: Oxford University Press), pp. 187–198, 250–272.

10. Schapiro, Leonard (1957) The Government and Politics of the Soviet Union (New York: Vintage), p. 114.

11. Aspaturian, Vernon V. (1967) "The Soviet Constitutional Order," in Roy C. Macridis and Robert E. Ward (eds.) Modern Political Systems: Europe, 3rd ed. (Englewood Cliffs, N.J.: Prentice-Hall), p. 575.

12. Juviler, Peter (1959) "The Functions of a Deputy to the Supreme Soviet," Ph.D. dissertation (New York: Columbia University), p. 10.

13. Berman, Harold J. (1963) Justice in the USSR (New York: Vintage) pp. 219, 269.

14. For a more detailed study see Vanneman, Peter (1974) op. cit.

15. Vyshinsky, A. Y. (1948) The Law of the Soviet State, Trans. Hugh W. Babb (New York: Macmillan), pp. 589–590, 683–685.

16. Berman, op. cit., p. 8.

CHAPTER 1

1. Billington, James (1970) The Icon and the Axe (New York: Vintage), p. xii.

2. Kovalevsky, Maxme (1903) Russian Political Institutions: The Growth and Development of These Institutions from the Beginnings of Russian History to the Present Time (Chicago: University of Chicago Press), pp. 14–16. See also Harry Dorosh (1944) Russian Constitutionalism (New York: Exposition Press), pp. 5–14.

3. Riasanovsky, Nicolas V. (1963) A History of Russia (New York: Oxford University Press), pp. 208–211; Billington, op. cit., p. 145; Kovalevsky, op. cit., p. 55.

4. Riasanovsky, op. cit., p. 209; Billington, op. cit., p. 99; each reflects a slightly different interpretation, depending on his period focus. Kluchevsky, V. O. (1912) A History of Russia, trans, by C. J. Hogarth (London: Dent & Son), vol. 1, pp. 288–322, and vol. 2, pp. 64–150, 193–221, provides a detailed account of the major meetings which helps clarify the ambiguity sometimes encountered in these works.

5. Aspaturian, Vernon V. (1972) in "The Soviet Constitutional Order," in Modern Political Systems: Europe, Roy C. Macridis and Robert E. Ward (eds.) 3rd ed. (Englewood Cliffs, N.J.: Prentice-Hall), p. 614.

6. Billington, op. cit., p. 100.

7. Utechin, S. V. (1963) Russian Political Thought (New York: Knopf), pp. 34, 79.

8. Riasanovsky, op. cit., p. 210. The Slavophiles were intellectuals who idealized Russian culture in the nineteenth century.

9. Ibid.

10. Raeff, Marc (1966) Plans for Political Reform in Imperial Russia, 1730–1905 (Englewood Cliffs, N.J.: Prentice-Hall), p. 16.

11. Kovalevsky, op. cit., pp. 99–100.

12. Ibid., p. 100.

13. Ibid., p. 79.

14. Levin, Alfred (1940) The Second Duma (New Haven: Yale University Press). The present analysis of the Duma experience is based on this work and on Levitsky, Serge (1956) "Legislative Initiative in the Russian Duma," Slavic Review, 3.

15. Levin, op. cit., p. 351.

16. This section of Russian legislation reflects Berman, Harold (1963) Justice in the USSR (New York: Vintage), pp. 171–277, as well as the author's legal training.

17. Berman, op. cit., p. 175.

18. This chapter relies heavily on the detailed and brilliant theoretical-institutional analysis of two scholars: Towster, Julian (1948) Political Power in the USSR, 1917–1947 (New York: Oxford University Press), pp. 3–119, 176–296; and Carr, E. H. (1950) The Bolshevik Revolution, 1917–1923, vol. 1 (London: Macmillan). On the Commune, see Jellinek, Frank (1937), The Paris Commune of 1871 (London: Victor Gollancz), pp. 390, 418–419; a somewhat disjointed account of a recent international conference on the Commune from a Marxist viewpoint, "The Paris Commune, 1871–1971," World Marxist Review, 14, 2 (February, 1971), 5; Cognoit, George (1971), "The First Workers' Government," New Times, 11 (March), 13; Carr, op. cit., p. 96; and Towster, op. cit., p. 177.

19. Harcave, Sidney, (1964) The Russian Revolution of 1905 (London: Collier-Macmillan), pp. 12–17, 177.

20. On Lenin's utopian faith in the people, see: Billington, op. cit., p. 529; and Barfield, Rodney (1971) "Lenin's Utopianism: State and Revolution," Slavic Review, 30, 1 (March), 45–56.

21. Carr, op. cit., pp. 15–259, but especially 238–259 which traces Lenin's evolving vision of the soviets.

22. Stalin, J. V. (1942) Leninism: Selected Writings (New York: International Publishers), pp. 278–279, as cited in Aspaturian, V. V. (1960) The Union Republics in Soviet Diplomacy (Geneva: Librarie Droz), p. 24.

23. Towster, op. cit., pp. 183–187.

24. Ibid., pp. 241–242.

25. Carr, op. cit., pp. 90, 91, 95.

26. Ibid., pp. 95–96.

27. Ibid., p. 100.

28. Ibid., pp. 122–133.

29. Towster, op. cit., p. 228.

30. Ibid., p. 227.

31. Turubiner, A. M. (1924) "The Organization of the Presidium of the CEC," Sovetskoye Pravo, 2, 126–128; Izvestia, June 22, 1918, p. 1.

32. Towster, op. cit., pp. 241–249.

33. Ibid., pp. 225–235.

34. Dobrin. S. (1956) "Some Questions of Early Soviet Legal History," Soviet Studies, 7, 4 (April), 353–371, describes the Democratic Centrists' efforts to strengthen the CEC and its Presidium.

35. Carr, op. cit., p. 157.

36. Ibid.

37. Ibid., p. 245.

38. Ibid., p. 250.

39. Little, Richard (1971), "Legislative Authority in the Soviet Political System," Slavic Review, 30, 1 (March), 59.

40. Towster, op. cit., p. 249.

41. Rabkrin is an acronym for Workers and Peasants Inspection. This body was the precursor of the Peoples' Control Commissions.

42. Carr, op. cit., pp. 230–234.

CHAPTER 2

1. Constitution of the USSR. English version, as amended in 1970 (Moscow: Progress Publishers, 1970).

2. Ibid.

3. The emphasis on law as an instrument for creating the material and technical basis of communism is evidenced in the following: Khalfina, R. O. (1970), "Law as an Impetus to Raise the Efficiency of Socialist Production," and Tolstoi, Yu. K. (1970) "Soviet Civil Legislation and Its Implementation, Promotion and Development," both in Sovetskoye gosudarstvo i pravo, vol. 11 (November).

4. Amendment of February 25, 1947, S.S. III/5/53, p. 327. The stenographic reports of the Supreme Soviet are published in Moscow by Izdanie Verkhovnovo Soveta SSSR, in a series of volumes entitled Zasedania Verknovnovo Soveta SSSR. Such references are abbreviated as above, meaning Supreme Soviet, third convocation, fifth session, published in the year 1953 at page indicated. Published reports in Zasedania are usually three years late; in the early convocations they were often later.

5. Chkikvadze, V. M. (1968) The Soviet State and Law (Moscow: Progress Publishers), p. 81.

6. An example of such treatment is: Chekharin, A. M. (1970) "Political System of Soviet Society: Some Theoretical Aspects," Sovetskoye gosudarstvo i pravo 9 (September).

7. Bovin, A. (1962) "From the State of the Dictatorship of the Proletariat to the All-People's State," Kommunist (March), pp. 20–30, is a succinct expression of the general line.

8. "Law and Legality at the Present Stage of Communist Construction" (1970), Sovetskoye gosudarstvo i pravo, 10, expresses the early line and does not seem to represent the present line.

9. Chkikvadze, V. M. (1966) "The Development of the National Essence of the Socialist State," Sovetskoye gosudarstvo i pravo, 10, 3–15.

10. Grigoryan, A. (1969) "Socialist State Power and Representative Form of its Realization," Sovetskoye gosudarstvo i pravo, 3, identifies state power with political power, distinguished only by a special organization, apparatus, and methods. G. V. Barabashev and K. F. Sheremet (1967), "The CPSU and the Soviets," Sovetskoye gosudarstvo i pravo, 11, mention that the Supreme Soviet constantly deals with political questions.

11. Platkovsky, V. V. (1970) "The Party as a Leading Force in the Socialist State," Sovetskoye gosudarstvo i pravo, 8; and Chekharin, op cit.

12. Chkikvadze (1971) op. cit., and Manov, G. N. (1966) "The Soviet State as a

Principal Instrument for Building Socialism and Communism," Sovetskoye gosudarstvo i pravo, 5, 81. In the guise of a polemic against anarchism Manov reiterates that the state is the center of the socialist political system.

13. Chkikvadze (1968) op. cit., p. 14 (emphasis added).

14. Andrianov, N. Y. (1964) "On Legislative Initiative," Sovetskoye gosudarstvo i pravo, 9.

15. For a recent discussion of the concept as the theoretical bulwark of socialist democracy, see: Chernobel, C. T. (1970), "The Concept of People's Sovereignty," Sovetskoye gosudarstvo i pravo, 8.

16. Vyshinsky, Andrei Y. (1948) The Law of the Soviet State, trans. by Hugh W. Babb (New York: MacMillan), p. 311.

17. Ibid., p. 337, note 6.

18. Chkikvadze (1968) op. cit., p. 81.

19. The interpretations presented in this section are a summary of many Soviet sources, the most rewarding of which are: Kuznetsov, I. N. (1968) Kompetensia organoz zlasti i upravlenia SSSR (Moscow), especially pp. 1–30, 46–60, and 99–104; Chkikvadze, V. M. (1968) op. cit., especially pp. 218–249; and Mitskevich, A. V. (1967) Akty organov sovetskogo gosudurstva (Moscow). Kuznetsov is a "middle of the road" jurist, if one may use such a term: neither a "reformer" nor a hard-line ideologue. His writings span the decade of moderate reforms, 1959-69; the above is his most recent work; see: Mitskevich, A. V. (1967) Akty vysskikh organov (Moscow), p. 98; Barabashev, G. V. and K. F. Sheremet (1965) Sovetskoye stroitel'stvo (Moscow), pp. 76–77, on coexstensive jurisdiction.

20. Bespaly, I. T. (1959) Prezidium verkhovnogo soveta sojuznoi respubliki (Moscow), pp. 8–10.

21. Kuznetsov, I. N. (1966) "Kompetensia prezidium verkhovnogo soveta SSSR i pravovye problemy ee reylamentatsii," Uchenye zapisi VNIISZ 1966, no. 8, p. 11; Kuznetsov presents this view rather clearly in this work. In his two other works, (1) Kuznetsov (1968) op. cit., pp. 99–127, and (2) "K voprosu o iuridicheskoi prirode ukuza prezidiuma verkhovnogo soveta SSSR i yego sootnoshenii zakonom," in Voprosy sovetskogo gosudarstvennogo (Moscow, 1959), pp. 235–238, written a decade apart, he is ambivalent. In the earlier work he seems to have backtracked from the 1966 view.

22. Kuznetsov (1966) op. cit.

23. Ibid.

24. Kuznetsov (1968) op. cit., pp. 99–127.

25. Kuznetsov (1966) op. cit., p. 11. Here Kuznetsov deviates from the main thrust of his writings in suggesting that, at least in one area, the Presidium has independent jurisdiction. In a very narrow sense, he yields to Bespaly, op. cit.

26. Barabashev and Sheremet, op. cit., pp. 76–77, is a recent expression of this view; Kravtsov, B. P. (1954) Verkhovni sovet SSSR, (Moscow), p. 78, is an older version of the same viewpoint.

27. Kuznetsov (1968) op. cit., pp. 140–152. See also, Bratus, S. N. and Samoshchenko, I. S. (1966) Obshehaia teoriia sovetskogo prava (Moscow), p. 144.

28. The classic statement of the alleged representative nature of the Presidium appears in Chkikvadze (1968) op. cit., p. 132.

29. Aspaturian, Vernon V. (1960) The Union Republics in Soviet Diplomacy (Geneva: Institute of International Studies), pp. 82, 127–128, and 200.

30. See Aspaturian, ibid., for a more complete discussion of the political as well as the legal complexities of Soviet federalism.

31. Chkikvadze (1968) op. cit., p. 222.

32. For a more detailed analysis of the Soviet hierarchy of laws see: Vanneman, Peter (1974) "The Hierarchy of Laws in the Soviet Communist Party-State System," The International Lawyer (April). Some partial Soviet attempts at classifying laws are: Denison, A. I. (1960) Vazhnyi etap razvitii Sovetskogo prava (VII u N), (Moscow). For a rather

sophisticated but brief exercise in legal classification, see Koslova, E. I. (1971) "Representative Organs of State Power in the USSR: Rules of Procedure," Sovetskoye gosudarstvo i
pravo, no. 1, 85–90. For a brief summary, see Shebanov, A. F. (1967) "The Various Forms
of Soviet Law," Sovetskoye gosudarstvo i pravo, pp. 22–31. A more detailed but rather
vague and ambiguous study is Mitskevich, A. V. Akty vysshikh . . . , op. cit. (Moscow);
Sadikov, O. N. (1971) "General and Special Norms in Civil Law," Sovetskoye gosudarstvo i
pravo, 1, attempts to clarify the distinction between broad norms and detailed implementive
laws. For a German effort see V. Meder, (1956) "Die Hierarchie der Rechtsquellen in der
Sowjetunion," Osteurope-Recht 2, 167–175.

33. Chkikvadze (1968) op. cit., p. 227.

34. Ibid., p. 232.

35. Two decrees of 1941 established commissariats (for rubber industry and for machine tool building), but the decrees were not confirmed by law of the Supreme Soviet until
its March 1946 session. Zasedania Verkhovnogo Soveta SSSR (Pervaya Sessia), Steno-
graficheskii Otchet (Moscow, 1946), pp. 33–37.

36. Barabashev, and Sheremet, op. cit. pp. 33–37.

37. Shebanov, op. cit.

38. Ibid.

39. See below, Chapter 8.

40. Ibid.

41. Zasedania Verkhovnogo Soveta SSSR: Sed'mogo sozyva, Third Session, Stenographic Report (Moscow: 1967), pp. 415–424.

42. Ibid. See below, Chapter 8 for a detailed discussion.

43. Ibid.

CHAPTER 3

1. The author wishes to thank Jerry Hough for permission to include these comments
from a forthcoming piece honoring Merle Fainsod. For a further relevant commentary,
which compares the relative roles of legislatures in legitimating political systems, see
Gilison, Jerome (1972) British and Soviet Politics (New York: Random House).

2. Rigby, Thomas H. (1953) "Changing composition of the Supreme Soviet," The
Political Quarterly 24 (July–Sept.), 309.

3. Ibid.

4. Ibid., p. 313.

5. Juviler, Peter (1959) "The functions of a deputy to the Supreme Soviet," Ph.D.
dissertation (New York, Columbia University), p. 131.

6. Clarke, Roger A. (1967) "Composition of the USSR Supreme Soviet: 1958–66,"
Soviet Studies 60, 1 (July), 58.

7. Bilinsky, Yaroslav (1967) "The rulers and the ruled," Problems of Communism 16, 5
(Sept.–Oct.), 23.

8. Clarke, op. cit., p. 63.

9. Chkikvadze, V. M. (1968) The Soviet State and Law (Moscow: Progress Publishers),
p. 1.

10. Carson, George Barr, Jr. (1955) Electoral Practices in the USSR (New York:
Praeger), is the most often cited.

11. USSR Constitution: Articles 47, 49d, and 54.

12. USSR Constitution: Articles 54, 47, and 49d.

13. Electoral Law: Articles 36, 40, 44, 48, and 51.

14. Kalinychev (1966) Soviet Socialist Democracy (Moscow), p. 87.

15. Juviler, op. cit., p. 505.

16. For a description of such a meeting and speech by a Western observer, see Black, Cyril (1958) "Soviet life today," Foreign Affairs 36 (July), 572–572.

17. Izvestia during the 1950 election campaign clearly reveals these three salient themes.

18. Aspaturian, Vernon (1967) "The Soviet Constitutional Order," in Roy C. Macridis and Robert E. Ward (eds.) Modern Political Systems: Europe, 3rd ed.

19. Schapiro, Leonard (1967) The Government and Politics of the Soviet Union, rev. ed. (New York: Random House), p. 107.

20. Gilison, Jerome (1968) "Soviet elections as a measure of dissent: the missing one percent," American Political Science Review (Sept.), 816.

CHAPTER 4

1. Most of this descriptive data on the sessions is gathered from Zasedania, which is rather unrewarding reading after one has read the reports of one or two sessions. Citations will be used whenever a specific event is alluded to which does not appear in most of the stenographic reports.

2. Kareva, M. P. and Fedkin, G. I. (eds.) (1956) Osnovy sovetskogo gosudarstva i prava, 3rd ed. (Moscow), p. 127.

3. Agranovsky, Anatoly (1971) "Soviet Parliament, A Working Body," World Marxist Review (May), p. 78.

4. Aspaturian, (1967) "The Soviet Constitutional Order," in Roy C. Macridis and Robert E. Ward, (eds.) Modern Political Systems: Europe 3rd ed. (Englewood Cliffs, N.J.: Prentice-Hall), p. 575.

5. S.S., II/1/38, p. 648.

6. This account and quotation appear in Agranovsky, op. cit., p. 85.

7. S.S., I/1/38, pp. 136–137.

8. Ibid., p. 153, carries Molotov's reply.

9. Saifulin, M. (1967) The Soviet Parliament (Moscow), p. 50.

10. Ibid.

11. Pravda and Izvestia, March 28, 1958, p. 1, provide an example of the first session paradigm, which since that day has hardly varied at all.

12. S.S., IV/1/54, pp. 8–9.

13. For example, in the "model" fifth convocation, Voroshilov nominated Khrushchev as Premier and the latter presented the government list later; Pravda, April 1, 1958, p. 1.

14. Smirnov, G. (1967) Pravda, December 4, pp. 2–3.

15. S.S., I/1/38, p. 7.

16. Ibid., p. 56.

17. Ibid., pp. 138–139.

18. Ibid., pp. 49–50, records both of the first two non-unanimous votes.

19. Ibid., and S.S. II/1/46, S.S. III/1/50.

20. S.S., I/1/38, p. 56.

21. S.S., I/2/38, p. 43.

22. Dohzhenko, A., M. Isaliev, and G. Tikhov (1956) "O sessiakh Verkhovnogo Soveta respubliki," Izvestia, February 9.

23. Editorial, "Za polnoe osushchestvovanie leninskikh printsipov sovetskoi demo-kratii," Sovetskoye gosudarstvo i pravo, 3 (May, 1956), 6.

24. Ibid., 6–7.

25. Ibid.

26. Pisotkin, M. I. (1956) "Obiodzhetnikh pravakh verkhovnogo soveta SSSR," Sovet-skoye gosudarstvo i pravo, 7, 16–21.

27. Ibid. See also pp. 146–147.

28. S.S., IV/4/55.

29. XX S'ezd . . . , Vol. I, 1956, p. 92.

30. Ibid.

31. New York Times, June 29, 1956, p. 10.

32. Romashkin, P. (1957) Pravda, March 8, pp. 1, 3.

33. The reports of leading officials to the 23rd and 24th Party Congresses continued to stress these same themes.

34. Agranovsky, op. cit., p. 79.

35. Podgorny, N. V. (1966) Izvestia, August 3, p. 3.

36. Planovoye khozyaistvo, 1970, No. 1, pp. 7, 8.

37. Voprosy ekonomiki, 1970, No. 3.

CHAPTER 5

1. Shorina, E. V. (1969) "Functions and Control in the Soviet State," Sovetskoye gosudarstvo i pravo, 11, 30–38; the abstruse official version of the "kontrol" concept is described here. See also Table 4.2, Chapter 4.

2. Izvestia, July 30, 1970, pp. 1, 3, discusses the concept of supreme "kontrol."

3. Ibid.

4. Vaciliev, V. I. (1970) "The Development of Soviets as a Social System" Sovetskoye gosudarstvo i pravo, 11, 92–100, presents the argument for further integrating the pyramid while expanding activities at all levels.

5. See, for example, Serenko, A. F. and N. G. Salisheva, "Law and Protection of People's Health," Sovetskoye gosudarstvo i pravo, 10 (1970), 19–27, which describes an example of the concurrent legislative process.

6. Izvestia, January 26, 1968, p. 3, describes how the Presidium of the Azerbaidzhan Republic Supreme Soviet exercises its control over local soviets, and how it is subject to the Presidium of the Supreme Soviet of the USSR.

7. Samsonov, B. I. (1961) "Deputatskaya deyatelnost v izberatelnom okruge," Sovetskoye gosudarstvo i pravo, 6, 94. Here the author, a deputy, portrays his role as a connecting link between the Supreme Soviet and local soviets.

8. Saifulin, M. (1967) The Soviet Parliament (Moscow), p. 137.

9. Krivenko, L. T. (1970) "The Standing Commissions and the Ministries," Sovetskoye gosudarstvo i pravo, 1, translated in Soviet Law and Government (Winter, 1970–71), 240.

10. Sheremet, K. Izvestia, February, 6, 1971, p. 2.

11. Izvestia, July 30, 1970, p.3.

12. Puusepp, P. Vice-Chairman of Presidium of Estonian Republic Supreme Soviet, Izvestia, January 25, 1959, p. 3.

13. Sheremet, K., loc. cit., p. 2. See also J. Hough, The Soviet Prefects: The Local Party Organs in Industrial Decision-Making (Cambridge: Harvard University Press, 1969).

14. Pravda, November 25, 1970, p. 3.

15. Stepanov, A. and V. Iunevichias (1963) "Years of Great and Fruitful Activity," Sovety deputatov trudyashchikhsya, 3, 9–12, describes the expansion from 1959–63; M. S. Binder and M. A. Sharif, "The Union-Republic Supreme Soviet and Guidance of the National Economy," Sovetskoye gosudarstov i pravo, 11 (1965), 11–18, suggests a greater budget role.

16. Avakyan, S. S. (1970) "Union Republic Supreme Soviets' Contribution to the Progress and Development of Legislation on Local Soviets," Sovietskoye gosudarstvo i

pravo, 5, 17–25, suggests that the lower supreme soviets should have exclusive power over local soviets.

17. "Deputaty i zhizn," Izvestia, December 29, 1966, p. 5.

18. Pravda, December 5, 1968, p. 2.

19. Izvestia, January 26, 1968, p. 3.

20. Lazarev, B. M. (1970) "Exclusive Powers of Local Executives," Sovetskoye gosudarstvo i pravo, 8, 101–118, describes the dual lines of authority.

21. Izvestia, April 30, 1968, p. 3.

22. Semin, V. P. (1969) "The Ministry in a Union Republic and Local Soviets," Sovetskoye gosudarstvo i pravo, 9, 19–30, describes aspects of ministry control over local soviets.

23. Brezhnev, L. I. (1971), Report to the Twenty-fourth CPSU Congress, Current Digest of the Soviet Press, 23, 14 (May 4), 4.

24. Sheremet, K., Izvestia, February 6, 1971, p. 2 (Emphasis added).

25. Towster, op. cit., p. 274.

26. Ibid.

27. Ibid.

28. Ibid,. p. 260.

29. Ibid., p. 252.

30. Ibid.

31. Ibid., p. 255–256.

32. Ibid.

33. Ibid., p. 259.

34. Novikov, S. G. (1963) "Uchastiye nauchnoi obshchestvennosti v rabote kommissii zakonodutelnykh predlozheny verkhovnogo soveta SSSR po podgotovke zakonoproektov," Sovetskoye gosudarstvo i pravo, 12, 56–60.

35. Krivenko, op. cit., p. 249.

36. Kolzhenko, A., M. Isaliev, and G. Tikhov (1956) (Kazakh supreme soviet deputies), Izvestia, February 9, p. 1.

37. Pravda and Izvestia, June 3, 1970, pp. 1–3.

38. Ukaz of the Presidium of the Supreme Soviet, July 1966, as described in Pravda, July 27, 1966, p. 1.

39. Izvestia, June 5, 1966, p. 5.

40. Article 49c, USSR Constitution; D. Richard Little, "Legislative Authority in the Soviet Political System," Slavic Review, 30, 1 (March, 1971), 63, argues that the power of interpretation (*dat tolkovanie*) is exercised only at the initiative of the Procuracy or the Supreme Court, but he does not cite any evidence to support this contention.

41. Pravda and Izvestia, June 3, 1970, p. 1.

42. Krivenko, op. cit., pp. 243–244.

43. Dolzhenko, A., M. Isaliev, and G. Tikhov, Izvestia, loc. cit. p. 1. This article called for more active "kontrol" of republic procurators by republic supreme soviets, and there is some evidence that activity did increase.

44. Chkikvadze, V. M. (1968) Sovetskoye gosudarstvo i pravo (Moscow: Progress Publishers), pp. 172–177.

45. Ibid.

46. Schwarz, Solomon (1962) "Is the State Withering Away in the USSR?" in Leonard Shapiro (ed.) The USSR and the Future (New York: Praeger), pp. 161–178, describes the evolution of this debate.

47. Kanet, Roger (1968) "The Rise and Fall of the All-Peoples State," Soviet Studies, 20 (July), 83–93, describes the evolution of this debate.

48. Chkikvadze, op. cit., p. 176.

49. Ibid., p. 177.

50. Varchuk, V. V. and V. I. Kazin (1968) Voprosy Filosofii, 4 (April), 134–143, is a

bibliography of the Soviet sources debating the relationship of the soviets to the mass organs. Compare A. Bawlin, Izvestia, March 1, 1959, p. 3. The former stresses the role of the mass organs, the latter that of the soviets as coordinators and directors of the mass organs.

51. The lengthy commentary of Brezhnev at the Twenty-Fourth Party Congress is ample evidence of the continued influence of the trade unions as an independent institution. Brezhnev, op. cit.

52. Pravda and Izvestia, June 3, 1970, p. 1.

53. Chkikvadze, op. cit., p. 235.

54. (1965) Vedomosti prezidiuma verkhovnogo soveta SSSR (Gazette of the Supreme Soviet of the USSR), No. 49, Article 718, December 15, contains the Ukaz; see also Chkikvadze, op. cit., p. 157.

55. Pravda and Izvestia, June 3, 1970, p. 1.

56. Krivenko, op. cit., p. 249. See also Agranovsky, Anatoly (1971) "Soviet Parliament, A Working Body," World Marxist Review (May), p. 84, where it is suggested that deputies have the right to demand access to People's Control files.

57. Kaluzhin, V. (Vice-Chairman of the USSR People's Control Commission) (1967) "People's Control and the Local Soviets," Sovety deputatov trudyashchikhsya, 12 (December), 18–24.

CHAPTER 6

1. (1970) Constitution of the USSR, English translation (Moscow), Articles 50 and 51.

2. There is some evidence despite Soviet authorities that the leading role of the LPC has been substantially curbed with the elevation of some former subcommissions to the status of full-fledged Branch or Sectoral Commissions.

3. Izvestia, October 13, 1967, p. 2 (zakon on the permanent commissions, Article 10).

4. See the discussion of the legislative function in the following chapter.

5. Izvestia, October 13, 1967, p. 2 (zakon on the permanent commissions), see both Article 11 and Article 13, Section 4.

6. Ibid.

7. Ibid.

8. Pravda, July 14, 1966, p. 1.

9. Izvestia, August 23, 1969, p. 1.

10. Saifulin, M. (1967) The Soviet Parliament (Moscow: Progress Publishers), p. 134.

11. Makhnenko, op. cit., pp. 56–66. Here in 1964 the author argues for that which was done in 1967—i.e., codification de jure of the de facto commission system.

12. The law creating the new sectoral commissions of the Supreme Soviet is published in Zasedania Verkhovnogo Soveta SSSR: Sed'mogo sozyva, Third session, Stenographic Report (Moscow: 1967), pp. 415–424. A translation is found in Current Digest of the Soviet Press, 19, 4 (November 22, 1967), 22–25. The law was also published in Izvestia, (Supplementary Edition), October 13, 1967, p. 2.

13. Izvestia, February 12, 1957, p. 1 (decree of the Council of Nationalities creating the Economic Commission of the Council of Nationalities), p. 2, lists the membership.

14. Ibid.

15. Ivashchenko, O. I. (1962) "The Activity of the Economic Commission of the USSR Supreme Soviet of Nationalities and Its Further Improvement in the Light of the CPSU Program," Sovetskoye gosudarstvo i pravo, 4 (April), 32–45.

16. A translation of Khrushchev's Central Committee Report to the Twentieth Party Congress in which he refers to the Economic Commission is found in Leo Gruilow, eds., Current Soviet Politics: The Documentary Record of the Twentieth Congress of the CPSU (New York: Praeger, 1957), p. 52.

17. Schapiro, Leonard (1967) The Government and Politics of the Soviet Union, rev. ed. (New York: Vintage), pp. 133–138, esp. pp. 134 and 138.

18. See the decree creating the Commission, Izvestia, October 13, 1967, p. 1, and compare the decree creating the Legislative Proposals Commission, Izvestia, February 27, 1947, p. 1, esp. Section 5.

19. Ivashchenko, op. cit., pp. 45–48.

20. Izvestia, August 3, 1966, p. 3, Podgorny discusses formation of the new Supreme Soviet commission system.

21. Kutafin, O. Ye. (1966) "Mutual Relations of the Standing Commissions of the Chambers of the USSR Supreme Soviet with the Presidium of the USSR Supreme Soviet and with the USSR Council of Ministers," Sovetskoye gosudarstvo i pravo, 4 (April), 32–40. This article initiated the debate soon joined by Mandelshstam, Izvestia, July 30, 1966, p. 3, who roundly criticizes Kutafin.

22. Kutafin, op. cit., pp. 37–40, provides the basis of the following discussion of the Economic Commission of the Council of Nationalities.

23. Ibid., and the decree creating the Legislative Proposals Commission, op. cit., Section 5.

24. Kutafin, op. cit., pp. 37–38.

25. See, for example, Izvestia, December 26, 1965, p. 2.

26. Kutafin, op. cit., pp. 32–40.

27. Solomentsev, M. S. (1967) Izvestia (Supplementary Edition), October 13, p. 5.

28. Makhnenko, A. Kh. (1964) "Increasing the Role and Improving the Activity of Standing Commissions of the Supreme Soviet in the Field of Drafting Laws," Sovetskoye gosudarstvo i pravo, 8, 55–58.

29. The official line on the drafting process is spelled out in an interview with R. N. Nishanov, Chairman of the Legislative Proposals Commission of the Council of Nationalities (seventh convocation), in Komsomolskaya Pravda, December 5, 1967, p. 1.

30. Saifulin, op. cit., p. 53.

31. Polyansky, D. S. (Chairman of Legislative Proposals Commission) (1962) Interview, Komsomolskaya Pravda, March 18, p. 2; Saifulin, op. cit., p. 134.

32. Smirnov, A. (1963) "The Organization of the Work of the Budget Commissions of the USSR Supreme Soviet," Sovety deputatov trudyashchikhsya, 3 (March), 96–100.

33. Novikov, S. G. (1963) "Participation of the Scientific Community in the Work of the USSR Supreme Soviet Commission of Legislative Proposals," Sovetskoye gosudarstvo i pravo, 12 (December), 56–66, describes the role of technical experts at every phase of the legislative process.

34. Ibid.

35. Ustinov, G. (1966) Izvestia, January 9, p. 2, describes an even smaller working group for the reformulation of draft bills than the subcommissions. These "editorial groups" apparently meet in secret.

36. Ibid., Article 5 (forbids members of Council of Ministers on commissions), Articles 25 and 35 (allow co-option of representatives of ministries, as well as experts from institutes, onto commissions).

37. Izvestia, January 9, 1966, p. 2, reports that a session of a subcommission of the joint Legislative Proposals Commissions was chaired by I. K. Mineyev, USSR Deputy Minister of Geology. The bill discussed related to regulation of the use of minerals. The report indicates that opinions were exchanged, but does not specify their content. The bill was ultimately referred to a smaller group within the subcommission, which presumably met in secret under Article 33 (sectoral commissions law, ibid.) which authorizes secret sessions. See also Izvestia, August 21, 1969, p. 2, which lists a considerable number of ministry officials taking part in the Commission on Construction and the Building Materials Industry.

38. Izvestia (Article 5), October 13, 1967, p. 2.

39. Ibid. (Article 35).

40. Ibid. (Article 26).

41. Chkikvadze, V. M. (1968), Sovetskoye gosudarstvo i pravo (Moscow), pp. 223–225.

42. Izvestia, October 13, 1967, p. 2.

43. Ibid. (Article 10).

44. Ibid. (Article 11).

45. Ibid.

46. Ibid. (Article 16).

47. Andrianov, Y. Ye. (1964) "On Legislative Initiative," Sovetskoye gosudarstvo i pravo, 9, 53–63; Chkikvadze, op. cit., p. 223.

48. Chkikvadze, op. cit., p. 223.

49. Andrianov, op. cit., pp. 57, 61.

50. Lepeshkin, A. I. et. al. (1962) Kurs Sovetskogo Gosudarstvennogo Prava, Vol. 2 (Moscow), 411.

51. Chkikvadze, op. cit.; Andrianov, op. cit.

52. Andrianov, op. cit.

53. See, for example, S. G. Novikov, "Uchastiye nauchnoi obshchestvennosti v rabote kommissii zakonodatelnykh predlozheny Verknovnogo Soveta SSSR po podgotovke zakonoproektou," Sovetskoye gosudarstvo i pravo, 12 (1963), 56–58.

54. Bratus, S. N. and I. S. Samoschenko (1964) "The Role of VNIISZ in Drafting Soviet Laws," Sovetskoye gosudarstvo i pravo, 4, 58–59.

55. Ibid.

56. Ibid.

57. Agranovsky, Anatoly (1971) "The Soviet Parliament, a Working Body," World Marxist Review (May), 78–79.

58. Ibid.

59. Saifulin, op. cit., p. 134.

60. Agranovsky, op. cit., p. 85.

61. Novikov, op. cit., pp. 58, 62.

62. Saifulin, op. cit., p. 134.

63. Ibid.

64. See, H. J. Berman, "The Struggle of Soviet Jurists Against a Return to Stalinist Terror," Slavic Review, 22 (1963), 314–319; Agranovsky, op. cit., p. 80 Novikov, op. cit.; Saifulin, op. cit., pp. 133–136.

65. Agranovsky, op. cit., pp. 80–81.

66. Schapiro, Leonard (ed). (1963) The USSR and the Future: An Analysis of the New Program of the CPSU (New York: Praeger), p. 298. Reporting of commission sessions is now frequent in the press; for a recent example, see Izvestia, November 19, 1970, which discusses activities at various commission sessions.

67. Saifulin, op. cit., p. 135.

68. Chkikvadze, V. M. (1968) Sovetskoye gosudarstvo i pravo (Moscow), p. 225.

69. Saifulin, op. cit., p. 130.

70. Spiridonov, I., Chairman of the Soviet of the Union (1970) "Socialist Democracy," New Times, 21 (May), 5.

71. Schapiro, op. cit., p. 315.

72. Polyansky, D. S., op. cit., p. 2.

73. Makhnenko, op. cit., pp. 56–66.

74. Novikov, S. G. (1966) "On Further Improvement of the Work of the Commissions for Legislative Proposals of the Chambers of the USSR Supreme Soviet," Sovetskoye gosudarstvo i pravo, 10, 16–24.

75. Kutafin, op. cit., pp. 38–40.

76. Izvestia, Editorial, August 23, 1969, p. 1., reviews the new commissions activities since their creation (1966–1969), stressing the monitoring function.

77. Zasedania, op. cit., Articles 1, 2, 22, 23, and 27 spell out the monitoring function.

78. Ibid., Article 24.

79. Ibid., Article 23. For a discussion of "proposals" and "recommendations" see L. T. Krivenko, "The Standing Commissions and the Ministries," Sovetskoye gosudarstvo i pravo, 1 (1970), translated in Soviet Law and Government (Winter, 1970), 240–256.

80. Krivenko, op. cit., p. 244.

81. Ibid.

82. Saifulin, op. cit., pp. 67 and 59.

83. Zasedania, op. cit., Article 37.

84. Kutafin, op. cit., pp. 37–38.

85. Mandelshstam, L. (1966) "Istina i domysly," Izvestia, July 30, p. 3.

86. Chkikvadze, V. M. (ed.) (1969) The Soviet State and Law (Moscow: Progress Publishers), pp. 119–127.

87. Ibid., p. 230.

88. Binder, M. A. and M. A. Sharif (1965) "The Union Republic Supreme Soviet and Guidance of the National Economy," Sovetskoye gosudarstvo i pravo, 11 (November), 11–18.

89. Zasedania, op. cit., Article 23.

90. For example, see the Armenian SSR.

91. Krivenko, op. cit., p. 242.

CHAPTER 7

1. (1970) Constitution of the USSR (English), as amended by the Seventh Session of the Seventh Supreme Soviet (Moscow: Foreign Language Publishing House).

2. Stalin, J. V. (1936) O Proekte Konstitutsii Soiuza S.S.R. (Moscow). Since the intelligentsia is not mentioned in the Constitution it has no formal legal status, although Stalin mentioned it favorably in the above.

3. Stalin, J. V. (1948) Report to the 18th CPSU Congress, translated in Julian Towster, Political Power in the USSR–1917-1947 (New York: Oxford University Press), p. 12: "We are going ahead toward Communism. Will our state remain in the period of Communism also? Yes, it will, unless the capitalist encirclement is liquidated, and unless the danger of foreign military attack has disappeared.... No, it will not remain and atrophy if the capitalist encirclement is liquidated and a Socialist encirclement takes its place. That is how the question stands with regard to the Socialist state."

4. Stalin, J. V., (1950) Leninism: Selected Writings (Moscow), pp. 278–279.

5. For a discussion of the representativeness of the Supreme Soviet's composition, see chapter 3.

6. Vyshinsky, Andrei Y. (1948) The Law of the Soviet State, trans. by H. W. Babb (New York: Macmillan), p. 311.

7. Ibid., p. 310.

8. For the history of the Zemsky Sobor see Chapter 1.

9. Vyshinsky, op. cit., pp. 352–356.

10. Ibid., p. 318.

11. Ibid., p. 309.

12. Ibid., p. 311.

13. Ibid., p. 326.

14. Stalin, J. V. O Proekte, op. cit., p. 40.

15. Aspaturian, Vernon V. (1968) "The Soviet Union," in Roy C. Macridis and Robert E. Ward (eds.) Modern Political Systems: Europe, 2nd ed. (Englewood Cliffs, N.J.: Prentice-Hall), p. 566.

16. Vyshinsky, op. cit., p. 325.

17. Fainsod, Merle (1953) How Russia is Ruled (Cambridge: Harvard University Press), p. 313.

18. Towster, op. cit., pp. 183–186, formulates and discusses the barometer concept.

19. Ibid., p. 186.

20. On this distinction, see Richard E. Dawson and Kenneth Prewitt, Political Socialization (Boston: Little, Brown, 1969); and Karl Deutsch, Science Review, 3 (September 1961), 493–514.

21. Schapiro, Leonard (ed.) (1963) The USSR and the Future: An Analysis of the New Program of the CPSU (New York: Praeger), pp. 170–171.

22. Ibid.

23. BSE (7) 1951, pp. 535–536.

24. Schapiro, op. cit., p. 298.

25. Ibid.

26. (1967) Zasedania Verkhovnogo Soveta SSSR: Sed'mogo Sozyva, Third Session, Stenographic Report (Moscow), pp. 415–424.

27. (1970) Article 51, Constitution of the Union of Soviet Socialist Republics (Moscow: Foreign Languages Publishing House).

28. Izvestia (Supplementary Edition), October 13, 1967, p. 2; see articles 26 and 27.

29. Vedomosti Verkhovnogo Soveta SSSR, No. 17, April 24, 1968, Item No. 145, pp. 248–249.

30. Ibid., Item No. 144, Article 16, p. 248. For text and commentary, see Izvestia, April 26, 1968, pp. 1 and 3. The commentary discusses the problems of red tape and bureaucracy.

31. Izvestia, June 3, 1970, p. 1.

32. Gellhorn, op. cit., pp 367–370, esp. p. 370.

33. Fainsod, op. cit.

34. Aspaturian, op. cit., pp. 201–203.

35. Smirnov, G., Pravda, December 4, 1967, pp. 2–3.

36. Kommunist, 10 (August 1956), 3–15.

37. Aspaturian, op. cit., p. 202.

38. Izvestia, May 7, 1960, p. 1; Pravda, May 8, 1960, p. 1.

39. Pravda, January 15, 1960, p. 1.

40. Aspaturian, op. cit., p. 203.

41. Istoriya Diplomatii, 3, 765.

42. USSR Constitution, Article 49.

43. Ibid.

44. Saifulin, op. cit., pp. 70–73.

45. Ibid.

46. Aspaturian, op. cit., p. 203.

47. Saifulin, op. cit., pp. 142–144.

48. Between December 1955 and March 1958, 1,302 deputies, or more than 96 percent, were members. "Otchet o deitel'nosti parlamentskoi gruppoi SSSR Mezduparlamentskogo Soiuza za period s 29 junia po 31 dekabria, 1955 goda," Biulleten' Parlamentskoi Gruppi SSSR Mezduparlamentskogo Souiza (henceforth, Biulleten) 1 (June 1956), 7. A. Lebedeva, Parlamentskoi gruppoi Sovetskogo Souiza (Moscow: Izdatel'stvo Instituta Mezdunarodnykh Ostnoshenii, 1958), p. 10. By the seventh convocation all Supreme Soviet deputies were members of the UPG, Saifulin, pp. 139–141.

The Belorussian and Ukrainian deputies did not join at first; they formed groups in their separate republics to maintain the fiction of their separateness. (Biulleten, 7–8). Apparently, dues have fallen from ten to one ruble (Biulleten and Saifulin, op. cit., pp. 139–141.)

49. (1958) "V Parlamentskoi gruppe SSSR," Pravda, December 27; and Biulleten, 4 (1958), 27.

50. Saifulin, op. cit., p. 141.

51. The 21-man commission elected in 1955 included: 10 central and the republic party

and state officials; 1 republic trade union official; 9 writers and academicians and administrative responsibility; 1 unknown. The commission elected March 29, 1958, totalled 32, including: 15 party and state officials above the district level; 2 republic trade union officials; 1 Komsomol official; nine academicians, writers (including one composer), all with administrative responsibilities; one kolkhoz chairman; one engineer; two foremen or workers; one teacher; "Obshchee Sobranie . . . 1958," Biulleten 4 (1958), 11–13.

52. Ibid., p. 140. For the UPG's answer to the questionnaire, see: Allan Kornberg, Democratic Participation and Institutions for Nation-Building: Report on the Feasibility of an International Program of Legislative Studies, prepared for AID, January 1971, under Contract No. csd-2607, p. 5 of appendix.

CHAPTER 8

1. The preceding discussion of the Presidium is based on V. V. Aspaturian, "The Soviet Union," in R. C. Macridis and R. E. Ward, (eds.) Modern Political Systems: Europe, 3rd ed. (Englewood Cliffs, N.J.: Prentice-Hall), pp. 615–618.

2. Loeber, Dietrich (1970) "Legal Rules 'For Internal Use Only'," International and Comparative Law Quarterly (January), 76. The full implications of this are analyzed further on.

3. Stalin on the Draft Constitution, as translated in J. H. Meisel, Materials for Study of the Soviet System (Ann Arbor: George Wahr, 1950), pp. 240–241.

4. Mikhailov, M. (1956) "Some Questions of Soviet Constitutional Practice," Sovetskoye gosudarstvo i pravo, 9, 6.

5. Saifulin, M., (1967) The Soviet Parliament (Moscow), p. 78.

6. Ibid., p. 78.

7. The published record from which the following description is taken appears in Izvestia, April 9, 1968, pp. 1 and 4.

8. Pravda and Izvestia, June 3, 1970, p. 1.

9. See Article 38 of the zakon creating the commissions, Izvestia October 13, 1967, p. 2; and Saifulin, op. cit., pp. 79 and 93.

10. (1970) USSR Constitution, Article 49, English translation (Moscow).

11. Ibid., Article 49, Section (c).

12. Ibid.

13. Shebanov, A. F. (1967) "Razvitie formy sovetskogo prava," Sovetskoye gosudarstvo i pravo, 9, 22–31.

14. Bespaly, I. T. (1959) Prezidium Verkhovnogo Soveta Soiuzno: Respubliki (Moscow), pp. 8–12, 105–108.

15. Barabaschev, G. V. and Sheremet, K. F. (1965) Sovetskoye stroitel'stvo (Moscow), pp. 76–77.

16. Bespaly, op. cit., pp. 8–12.

17. Ibid., pp. 12.

18. Mitskevich, A. V. (1967) Akty Vysshikh organov sovetskogo gosudarstva (Moscow), p. 98.

19. Statute of Procuracy of the USSR of 1955 (VVS SSSR 1955, no. 9, item 222; English translation, 1956, 4 Highlights 83–99), Art. 10. From the literature see: S. G. Berezovskaia, Prokurorskii nadzor v sovetskom gosudarsvennom upravlenii (Moscow, 1954) pp. 52–53; S. G. Berezovskaia, Prokurorskii nadzor za zakonnost'iu pravovykh aktov organov upravleniia v SSSR, (Moscow, 1959), p. 36; S. G. Berezovskaia, Okhrana prav grazhdan sovetskoi prokuraturoi (Moscow, 1964), p. 49; I. N. Pakhomov (1956) 8 Sovetskove gosudarstvo i pravo, 135–137 at 136; I. N. Pakhomov (1958) 2 Pravovedenie

37–42 at 38; I. I. Kuznetsov, in Teoreticheskie voprosy sistematizatsii sovetskogo zakono-datel'stva (Moscow, 1962), pp. 86–144 at 140.

20. Gellhorn, Walter, in Columbia Law Review, 66, 1051–1079 at 1062, note 36.

21. Kutafin, O. Ye (1966) "Mutual Relations of Standing Commissions of Chambers of USSR Supreme Soviet with the Presidium of the USSR Supreme Soviet and with the USSR Council of Ministers," Sovetskoye gosudarstvo i pravo, 4 (April), 34.

22. Mandelshstam, L. (1966) "Istina i domysly," Izvestia, July 30, p. 2.

23. Chkikvadze, V. M., ed. (1968) The Soviet State and Law (Moscow: Progress Publishers), pp. 132–133.

24. Little, D. Richard (1971) Legislative Authority in the Soviet Political System, Slavic Review, vol. 30, no. 1, 65–66.

25. Ibid.

26. Mitskevich, op. cit., p. 101.

27. Kravchuk, S. S. (1966) Voprosy razvitiia Sovetov, na Sovremennom Etape (Moscow), pp. 44–46.

28. Mitskevich, op. cit., p. 102.

29. The Presidium of the Supreme Soviet not only has a distinct administrative staff but it also apparently has the authority to create ad hoc commissions of its own without any approval of the Supreme Soviet. Often the jurisdiction of these commissions includes preparation of very important legislation, affecting the powers of the Supreme Soviet itself. For example, in May 1967 the Presidium of the Supreme Soviet created the Commission for the Preparation of Proposals on Expanding the Rights of Rural and Settlement Soviets (Izvestia, April 9, 1967, pp. 1 and 4). The Commission was chaired by a vice-chairman of the Presidium and member of the CPSU Central Committee, and included representatives from the ministries, the union republics, and local soviets.

30. Kutafin, op. cit., p. 34.

31. Ibid. The zakon on commissions arguably weakens the legal control of the chambers over the commissions. Kutafin may have been seeking to forestall its passage.

32. See Pigolkin, A. S. (1968) "Technicians in the Drafting Process," Sovetskoye gosudarstvo i pravo, vol. 1.

33. Novikov, S. G. and Sharif, M. A. (1966), "Problems of the Organization of the Work of the USSR Supreme Soviet at the Present Stage," Sovetskoye gosudarstvo i pravo, 12, 26–28.

34. Kutafin, op. cit., pp. 33–34.

35. Ibid., pp. 32–35.

36. Mandelshstam, op. cit.

37. Podgorny, N. V. Izvestia, August 3, 1966, p. 3 (emphasis added).

38. Solomentsev, M. S. Izvestia, October 13, 1967 (supplementary edition), pp. 5–6. The word "assist" suggests a secondary role for chamber chairmen.

39. Saifulin, op. cit., p. 54.

40. For a recent example, see Izvestia, June 3, 1970, p. 1. This account of a Presidium session illustrates how the permanent commissions report to the Presidium on their findings, which the Presidium than converts to an order binding on the ministries, or a recommenda-tion which is not binding.

41. Podgorny, N. V., Izvestia, August 3, 1966, p. 3.

42. Izvestia, August 23, 1969, p. 1.

43. Krivenko, L. T. (1970) "The Standing Commissions and the Ministries," Sovetskoye gosudarstvo i pravo, vol. 1.

44. Ibid., and Izvestia, June 3, 1970, for a specific example of a Republic presidium exercising its authority over the Procuracy and People's Control Commission. The People's Control Commissions were so-called "voluntary" organs established by the CPSU to super-vise execution of its policy. Their powers declined after 1964.

CHAPTER 9

1. Kerimov, D. A. (1961) "The guiding role of the CPSU in the law-making activity of the Soviet state," Sovetskoye gosudarstvo i pravo, 10 (October), 77–85.

2. Barabashev, G. V., and Sheremet, K. F. (1967) "CPSU and the Soviets," Sovetskoye gosudarstvo i pravo, vol. 11.

3. Ibid.

4. Ibid.

5. Ibid.

6. Ibid.

7. Pravda, October 31, 1967, p. 1; Izvestia, November 1, 1967, p. 1.

8. Ibid.

9. Ibid.

10. Izvestia November 22, 1969, pp. 1 and 2.

11. Romashkin, P. S., (1960) "A new stage in the form of the Soviet government," Sovetskoye gosudarstvo i pravo, vol. 10.

12. Kalinychev, F., (ed.) (1968) Sovetskoye Sosialisticheskaya Demokratiya (Moscow: Progress Publishers), p. 251 (emphasis added).

13. Lobanov, P. P., (1958) "Socialist democracy and the law-making of the Supreme Soviet," Sovetskoye gosudarstvo i pravo, 3, 24.

14. Pravda October 2, 1965, pp. 1 and 3.

15. Kerimov, op. cit.

16. Organov, N. N., (1961) "The party and the Soviets," Sovetskoye gosudarstvo i pravo, 10 (October), 13–25.

17. Lepeshkin, A. I., et. al. (1962) Sovetskogo gosudarstvennogo prava, vol. 2 (Moscow), pp. 418, 429. The definition of legislated initiative appears in Chkikvadze, V. M. (1968) Sovetskoye gosudarstvo i pravo (Moscow), p. 223.

18. Adriannov, N. Ye. (1964) "On legislative initiative," Sovetskoye gosudarstvo i pravo, 9, 55–63.

19. See Chapter 6 on legislative process.

20. Lepeshkin, op. cit., pp. 418–429.

21. Pravda, July 15, 1970, p. 2.

22. Aspaturian, V. V., (1968) "The Soviet Union," in R. C. Macridis and R. E. Ward, eds., Modern Political Systems: Europe, 2nd ed. (Englewood Cliffs, N.J.: Prentice-Hall), p. 569.

23. Saifulin, op. cit., p. 156.

24. Clarke, op. cit., p. 56.

25. Ibid., p. 54.

26. Saifulin, op. cit., pp. 19 and 20.

27. Aspaturian, op. cit., p. 577.

28. Ibid., pp. 577–578.

29. Juvilier, op. cit., p. 118.

30. Ibid., p. 117.

31. The statistics and computations in the following tables in this chapter are compiled from the following biographical sources, plus lists published in Pravda and Izvestia: Edward L. Crowly, Andrew I. Lebed, Heinrich E. Schulz, eds. (1969) Party and Government Officials of the Soviet Union: 1917–1967 (Metuchen, N.J.: Scarecrow Press); Crowley, Lebed and Schulz, eds. (1968) Prominent Personalities in the USSR (Metuchen, N.J.: Scarecrow Press); Lebed, Schulz, and Stephen S. Taylor, eds. (1966) Who's Who in the USSR, 1965–1966 (New York and London: Scarecrow Press); Deputaty Verkhovnogo Sovet (1966), the official Soviet biographical source (Moscow: Sedmoi Soyz); and Directory of Soviet Officials (1966) vol. I, USSR and RSFSR (February), and Revisions to Directory of Soviet Officials (1968) January.

32. New York Times, April 10, 1971, p. 1.

33. They are Brezhnev, Podgorny, Kunayev, Shelest, Grishin, Demichev, Mazurov, Mashcrov, and Rashidov.

34. Saifulin, op. cit., pp. 46 and 51.

35. Ibid., p. 46.

36. Ibid., pp. 41 and 56.

37. Billington, James, (1966) The Icon and the Axe (New York: Vintage), pp. 203, 370, 469.

38. Aspaturian, op. cit., pp. 169–175.

39. Skilling, H. Gordon, and Griffiths, Franklyn, (1971) Interest Groups in Soviet Politics (Princeton, N.J.: Princeton Univ. Press); Griffiths' unique approach appears at 335–379.

40. Verkovni Soviet SSSR: Vosmoyo Soziva (Statustucheskii Sbornik) (1970) Moscow, p. 50; and S. Vorovitsyn (1969) "The present composition of the Party Central Committee: A brief seriological analysis," Bulletin 16 (June), 23.

41. Verkovni Soviet SSSR, op. cit.; and Bulletin, op. cit., p. 23.

42. Saifulin, op. cit., p. 158.

CHAPTER 10

1. Podgorny, N. V. (1966) Chairman of the Presidium of the Supreme Soviet, Speech to Joint Session of the Supreme Soviet, Pravda, August 3, p. 3.

2. Pospielovsky, Dimitry V. "Ideological Theses and Constructive Political Proposals of the Democratic Opposition," Bulletin 26; the author reviews samizdat, which are mimeographed and circulated by dissenters.

3. Ibid.

4. Ionescu, Ghita (1967) The Politics of the European Communist States (New York: Praeger) p. 253.

5. New York Times, December 23, 1965.

6. East Europe, January 1967, p. 38.

7. Gamarnikow, Michael (1969) quoted in "Problems of Communism," March–April, p. 18.

8. World Marxist Review, August 1971, pp. 23–24.

9. Ibid., p. 36.

10. Ionescu, op. cit., p. 259.

11. Ibid., p. 262. The power of government, theoretically and structurally, is centered in the Yugoslav Legislative Assembly system. See Fisk, Winston M. (1971) "The Constitutionalism Movement in Yugoslavia," Slavic Review, June, p. 288.

12. Ionescu, p. 258; and Stehle, Hans Jakob (1965) The Independent Satellite: Society and Politics in Poland Since 1945 (New York: Praeger) p. 194.

13. Stehle, op. cit., pp. 178–79; (1965) "Problems of Communism," March–April, p. 130.

14. World Marxist Review, op. cit. p. 21.

15. A whole literature revolving around this subject has emerged. For example, see the critical bibliography of Varchuk, V. V., and Razin, V. I. (1967) Voprosy Filosofii, 4, (April) pp. 134–143. See also Izvestia, March 1, 1959, p. 3.

INDEX

Aspaturian, Vernon, 16, 64, 172, 222

Bespaly, I. T., 192–195
Bolsheviks, 22–26, 29, 31, 102
Brezhnev, Leonid, 99, 108, 145, 178, 205, 213, 218, 232
Bulgaria, 228

Central Committee, 13, 34, 71, 85, 90, 93, 99, 106, 131, 171, 184, 186–188, 201, 203, 210, 211, 215, 217–219, 224, 232, 235
Central Executive Committee, 26–34, 109, 152, 183, 207
Congress of Soviets, 26–30, 109
Constituent Assembly, 27
Constitution of 1918, 26, 28
Constitution of 1922, 28
Constitution of 1936, 13, 38, 61, 81, 106, 109, 155, 163, 204; Article 1, 38; Article 14, 39, 47, 106; Article 15, 49, 106; Article 21, 122; Article 22, 122; Article 24, 121; Article 30, 37, 42, 45; Article 32, 37, 45, 47, 95, 136; Article 46, 52, 191; Article 47, 51, 52, 86, 189, 191; Article 49, 46, 52, 57, 112, 179, 182, 189, 190, 192–194, 197; Article 51, 58, 110, 163; Article 53, 52, 86; Article 55, 86; Article 56, 51; Article 64, 47, 109; Article 65, 48, 108, 147; Article 66, 48; Article 71, 59; Article 73, 109; Article 98, 106; Article 101, 106; Article 105, 111; Article 113, 113; Article 114, 113; Article 126, 14, 126, 153, 205
Constitutional Democrats, 20
Constitutional order, 12
Council of Elders, 13, 29, 81, 85, 89, 90, 137, 187, 201, 220, 223
Council of Ministers, 13, 45, 50, 58, 72, 90, 94, 107–110, 113, 118, 126, 137, 143, 162, 166, 168, 177, 178, 180, 186, 198, 206, 232, 234
Council of Nationalities, 51, 66, 70, 71, 77, 86, 124, 127, 145, 146, 154, 155, 160, 215, 218, 220; Economic Commission, 52, 71, 92, 95, 96, 162

Council of People's Commissars. *See* Sovnarkom
Council of the Union, 51, 70, 77, 154, 206, 215–217, 220
Czechoslovakia, 231

Deputaty, 63

Fedorenko, N., 99

Gelhorn, Walter, 193
Gorkin, A. F., 113
Griffiths, Franklyn, 222

Hungary, 229, 230

Inter-Parliamentary Union, 169, 172, 173
Ivan IV, 16, 19
Izvestia, 62–63, 82, 103, 147, 183, 187, 197, 198

Juviler, Peter, 66

Kalinin, Mikhail, 179
Komsomol, 117, 209
Kontrol, 98–100, 102–105, 107, 111, 112, 114, 117, 120–122, 169, 170, 178, 189, 204, 214, 228; evolution, 145, 146, 163–166; legality, 146–150, 181
Kosygin, A. N., 186, 213, 232
Kruschev, Nikita, 16, 40, 41, 93, 94, 96, 97, 115, 127, 145, 163, 178, 180, 195, 205, 215, 216
Kutafin, O. Ye., 195, 196
Kuznetsov, I. N., 46–48

Legislative Proposals Commission, 107, 112, 117, 120, 124, 127, 131, 135, 139, 144, 160, 186, 187, 217–219
Lenin, V. I., 22–25, 27, 31, 140, 153, 232, 233
Litvinov, M. M., 87, 91, 93

Malenkov, G., 93, 94, 96, 100
Marx, Karl, 22, 23, 153, 232, 233
Mensheviks, 23, 27, 31

Mikoyan, Anastas, 179
Molotov, V. M., 88

National State Duma, 20
New York Times, 96
Nicholas II, 20
North Atlantic Treaty Organization, 172
North Vietnam, 230

Pakhomov, N. I., 91
People's Control Commission, 112, 117,
    118, 167, 187
Pisotkin, M. I., 95
Planning and Budget Commission, 124, 131,
    137, 146, 196, 217
Podgorny, N. V., 98, 148, 179, 197, 198,
    213, 227
Poland, 229, 230
Politburo, 13, 179, 180, 186, 201, 212,
    213, 232
Pravda, 62, 63, 82, 183
Presidium of Central Executive Committee,
    29, 30
Presidium of Supreme Soviet, 13, 14, 56,
    85, 89, 90, 93, 104, 112–114, 137, 147,
    170, 177–199, 232, 234; election,
    75–79; jurisdiction, 44–52
Procuracy, 43, 112, 120, 145, 167, 182,
    190, 191, 193, 199
Procurator General, 13, 113, 114, 134, 187

Rudenko, R. A., 114

Second Duma, 20, 109
Shvernik, Nicolai, 179
Sobornost, 43

Socialist Democracy, 153, 158
Socialist Revolutionaries, 27
Solomentsev, M. S., 197, 218, 219
Soviet of the Nationalities, 11, 153, 154
Soviet of the Union, 11
Sovnarkom, 24, 25, 28, 30–34, 109
Stakhanovites, 66, 67
Stalin, Joseph, 19, 28, 40, 47, 77, 83, 87,
    92, 93, 130, 133, 152, 153, 155, 178,
    183, 207
State Duma, 22–24, 152, 153
Supreme Court, 13, 29, 111–113, 134, 135,
    149
Supreme Soviet Commission System, 103
Suslov, M. A., 216, 218
Sverdlov, Ya., 27

Time of Troubles, 17

Ukaz, 21, 22, 95, 112, 121, 156, 187, 190,
    191, 199; legality, 56–59

Veches, 15, 17, 23
Voroshilov, Marshal, 96, 179
Vyshinsky, I., 51, 109, 154

Yugoslavia, 95, 229, 230

Zakon, 21, 49, 54, 104, 112, 120, 124, 148,
    156, 160, 188, 190, 191, 198; initiation,
    134–137
Zasedania, 62, 63, 82, 87
Zemsky Sobor, 15–19, 22, 24, 101, 152,
    153, 233, 235
Zhdanov, A. A., 87, 91, 93